# Praise for

"With wit, intelligence and gut-wrenching honesty, Perry reminds us that the path to real love is often rocky, but that the destination is perhaps the most glorious one we can achieve in life."

—Robert Epstein, Ph.D., editor in chief, *Psychology Today*

"Perry explores the complex nuances of and challenges to achieving intimacy through an in-depth exploration of the experiences of real people. This book [is] an enlightening and inspirational touchstone."

— Jeremy P. Hunter, Ph.D., research director, Quality of Life Research Center, Peter F. Drucker School of Management

"A remarkable book—a wonderful mix of pointers, anecdotes, suggestions, reassurances, and hints. Perry uses a large dollop of humor to guide you along the ins and outs (and do's and don'ts) of how to make love work. Highly recommended."

—James C. Kaufman, Ph.D., California

"Perry has come up with some really useful suggestions, and her writing is soothing and refreshing. It's a book worth any ten on the same subject on the shelves. *Loving in Flow* is a thoughtful, stimulating and potentially dynamite bestseller!"

—Mihaly Csikszentmihalyi, Ph.D., author of the *New York Times* bestseller FLOW

# Loving in FLOW

# Loving in FLOW

## How the Happiest Couples Get and Stay That Way

### Susan K. Perry, Ph.D.
author of *Writing in Flow*

SOURCEBOOKS CASABLANCA™
AN IMPRINT OF SOURCEBOOKS, INC.®
NAPERVILLE, ILLINOIS

This publication is designed to provide accurate and authoritative
information in regard to the subject matter covered. It is sold with the
understanding that the publisher is not engaged in rendering legal,
accounting, or other professional service. If legal advice or other expert
assistance is required, the services of a competent professional person
should be sought.—*From a Declaration of Principles Jointly Adopted by a
Committee of the American Bar Association and a Committee of Publishers and
Associations*

Published by Sourcebooks, Inc.
P.O. Box 4410, Naperville, Illinois 60567-4410
(630) 961-3900
FAX: (630) 961-2168
www.sourcebooks.com

Library of Congress Cataloging-in-Publication Data
Perry, Susan K.
  Loving in flow : how the happiest couples get and stay that way / by
Susan K. Perry.
     p. cm.
  ISBN 1-4022-0065-X (pbk. : alk. paper)
  1. Marriage. 2. Couples. 3. Love. I. Title.
HQ734 .P472 2003
306.81—dc21

                                                              2002153438

        Printed and bound in the United States of America
            BG  10  9  8  7  6  5  4  3  2  1

For Stephen

# ACKNOWLEDGMENTS

To all those who shared their intimate lives with me so others could learn from their hard-won insights; to Mihaly Csikszentmihalyi for his encouragement; to my agent, Sheree Bykofsky Associates, and especially Janet Rosen, for making this happen; to Jon Malysiak and Laura Kuhn, my editors at Sourcebooks, for making it painless; to my parents, for whom my love is as enduring as theirs has always been for me; to my sons: may they make fewer and smaller mistakes than I did; and to Stephen, for offering exhilarating conversation and careful critiquing, for vanquishing my malignant computer codes, and for allowing me, with such exquisite generosity, to share our story here: all my love always.

# TABLE OF CONTENTS

# *Introduction*
# THE GARDEN OF DORIAN GRAY

The first thing you notice is the white picket fence. Then the roses: miniature trees in rainbow profusion, red blooms thrusting through the slats, vines climbing to the tip of the Spanish-tiled roof. Neighborhood walkers often stop to admire the garden. With its delicately white-flowered bower and curvy brick walkways, it has a fairy tale quality.

I call it the Garden of Dorian Gray. Admittedly, we inside the house aren't growing increasingly hideous the more the daylilies bloom. At least, not anymore. Right now will someday be the good old days I'll look back to with fondness. But my husband and I had to make it through relationship hell in our two decades together to reach the happy place we're in now.

It is often that way: further down your own block, or around the corner, there may be a couple who appear joyful in one another's company, yet who weren't always that way. All satisfied couples have histories, and some of those histories hide more agony than you might imagine. In this book, I will share with you some of my secrets and the secrets of more than three dozen couples I interviewed. How some couples move from the gloom of their own dark ages to much sunnier times—to loving in flow—is what you'll discover in the following pages.

# WHAT IS "LOVING IN FLOW"?

> Like any other marriage, the MacAllisters' had had its lean years and its fat, but it seemed capable of recurring refreshment, a spring that sometimes trickled and sometimes gushed but that had thus far proved inexhaustible.
>
> —William McPherson, *To the Sargasso Sea*

Relationships come and go. Some manage to hang in there, if just barely, but so what? Truth be told, what everyone wants is a relationship where, after decades, you can still get goosebumps at the sight of each other. A loving in flow relationship rises above the ordinary, beyond tit-for-tat. In this book, I'll show you how the best marriage is having someone with whom to transcend aloneness in a random chaotic universe. I'll prove that real couples with real flaws and inadequacies can indeed find exceptional joy together.

My husband and I spend a lot of time in flow these days. It happens when Stephen makes one of his trademark bantering comments, many of them salacious, such as when he notices me leaning over the tub to wash my hair and says, "Oh good, chimps at the stream," and I know he's referring to the helplessness of a primate bending to get a drink. And I'm aware he's showing me how delightful and sexy my everyday habits are to him. At such times the bond between us feels timeless and irreplaceable.

That's called flow. It's the same as being "in the zone," as athletes have long referred to the mindset. For couples, it means an intense engagement unlike what either of you has with anyone else. Such flowing interactions are profoundly and endlessly refreshing, keeping us far from bored. If that sounds a bit dull to those who wish the frantic early days of emotional white-water-rapid highs could continue for a lifetime, rest assured: it's no duller than transcendence itself.

Anyone can learn to enter flow. According to the findings of flow pioneer Mihaly Csikszentmihalyi, as well as my own nearly decade-long research, flow happens when you're so engaged in whatever you're doing that time seems to stop. You want to keep on doing it simply because it pleases you. It's easy to grasp that reading a compelling novel, playing a spirited game, or composing a song could propel you into such an altered state. But what does it mean for lovers to spend time together in flow?

"I think the most intimate time is when we're both very happy to be with each other," said one of the happily married men I interviewed. "There's nothing the matter with our relationship in a major sense, we're relaxed and calm, and we're just feeling good being together. It's a relationship flow."

When you and your mate are in flow together, you lose your usual self-consciousness and feel part of something larger—a system of two, an "us." The flow metaphor is especially apt for a relationship because two people moving through life together is anything but a static structure that can be taken for granted. Such a relationship "focuses not so much on the other individual, nor on oneself," the great humanistic psychologist Carl Rogers observed, "but on the immediate relationship of loving and living which exists between the two."

One of my long and very agreeably married interviewees explained it this way: "He's my soulmate, at least after those first seven years." Here she laughed aloud, because we'd already talked about how hard those early years were. As is typical, that much-desired sense of intense connection didn't come automatically to this couple. "We talk about this so often, about how there is no question that we were meant to be with each other. Call it pre-destined, made in heaven, metaphysical, whatever you want to. There is no question in either of our minds that we are much more together than either of us would have been separately or with anyone else."

Those who have found a connection like this experience something beyond a simple us-against-the-world mentality. It is more like a fully actualized us-*in*-the-world. That's what I mean by loving in flow. In the following chapters, I'll show you how to be among those lucky couples who find flow together.

# THE PUZZLE OF HAPPY RELATIONSHIPS

> Words on black leather Made-in-Korea key chain ($1.95) seen at locksmith shop: "Opening the Door to Happy."

Over the past couple of generations, the "door to happy" seems to have moved and left no address. Ever since societies in the more developed countries made divorce a relatively easy option for couples to choose, choose it they do. No longer tied unquestioningly to their first partner, about half of those who marry opt to try another match, often more than once.

For some years now, researchers have been trying to decipher what makes some marriages succeed better than others. You could look at the high divorce figures another way: with a task as complicated as two people getting along for a lifetime without wearing out each other's nerves or boring each other to death, it's a wonder so many make it. We might keep in mind the vast complexity possible in any two humans. Biological gender is one of thousands of variables in operation that differentiate us. Count the bits of DNA, add in every experience we've each ever had. The possible combinations are astronomical.

And yet some of us find a mate and transcendent, lasting happiness. When I began looking for very happy couples to interview, almost everyone I spoke with suggested one couple who might qualify, but rarely more. And even a few of these supposedly happy couples confessed that they didn't view themselves as all that exemplary. This would seem to dispute the findings of a recent study that 63 percent of married Americans age 18 and older reported having "very happy" marriages.

I believe there's a serious problem with most such studies. When a researcher asks (and these days such studies are sometimes performed in cyberspace), "Is your marriage Very happy? Happy? Average? Unhappy? Very unhappy?" the results will inevitably be less revealing than what you'd get by way of an authentic conversation.

## ABOUT THIS BOOK

Relationship and marriage books abound, traditional how-tos that purport to offer a certain number of oversimplified rules for bliss. I see this book as a counter, for instance, to those that advise women to give up their identity in order to get their husbands to buy them trifles and take care of them, as well as to those recommending marriage because it's healthier, as though coupled life were a prescription. Would we ask people to *surrender* to winning the lottery? Instead, this book—part of the movement toward a more positive psychology—shows how a superior relationship, one in which you have learned to love in flow, is achievable if you both want it enough.

In my research, I delved deep into the relationship literature and then interviewed a series of fulfilled couples to find out how they got through the worst parts to the best parts of their joint lives. I sought to distinguish what qualities separate those couples whose relationships survive crisis (infidelity, severely ill child, loss of livelihood) from those that don't. What makes a resilient marriage? What can you do to be in harmony, stay together, resist the forces that pull you apart, actualize yourself while you support your partner's self-growth at the same time? How can you learn to love in flow, even when your partner sometimes exasperates you?

I did with couples what psychologist Abraham Maslow did with self-actualizing individuals: studied the best. As William James wrote, "Interesting as the origins and early stages of a subject always are, yet when one seeks earnestly for its full significance, one must always look to its more completely evolved and perfected forms."

I sought out, by a variety of means—what's called a convenience sample—couples who had been married (or in a committed relationship) for at least ten years (most for many more than that) and who identified themselves as extremely happy, those who would rate their satisfaction near the top of a scale of one to 100. I asked them a lot of personal questions to find out how they got there.

Throughout this book, when I refer to someone by first name only, it's a pseudonym; other identifying features have also been changed to protect the anonymity of those who requested it. Where surnames are given, those stories are true in every detail. I use the terms "relationship" and "marriage" interchangeably. I use the term "partner" frequently; I like that it includes all genders and carries within it the seal of equality so crucial to loving in flow.

This book also contains much personal material. By sharing my own experiences, I hope you'll be able to identify with some of my shortcomings, and perhaps find resonances to your own relationship struggles. When you realize your concerns are nearly universal, then you can stop the blame and guilt and get on with solving the problems.

I'll begin by examining some of the words that are so important to a new couple—fear and love—and other issues that come up again and again. By backtracking, we can make better sense of current frustrations. I'll explain the inevitable changes that time brings to a romantic relationship: disillusionment, conflict, and learning how to talk to and deeply understand one another. Next comes dealing with those irritating behaviors that can be either trivial or relationship-threatening, followed by an investigation of sexuality in a good relationship.

I'll share the way back up from the apogee of my own marriage, along with the stories of other enduring couples who made it through a range of changes and traumas. I'll also discuss the role of fairness in a flowing relationship. After that, I'll delve into how couples are intimate and separate in an easygoing balance, the crucial roles of play, novelty, and appreciation, at last arriving at a feeling—this time based on genuine knowledge—of being made for each other. In the last chapter, I'll show why a mindful awareness of time's speedy passage can be the catalyst for the best possible lifelong love. An epilogue summarizes eight insights that have been learned and lived by my group of happiest couples.

Now let's begin at the beginning.

# Loving in FLOW

# 1
# IN THE BEGINNING
# ARE THE WORDS

I'm turned on by ideas, intensity, my self evolving, laughing in
bed, honesty, men who value my uniqueness. Writer, 36, 5'3",
120, brown hair/eyes, attractive, M.A., Jewish atheist, non-materialistic. *Very warm*, need to touch, give, share. You're *intelligent*,
funny, communicative, sensuous, creative, liberal, not selfish,
seeking best friend.

All relationships begin in their own quirky way. Ours, pre-
computer age, began with the above words in a singles magazine.
I was lucky: the ad brought an exceptional man to my doorstep.
What I couldn't know then was that all the elements were already
in play, all the bits and pieces of ourselves that would lead us
from the usual first-blush typical euphoria through the kind of
despair that turned us inside out, to what I call loving in flow.

Delving into how relationships start gives clues to what
makes them work well. Who you both are is a vital ingredient of
what makes for a zestful relationship. That includes whether you
both have a flexible set of attitudes, including open-mindedness
and resilience and the willingness to take emotional risks.
Turning your attention back toward how you and your current
partner met—what you were looking for and what you think you
found—can lead you toward understanding what keeps you in or
out of flow today.

As I began interviewing other couples, I also reread my old
journals and love letters. These offered tantalizing lessons, not
only to the incredible fallibility of memory, but to how we might

have done things differently, or sooner, or more wisely. At times it felt like my husband and I were two arthritic, nearsighted mice bumbling our way along the edge of a series of scary precipices with no sense of direction. When I share such excerpts as an adjunct to the recollections shared by my interviewees, it's in hopes that others might avoid some of the more common dead-end pathways.

## SENDING SIGNALS

Before we commit to a permanent match, most of us have a mental image of the partner we'd prefer. Often, we hang onto this image *afterward*, too, and therein lies the problem. For some, that image might be visual, such as a woman who looks like Catherine Zeta-Jones, or a man whose arm muscles bulge like those of a former roommate's sexy boyfriend. Or the image you carry around with you may be a composite of dozens of impressionistically vague traits. Now that we're in the era of singles ads, it's easy to discover what a lot of people hope to find in a mate. But even if they find what they're seeking, many of the relationships that result from such ads will end up in trouble due to an obsession with what just doesn't matter.

Can you recall the list of qualities, perhaps never brought fully to consciousness, that you sought in a lifemate before you met your partner? If so, how meaningful did each item turn out to be? No one can build a life based on the fact that both partners like natural fibers or believe in tax breaks for businesses. Think for a moment about which items on your mental list were expendable, merely shifting tastes, and which reflected more essential values. Are there any that make you slightly melancholy even now because your partner doesn't have them? Does each trait you relinquished, however unwillingly or unsuspectingly, have another, equally valuable though not necessarily analogous, to take its place? In flowing marriages, each partner can compile such a list that balances out losses with wins.

The ad at the start of this chapter was the one I placed twenty years ago in a now-defunct glossy singles magazine named *INTRO*. If I were to write one today, it would be very similar. (Obviously, I'd still have the sense not to tell the *whole* truth, meaning I'd still leave out that I can be pitbull-tenacious about minor details, which can feel to whoever's on the receiving end like nagging or nitpicking, or worse. Or so I've been told.)

I'd been divorced for about nine months after a 13-year marriage and had been devoting myself frantically to earning a living and caring for my two sons when I realized I was ready to begin sharing my life again. Meanwhile, Stephen had placed the following ad:

Professional poet: Intelligent (can be disconcerted if my date confuses Plato with a Walt Disney character); MA in Literature. 31, 138, 5'5". Quintessentially cute. Love all the arts; especially music (Bach, Chopin). Widely read. Like philosophy, but have my more primal side also. Sensuous, sensitive, caring, passionate, honest and open, somewhat shy in groups, but vibrant and playful one-on-one. To know me is to have read Yeats' "The Song of Wandering Aengus." Desire short, slim, pretty Sprite with lively sense of humor—who seeks intense *communication* with equally unique soul. (23-36). Photo appreciated.

You can learn a lot about yourself by noticing how you read such ads. Grab the nearest singles ads (it's okay, this is research), skim through them, and note which are total turn-offs. Why do you react this way to those in particular?

I didn't respond to Stephen's ad, but he answered mine. Here's part of his initial letter, written on a card with a photo of a ballet dancer on the front:

*Bonjour:*
You seem a perfect echo. If I ever need an aorta transplant, I'll know who to turn to. Our hearts seem to beat to the beat of the same drummer.

Let's see. I'm also a writer. Mainly poetry. I'll be 32 in December, M.A. in Literature. Atheist with a penchant for comparative mythology à la Joseph Campbell.

Non-materialistic. How do you communicate to someone that there's more to life than a Mercedes and designer jeans? Very warm, also.

I am quite liberal. Am very open-minded. Which comes from being a philosophical Skeptic. The world has circumference enough for many realities.

Anyway, I like: Bach's double-violin concerto; Chopin, particularly the *Barcarole*;...a good vintage of California wine by candlelight; exploring feelings, the deep corridors of two personalities, etc.

Brown hair/eyes. Like *curious* people. Hope you find enough echoes here to call.

Sincerely, Stephen

His talk of feelings was a seductive hint of an open emotional life. He'd enclosed the Yeats poem "The Song of Wandering Aengus," about a "glimmering girl" worth searching for forever, which concludes with the evocative lines: "And pluck till time and tides are done / The silver apples of the moon / The golden apples of the sun." I should have known then that he was a romantic at heart, and surely I did, but I didn't understand yet how that might play out in our struggle for connection through the years to come. The way we use words as often leads to obfuscation as to clarity, especially when we don't know *ourselves* well.

## A LIFE IN LISTS

But then if you get to where you, you know, love a person, everything sort of reverses. It's not that you love the person because of certain things about the person anymore; it's that you love the things about the person because you love the person. It kind of radiates out, instead of in.

—David Foster Wallace, *The Broom of the System*

Years ago, I worked for a computer dating firm. We'd often resort to hand-matching clients in order to provide them with at least one or two dates since so many people sent in long lists of traits they demanded in a partner, making them unmatchable by machine. Their specific requirements included everything from height, weight, and eye color to educational level and leisure preferences (must play the kazoo and enjoy ice hockey). Compiling such shopping lists of superficial traits invites us to see people as mere collections of attributes. Even today, on Internet matchmaking sites, someone could match each and every physical spec, right down to earning the "right" amount, and still be a disappointing date, much less a suitable life partner. Some singles ad afficionados go mad with the multiplicity of choices, never sure they've settled on the right one, and constantly on the lookout for someone better.

Once you know someone, though, you could be irritated by numberless maddening idiosyncrasies and still be simpatico. There's something much more ineffable about who we are (even if someday brain research will pinpoint, literally, where our existential crises reside).

None of the matchmaking services ask what you would do if your partner lost his job and decided to commit to years of costly education with no income. Some traits mean proportionately a thousand times more than others: how you approach adversity versus your toenail-cutting finesse, or whether you're there for your friends versus how often you forget to recycle your cans. Besides, a bit of thoughtful narrative conveys more about who we are than do short phrases. Compare the familiar and generic "I like to walk on the beach" with "I enjoy exploring isolated beaches for odd-shaped driftwood while bed-and-breakfasting in Mendocino."

I bring up this trait-listing behavior in some detail because it's not done only when hunting for a partner in the first place. Some people do it obsessively, constantly dissatisfied with the little boxes their current partners wouldn't be able to check. One of the people I interviewed told me ruefully that in order to be closer to "100" in her satisfaction level, her husband would have to be just like her. I shared this surprising tidbit with Stephen, adding, "I don't think I'd like to be with someone exactly like me."

"You'd drive you crazy," he agreed.

Gain some insight by designing an ad about yourself, even now: don't forget to list your most adaptable qualities, and then go back and remove everything superficial and focus on those qualities that could conceivably endure for a lifetime, such as tolerance, loyalty, and compassion.

At times, listing qualities *can* be useful—so long as you're not adding up superficialities. When our marriage was undergoing a serious reevaluation (by Stephen) some years later, it helped him regain rationality when he was at war with himself, the war of hormones over cognition. By forcing his mind back to reality with the rigorous task of listing positives and negatives, he was able to make a sane decision.

## FIRST MEETINGS

> After all this time I still find it remarkable that people do come together, that they carry out their imaginings, sometimes exactly as they have hoped. It surprised my mother, that year of Richard Polloco, that she wished, and months passed, and she wished some more, and what do you know—he appeared before her, eating crackers and cheese.
>
> —Jane Hamilton, *Disobedience*

Some of life's biggest changes have a way of sneaking up on you. You can't know, for instance, when you meet someone new that this is going to be the person you'll want to wake up next to every morning until the day one of you doesn't wake up anymore.

Think about your own initial impressions of your partner-to-be. We know so little about each other when—for many of us—our hormones begin to take over. How effectively we are able to determine whether a relationship has genuine potential—whether this time it's "real"—is one of the lynchpins of relationship success. All of my happily married interviewees managed to keep their higher brains operating so as to counteract too swift a fall into mere infatuation. Luck (even science agrees) plays a role, too.

Consider writing up your own initial meeting with your partner. Make it as detailed as you can. Here, as an example, is an abbreviated version of events surrounding my first date with Stephen:

As soon as I got Stephen's card, we spoke on the phone for three hours. I recall most vividly his describing what he called his "hierarchy of love." At the least intense end of the list were "fucking buddies" (he had one—someone to fill in the gaps between serious relationships), and at the top would be love that's "cosmic." Of course, his definition of cosmic and what I pictured weren't—couldn't be—identical, and that disjunction would later come to matter a great deal.

Stephen surprised me by calling again the next night, and we spoke for three more hours. I had another date planned that night, but while Stephen and I were talking on the phone, the other fellow called to postpone. I invited Stephen over. A couple of hours later, after getting lost in the rain due to my poor directions, he arrived at nearly 10 p.m. When I opened the door, we were both struck with sudden shyness. He wasn't much taller than me, but I knew that already. His hair was longish, which was a sexy plus for me. I let him in and then noticed that he was carrying a closed paper bag, which struck me as odd. I asked what was in it, and he said, "I'll tell you later." This gave me pause. I served him cold chicken, one of my favorite meals. Later he poked fun at this, my first love offering. I had selected some records to play that I thought would please him, and he sorted through my paltry collection and chose less heavily classical ones, which surprised me. We sat on the couch in the living room.

Filling the silence in the time-honored manner, we began

kissing. After a while of this, he asked, "Do you have a bedroom?" Not one to attempt to hide such an obvious home accoutrement, I led him there. He instantly (he says "innocently") came up with this line (later shared with our best friends to great hilarity): "I always feel more comfortable naked." I can't say I agreed with him, but by then I was ready to connect on deeper levels.

In the morning he opened that paper bag and pulled out some poetry books. A bit anti-climactic (which was fine, all possibilities considered), but his reading of Wallace Stevens's "Sunday Morning" was unlike any other date finale I'd ever had.

When you reminisce with your partner about your first few dates, are your memories of those earliest hours, days, and weeks at odds, or similar? What did you think of your partner the first time you saw him? Did you honestly enjoy that first meal you shared, that first movie you saw together? What disappointed you, what excited you, what is most memorable to each of you?

## RIDING THE EMOTIONAL SEE-SAW

If endless love was a dream, then it was a dream we all shared...and if anything set me apart it was not my impulses but my stubbornness, my willingness to take the dream past what had been agreed upon as the reasonable limits, to declare that this dream was not a feverish trick of the mind but was an actuality at least as real as that other, thinner, more unhappy illusion we call normal life.

—Scott Spencer, *Endless Love*

The dating patterns of most new couples are quickly established. The more time you allow for building intimacy, the better your odds of connecting with a genuine person, not an imagined image. Stephen and I, for example, spent from Friday night to Sunday night together (my ex-husband entertained our two sons every weekend), and I attribute our getting to know each other so well to those intensive and exhausting periods of time, going out somewhere each weekend but mostly just hanging about, talking and touching. When I speak with other dating couples today, I'm surprised at how little some of them share. When you choose structured activities like dinner and a movie, it sometimes serves to keep intimacy at bay, and I don't mean the physical kind.

What passes for love early on often has such a volatile quality, more lust than anything else. This vacillation and initial instability seem to be nearly universal. At one moment Stephen was more the high Romantic in search of Yeats's "glimmering girl," and then it would be my turn to put all reason aside. Years later, we rode the giddy see-saw again in a way that imitated this early period. Both individual and couple development are cyclical, and if you don't learn what you need to grasp the first time, you get to try again later. Karma and reincarnation, all right here and now.

Like all couples, we began testing each other for trustworthiness. The more you disclose about yourself, the more you discover how much you can trust the other person to handle your disclosures with sensitivity. Among the primary attitudes you can adopt that will help you enter flow more often in a relationship are openness and a willingness to take emotional risks, which we'll talk more about in a later chapter.

I once had a student with an erratic dating history who insisted that he couldn't tell a new dating partner his religion for fear of her prejudice. Then when he finally did tell her, and she reacted in the prejudiced way he'd hoped to avoid, he felt reinforced for not being more forthcoming earlier about his most personal beliefs. But one of the main purposes of intimate honesty early in a relationship is to find out if the receiver of your confidences can love the fullness of who you are—and if not, it's time to move on and find someone who can. To delay those moments of truth doesn't usually accomplish what you hope it will.

One of my interviewees told me the main reason she chose her husband—even though she'd been more sexually excited by a previous lover—was that "there was a tremendous honesty." Harriet had been engaged a couple times before, but each time realized that either the young man wasn't someone she could count on, or he was a person that, "every time he went near me I cringed." (She'd gotten engaged, she says, because her neglectful mother wanted her out of the house.) When she met an honest fellow, "the only thing I knew was that I couldn't let him go."

## CLUE-COLLECTING AND PROJECTING

> It is the terrible deception of love that it begins by engaging us in play not with a woman of the outside world but with a doll inside our brain—the only woman moreover that we have always at our disposal, the only one we shall ever possess...an artificial creation which by degrees, and to our own hurt, we shall force the real woman to resemble.
>
> —Marcel Proust, *In Search of Lost Time*

Projection—how we sometimes see in someone what isn't there—is another fallacy that begins (but doesn't end) when you're new together. Understand that you aren't in your right mind when you're lusting after and romanticizing someone. Those feelings are a reflection of your body's intense desire to connect with another body, not necessarily a reflection of the day-to-day reality of living with someone. Thus we rationalize that our beloved is exactly right for us. You may or may not be aware of how much a role such considerations played in your relationships, both present and past. When you're projecting, you're missing the actual person in front of you.

One of the key aspects of loving in flow is that who you are as individuals and who you can become over time, both separately and together, forms a complementary unit. Your personalities, attitudes, and values mesh, if not at first, then eventually. Therefore, we all tend to go through a detective stage to determine who this other person *is*. No need to hire a private eye, though. Assuming your beloved isn't a clever serial killer, most of what you're seeking to determine will show up if you stay alert and avoid distorting what you see into what you *wish* it were.

Or you might be overlaying what you most fear. Take a clear-eyed look at your partner's same sex parent, but also examine the other parent's marital interactions. This can provide you with vital clues to your loved one's current behavior—or partial truths. For instance, your partner may expect you to behave like his opposite sex parent, and thus will interpret a miniscule similarity as foretelling doom. In our case, my tendency to carry on some of my father's critical behaviors caused Stephen, whose mother had the same critical streak, to worry about what he called my negativity. Though the issue first came up only a month into the relationship, it took on a huge importance some time after we were married, leading us inexorably toward the worst part of our marriage. More on this later.

One of my interviewees told me she and her husband were engaged within two weeks of meeting each other. "I'd always dreamed of having a life of peace, because I was raised in a family where my father was a rager. I hated it. Who knew I was marrying one?" Still, as we'll see later when we get to the chapter on dealing with major crises, this couple managed to do what so many try and fail to do: deal effectively, once and for all, with the issue that subconsciously compelled them to choose someone just like dear old Mom or Dad.

Being the *object* of such deep analysis can be disconcerting—and may bring up personal issues that are hard to face. From one of my journal entries: "I'm feeling stripped naked to the bone. Stephen is so aware of who and what I am; he's been analyzing me down to my very soul. Am I intelligent enough? Am I scintillating enough? And worse, he suspects I'm holding back because I'm not vocal during lovemaking, but that's the way I *am* and now I fear my own self-consciousness more than ever." Eventually, he forgot those extroverts he used to date and grew to appreciate my distinct style.

In retrospect, my whole life was decided by the way Stephen ate a Tommy's burger. We took my preteen sons to the original Tommy's on Beverly Boulevard in Los Angeles, where patrons stand at high counters, pull down handfuls of paper towels, and eat sloppy chili burgers. Stephen, who in those days would order two double chili cheeseburgers, ate the leftovers from my kids. I thought it meant one thing—that he would accept my kids wholeheartedly—but it meant much more (and less). Yes, he wasn't a fussbudget about germs and such, and would take on my kids as though they were his own. That was true. But his hearty and carefree eating style mainly meant he was a hearty and carefree eater. (Later, ironically, I would struggle to change this about him.)

So much of what goes on in the early part of any relationship involves overactive wish-fulfillment, which can get in the way of accurate clue-gathering. When I wrote to him after three weeks, "Sometimes I talk to you in my mind—you're a good listener," did I imagine I could fill in his part of the conversation? *Now* we can both do that with startling accuracy. Stephen often falsettos his voice and pretends to be me: "Why are you having a Coke now when it's so close to bedtime? You *know* you won't be able to sleep." Then he responds to "my" voice in his own voice, "Yes, I know, but I need a little boost now, so don't worry." I listen to both parts of the "conversation" and think about two-year-olds who say, "No, no, no," as they reach for a cookie before dinner. Sometimes I can't help but think deep thoughts about incompletely integrated consciences, but more often, I'm amused.

Stephen so longed to spend his life with an artist of some sort. It was no wonder, then, that he turned me into an artist, too, in a brilliant example of projection: "My dear Susan: What a wonderful letter. Who says you're not an artist?" Which is not to deny that his projections had their effect on me: over the years I've found myself evolving more and more into what he once thought I was—was he prescient, or am I simply malleable?

Perhaps when we project, we're tuning in subliminally to less obvious aspects of the other's personality. When that's the case, the results are quite positive, as we'll see in the next chapter when we deal with the value of seeing the best in our partner.

## QUALITIES FOR KEEPS

We can't predict precisely which characteristics are going to be called for in any particular set of future experiences. A metaphor that applies (and might appeal to the technologically conversant) is to think of the two of you in terms of television sets as-yet-untuned to the local channel lineup. But rather than checking the instruction manual to see which channels your partner gets, you have an opportunity to set your channels in unison as you grow, develop, and share experiences together. Just so long as you determine in advance that your lifemate-to-be is cable-ready for a vast number of channels, including some as yet unnumbered, perhaps not to be needed for decades (such as the one that dictates behavior when one partner has a terminal illness). But take heart: if you're already part of a couple, you and your partner can upgrade yourselves at any time. The human personality is hugely adaptable, in spite of the folklore suggesting we can't change. We can indeed change *ourselves* (slowly and with great difficulty, and only if strongly motivated—but we can do it).

And so, eventually, during our first year, Stephen and I began relating in ways that foreshadowed our present sense of flow. "Do you remember," I wrote to him after a few months of dating, "when I said that you shouldn't lean so hard that I fall over? Well, now I feel more of a balance is being achieved: I need your support very much and you obviously need mine too, and sometimes we need each other's help at exactly the same moment, but there isn't really a serious conflict." One of the aspects of loving in flow is exactly this give-and-take equilibrium, one that is not achieved once and for all, but must be recalibrated as circumstances change.

Eventually, all this emotional back-and-forthing may result in a marriage proposal or some similar expression of commitment. In our case, Stephen chose June 16 to propose to me, because that's Bloomsday, when Bloom proposes to Molly in James Joyce's *Ulysses*. We were to be married in the fall, and as the engagement proceeded, though some bothersome issues continued to surface, we were mostly insipidly cheerful. Once you're engaged, you've gotten just what you wanted. Or have you?

# 2
# INTIMATIONS OF REALITY

My first husband was a dog, all snuffling, clumsy, ardent devotion. At first (to be fair to him) we were a couple of puppies, gamboling and frisking in our love for each other and collapsing in a panting heap on the bed every night. But time and puppyhood passed, as it tends to do, and as he grew into a devoted, sad-eyed, rather smelly hound, I found myself becoming a cat.... I became more and more irritable, until everything he did displeased me. Finally, even the sound of his throat-clearing sigh when I had rebuffed him once again would make my fur stand on end.

—Lisa Tuttle, "Husbands"

We enter our committed partnerships starry-eyed. This is *it*, or we wouldn't have pledged ourselves (official ceremony or not). Now's the time to shove our doubts aside. Like the majority of couples, we are so sure we'll beat the odds and enjoy everlasting joy and happiness because, after all, we're not like any other couple that ever existed. You don't have to believe in the concept of soulmates to think this way. You have *chosen* to be soulmates and the rest flows from that—or so goes the expectation.

And then, after the rice is swept off the floor, but often before the photos are placed in the wedding album, reality begins stealing in through the keyholes. For some it takes the form of the realization that they'll never be allowed to have sex with anyone else as long as they live. For others it's more about noticing the odd noises their partner makes when slurping soup, or realizing that now, in this one life they've chosen, they will never have a partner who shares their passion for music. Rather, they've permanently sutured themselves to someone who has a tendency to chatter throughout the blindingly beautiful second movement of Beethoven's *Seventh Symphony*.

The internal natterings of disillusionment may begin almost imperceptibly, or with a shout. As you read this chapter, see if you can recall the doubts, trivial or otherwise, that you repressed when you decided to commit to your mate. Did any of them come back to plague you later? How soon, and how persistently? It's been said that the honeymoon period lasts from six months to two years. What was your first realization that your partner wasn't perfect? Or that this relationship wasn't what you thought it was going to be?

As we've already seen, the type of person you are matters when it comes to flow potential. In the disenchantment period, the best attitudes to have are flexibility, resilience, humor, open-mindedness, reality-groundedness, and loyalty. Now is also when your motivation begins to count. How committed are you to this relationship? If the answer is not enough, the obstacles will seem too hulking to overcome.

## THE FIRST FIGHT

It doesn't necessarily signal anything momentous, but your first pitched spat is often the earliest sign of disenchantment. You may agonize at the time that this early strain foreshadows some deep incompatibility. More likely you'll get some useful clues to how you both deal with conflict and what you need to learn to do better.

Some couples enter the sparring ring very soon. When Tina Tessina, a psychotherapist in Long Beach, California, met Richard Sharrard, a ballroom dance instructor, at a self-development retreat, they were both in their mid-thirties and had both been married before. Now married for nineteen years, Tessina, the author of relationship books such as *How to Be a Couple and Still Be Free*, tells me that their worst-ever fight took place coming home from their honeymoon. She says this was the only serious "I'm leaving you" kind of fight they've ever had. She attributes it to the stress of planning the wedding, when his mother and two aunts stayed at their home and six people were sharing one bathroom. But not only that, the newlyweds were struggling to put their respective businesses on hold so they could get away for a week.

"We went on the honeymoon," explains Tessina, "and coming home, we had just had it. I threatened to jump out of the car on the freeway. It was one of those dramatic things, to do with his not paying me the right kind of attention. Stupid stuff. I was screaming at him, but when the phone rang, I answered in my therapist's voice, and that showed me that I didn't have to be screaming at him. From that point on, we started to fix the fight."

George Seeds Sr., a retired psychiatrist, claims he and his wife Norma only had a couple of misunderstandings and "that was right after that first year of madness." Seeds recalls that during the most furious argument they ever had, he said to himself, "Get out of here." So he left the house and jogged up and down an adjacent alley in Beverly Hills, "up and down, up and down until all the anger was gone. And then I came back home. That was the maddest I can ever remember getting. And I don't remember at all what it was about."

In my own marriage, it took three months of dating to reach this scary-at-the-time milestone. It was our first holiday season, when expectations run unnaturally high anyway.

A bit of background: it is difficult for me to make decisions about gifts. No one ought to respond to my question of "Should I get this?" with a casual "Why not?" I can think of dozens of reasons "why not" to every possible selection. It's too expensive, he'll be allergic to it, he'll think I got it at a bargain store, he has one, he never wanted one, it's the wrong size, color, shape, brand, and on and on. (Deeper background: growing up, I could never seem to buy the perfect gift for my parents, and they'd as often return what I bought for them as keep it. We're all practical in my family.)

Thus, shopping for Stephen's Christmas gift precipitated a more-than-minor trauma. As should befit a remarkable relationship, I wanted it to be an astonishing gift. But with no child support coming in, my freelance writing was barely keeping my two boys in Cheerios. On an impulse, I drove over to Farmer's Market, a place I never shop. I saw a $75 snakeskin wallet, so soft to the touch, but $75 was more than I'd ever spent on a gift for anyone in my life. It was more than I could afford. But Stephen wouldn't already have one (I'd seen how tattered his old wallet was). Tortured by indecision, I finally bought it as the store was about to close.

Stephen gave me some sweet little crystal wine glasses. He seemed to like the wallet and began using it. When he arrived at my house the next weekend, he tossed his laundry into the washing machine. Later, when I took his sopping clothes out to put them into the dryer, there was a suspicious—and drenched— lump in a pocket.

"Is this all you think of my gift?" I asked, perhaps ungently.

Rather than responding sheepishly, he made some irrelevant comment about the paucity of nice things in my house. I already felt inferior when it came to aesthetics, so I tossed some barb about his stupid wine glasses, which I said he'd obviously purchased with selfish intent—after all, he's the drinker with his mental pinky in the air. He took his hurt feelings and withdrew. Somehow, I didn't know what I'd done wrong (using hindsight, I have no trouble figuring it out), and I was afraid to ask until the next day. We spent an evening under a damp cloud of confused silence, with me desperately trying to find a way to reconnect. It was my first experience with withdrawal as a conflict strategy. I felt like I was hugging a ghost.

We tried to talk about the problem the next day, but he said I was a bundle of neuroses when I tried to explain the problem I have with money and gifts. It was scary because I remembered that one of his bigger fears for our future was that what he called my negativity would drag him down.

Only a day or two before this fight, Stephen had said he loved me more than he's ever loved anyone, but now the tension was horrible. Our usual connectedness didn't fully return for days. We realized we had a lot to learn about seeing each other's point of view and disagreeing fairly and effectively. In spite of how much we thought we knew about each other, what we were learning about one another's sensitivities was disillusioning. It can seem as though the other person's tender spots are due to hyper-reactivity (which they are, in effect, but that presupposes that there is a "right" amount of reaction one should have to any behavior).

Of course, we didn't know we were a cliché even then. Author Mimi Schwartz describes her dismay at her own first fight in her frank memoir, *Thoughts from a Queen-Sized Bed*:

> Our first knock-down-drag-out battle took place six months after our honeymoon, and I was shocked. We both were. It was my first cooking victory other than franks and beans or spaghetti, and I brought it to the table as if it were beef Wellington for King Louis. But new wife or not, Stu wasn't about to fake it.
>
> "What's this?" He pulled away from the casserole as if it were the plague.
>
> "Macaroni and cheese!" I beamed, heaping three scoops onto his plate. I was so into my accomplishment I didn't notice how the voice dropped, the shoulders hunched, the jaw set.
>
> "I don't eat the stuff!" he said. "What else do you have?"
>
> "Jake's Bar down the block, you jerk. I spent two hours on this. This is from scratch."

Then she describes how they argued: macaroni flew around, he stormed out, and she cried. I think there are two striking aspects to Schwartz's description. The first is that I could readily write diverse endings to the same fight (as, of course, I could to my own): apologies all around, mature problem-solving (she freezes the macaroni and he eats cold cereal and they laugh about how much they still have to learn about each other), and so on. The second aspect, more surprising, is that, after many years together, she tells us, they're still having the same fight. He doesn't always like what she makes for dinner and says so, and she gets silent and he gets mad, and then they fight over something trivial and unrelated, eventually making up by wrapping themselves around each other in the middle of the night. Deeply connected and loving, they still haven't found ways to get around these disputes without going through the entire routine.

You and your partner may be able to begin to find common ground by describing your first long-ago fight in as much detail as you can retrieve. Either write your accounts separately or talk it over together. What precipitated it? What did you discover about each other? Do you still fight over the same issue? How did this argument fit into your relationship: did it precipitate the start of disillusionment, or was it over and done and rarely or never mentioned again? Can you laugh about it now? Why or why not? Are you laughing at yourself, at your interaction, or at the impossibility of agreeing on what happened? By going over the answers to such questions, you may gain sudden insight into the deep roots of some of the more repetitive annoyances of your lives together today.

One of the first times my insistent practicality frustrated Stephen was all the way back when we shopped for our wedding rings. The choice felt momentous to both of us, making the occasion very stressful. That evening we were both exhausted. Suddenly Stephen turned silent. He later said, "It's all so ordinary. You're so damn pragmatic."

Our values had clashed: my own panic, picked up from my parents due to their own beginnings, and nurtured by having never had enough money in my first marriage and barely enough to survive on in my post-divorce months, versus Stephen's persistent romanticism, his deep belief that one shouldn't think of money when choosing a symbol of eternal love. He wanted to believe I was just like him, but reality kept getting in the way of his fantasies.

# PUTTING YOUR BEST KNEE FORWARD

"Oh," he said, "it's not what I expected love to be like. I always imagined it would be like a Carnegie Hall début. That would be the day when everyone would recognize how great you were, what a genius. The applause would be deafening; some ladies would weep. You're more like what happens every day, practicing alone in a deserted settlement house." I'm sorry I asked, Wanda said, more than a little hurt. For he was definitely her Carnegie Hall. "Hold on, let me finish. You're practicing there, see, it's cold and damp and you wonder what in the hell you're doing there, knocking yourself out day after day. Then you listen, you hear. It's the music, the same music. It really doesn't matter where you play it, does it?"

—James Wilcox, *Guest of a Sinner*

Relationships that begin with each person feeling overwhelmingly cherished often become less engulfing and more sustainable once the honeymoon period is over. If you're not expecting *any* change, though, disappointment can hit perversely hard. Are you resilient? It's a personality attribute you can strengthen with effort and knowledge. Is your motivation sufficiently powerful to override the blow that your partner is only human? When you recognize imperfection, do you *care* enough to continue?

In the getting-to-know-you phase of a relationship, we tend to wear our best selves. It's not that we're lying or actively covering up, but we want this person we're falling in love with to like the self we're exhibiting, so we pick the most desirable one we've got in our repertoire. It works both ways, of course: those of us with a self-esteem deficit especially tend to over-idealize our beloved. We *need* to idealize the one we love—he represents the sum of all our longings. But even though our partner is made up of some superb qualities, can they *all* be that positive?

It's only at the end of the so-called high romance—the end of that period of idealizing based on repression of the negative—that a real relationship can begin. That's when you've reached a place where you're able to negotiate your weaknesses, neediness, and differences. You can be honest, no longer feeling you'll be rejected if the cracks in your pedestals show. A tiny example: that whole year that Stephen and I were dating and he was spending Friday and Saturday nights at my house, I hid my knee pillow in the closet. Due to an achy lower back, I'd gotten in the habit of sleeping with a small pillow between my knees, but I didn't feel this was sexy and didn't want him to see me using it.

As we gain trust and security in the relationship, we allow more aspects of our personalities to be seen—bringing our knee pillows out of the closet—as a way, consciously or not, to find out for sure if our partner will still love us after he discovers who we "really" are. It's a possibility that by showing some aspect of yourself that you'd kept out of sight, you may disillusion your mate. When your partner expresses a bit of surprise or disappointment at a revelation, that may feel disillusioning to *you*. After all, weren't you promised unconditional love, no matter what?

Perhaps you too hid parts of yourself in the closet during courtship or early marriage. What happened when you stopped hiding? Were the disclosures disconcerting or did they add to your intimacy? If you're still holding some pieces of yourself back, what are you afraid of? Do you believe your partner has let you see all of himself by now?

Not everyone thinks of this adjustment period in terms of disillusionment. Zhita Rea, an educator and librarian in Los Angeles, has been married for more than eighteen years to Jim, a 66-year-old retired electrician. She says she never experienced a disillusionment period. "It was pretty wonderful. There was such a sense of being able to be a person." She does admit, though, that during the first year she "had to get over the feeling that somehow he'll discover what I look like in the morning, and was it safe for me to be upset and get angry?" The relaxation of true flow can't happen until we've let ourselves be fully experienced by our partners.

# WHAT HAVE YOU DONE FOR ME LATELY?

> The more I had come to know about her, I thought, the better I knew her, although the opposite might well have been the case. For all I knew, there might well be even more to know. A bottomless thought. I couldn't remember when I had stopped imagining her secret, hidden sides, when I had grown used to her.
>
> —Jens Christian Grondahl, *Silence in October*

Another fact of life post-honeymoon is that the thrilling emotional highs you've gotten accustomed to begin diminishing. It's more what you each *don't* do—or no longer do—than what you do. When you know each other and become comfortable, you begin to become predictable to each other, so that you no longer get the reaction that comes from *rising* intimacy. Social psychology tells us that once we're accustomed to a certain level of intimacy, we no longer react emotionally except to a noticeable increase or decrease.

What might be surprising is that we do this leveling off on purpose (if not consciously) to keep our emotional lives manageable. By selectively ignoring the aspects or behaviors of our partner that used to ignite our passion, we keep the positives down, as well as those less desirable negatives. Whereas we once saw our beloveds as extraordinary, later on we rebuild our images of them as ordinary, human, and in fact, quite imperfect. Such a switch does keep us from being surprised in a negative way, but it can also result in our feeling let down. We start to wonder, is this all there is?

We would all like to be loved unconditionally. Unconditional love is what we might have gotten from our parents (if we were lucky), and have been seeking to replicate (or experience for the first time) ever since. Clearly, we're happiest when our partners value and accept us in spite of our flaws. But what a bother it can be to keep behaving as we did during courtship, doing those very things that may have contributed to making you appear so lovable, including, as Robert C. Solomon puts it, to "maintain conversation at such an exalted level ('When was the last time we talked about the importance of Proust for the existential-ists?')." That entire afternoon we spent in bed deconstructing the first page of *Ulysses* is a high point that has never been repeated. (But, honestly, neither is it likely to have the same power to turn my innards to jelly as it did then.)

What activities did the two of you enjoy when you were first together that you no longer do? Which of those do you miss and wish you could do again? Discuss what's stopping you, whether it's money, time, energy, age, children, or plain habit. Or, tell the truth—do you want to do those same things, or is it that you want to duplicate that sense of exciting newness? If the latter is the case, searching out fresh activities to share would be more likely to get you both what you crave. I'll talk more later about the importance of novelty and complexification in keeping a relationship growing and flowing.

In the post-honeymoon months, you might also find yourself disillusioned by how you feel day to day. Those everyday moods may change from high to ho-hum, even if you still have mainly positive feelings about the specialness of your partner.

Stephen and I had only been married about nine months when the tediousness and frustration of real life got to me (especially real life in a reconstituted family with nearly-teenaged boys), and I began to resent that Stephen wasn't as attentive as he had been when it was just him and me playing all weekend alone together.

This is what I wrote at the time: "I'm feeling a lot of repressed frustration. On weekends when both kids are here, I am never free to do anything I want to do. After a day of being interrupted by household demands (take me here, buy me that, do the laundry, make breakfast, lunch, dinner, how do you spell—, stop bothering him already!), I feel like a maid who's also being asked to earn half the money. How can I do it all? And why should I? It's like Stephen's not here for me. He's playing the piano and drinking wine."

# SLIPPING BACK TO NORMAL

What is missing is that ecstatic sense of being dragged screaming toward one's destiny.

—Gail Godwin, *Violet Clay*

How compatible are your expectations of togetherness?
Differences in the amount of separation you each prefer can
affect the pleasure you take in and out of each other's company.
Some couples do almost everything together. My parents are
like that, and Stephen and I followed that pattern at first. But
then this unexpectedly changed. One day, just like that,
Stephen decided to go out to the garden and spend a billion
hours without me (I hate gardening). Then he bought an elec-
tronic chess game and spent every waking hour with it, even
taking it to bed. (Later he discovered computers and all was
lost, to my tilted reckoning.) These initial forays into separate
lives hit me hard, I'm embarrassed to admit. I took them personally. How could he spend so much time amid flowers and
weeds when he had *me* sitting alone upstairs? It must mean he
was bored with me.

One partner typically is the first to drift—or leap—from total
oneness toward some individual interests. What some couples
have at first may be an unhealthy enmeshment. To some this
feels comforting, but to plenty of others it is suffocating.
Eventually a balance needs to be found. Initially, I tend to put my
own interests on hold when I'm in love. Stephen must have also,
but as soon as the newness simmered down, he reconnected with
himself, which is ultimately positive. But I was not prepared, and
I felt at a loss for a long time. I missed the early closeness and
complained so that he would feel guilty for abandoning me.

The disenchantment period is one of ups and downs, especially
in a relationship that is destined to persevere (as opposed to those
that go straight downhill, never recover, and result in flaming
divorce within the first three years). A few months after we were

married, I wrote, "It's been great between us for two-and-a-half weeks now. It's a good feeling being able to recapture that original intimacy. The sense of being free to be myself keeps growing." Odd that I so much enjoyed being able to be myself but couldn't make the connection that I needed to offer Stephen the same freedom.

And then, a little over a year after we were married, another dip: "I'm feeling peevish again. Stephen is playing backgammon with Simon, and Kevin is attempting to perfect a 'bomb.' On Friday night Simon picked up a lighter and promptly set his hair on fire. I'm bored. I could clean something; but I'd resent that Stephen hasn't cleaned in ages. He's been spending all his time on the front garden project. Just like the old days in my old life. There doesn't seem like any time for fun."

My error was comparing this relationship to my previous marriage, in which duty and work took precedence over pleasurable shared times, and then jumping to the conclusion that the way I lived now wasn't improvable.

"Even in the best of marriages," point out authors Richard Schwartz, M.D., and Jacqueline Olds, M.D., "people are almost always moving closer together or further apart." As comforting as it might be to imagine we will settle down into a fixed level of closeness, it often doesn't happen smoothly.

Suspecting that life together isn't matching your expectations is one thing. Talking about it is another. For some couples it takes years—years filled with children and work and busybusybusyness—before a full and frank discussion about disillusionment ever takes place. When psychologist Karen Kayser studied fifty couples in which spouses were no longer in love with their partners, she discovered it was the piling-up of the effects of various stress points that led to such a high level of disaffection. And that took anywhere from one year (60 percent expressed doubts about their marriage during the first year) to thirty-eight years, with an average of eleven years. More than half the respondents reported that they kept silent, and a third used denial as a coping mechanism. Neither method worked in the long run. She found in those marriages that came apart, the disillusionment phase was followed by hurt and anger phases, before the marriage crumbled from utter lack of affection.

We can see how disillusionment builds toward trouble in the life of Susan Tyler Hitchcock. The fifty-one-year-old Charlottesville, Virginia, writer detailed her own marriage's changes in a memoir, *Coming About: A Family Passage at Sea*. Married twenty-one years now, she awards her relationship with her engineer/project manager husband David a high satisfaction level. But ten years into their marriage, it had become clear that neither of them was untroubled.

"David comes from a family of six children and a very solid devoted parent dyad," explains Susan. "I come from a family where my parents divorced when I was twelve, and they were never happy together in all my memory. Our expectations of togetherness were so different."

Their disenchantment started when she became immersed in having babies, says Susan. David was running his own business, starting with five hundred dollars, building it to a million dollars. "He would come home at nine o'clock and wonder why I couldn't even keep up a conversation," she says. "I was exhausted." It took him a couple of years before he began talking about it, other than some "little grumbles," she concedes.

When he finally spoke up, it was the classic, "This isn't what I thought marriage would be." He complained that he and Susan weren't doing things together, that they were "parallel parenting," taking turns being with their two young children. There wasn't enough sex in their marriage, either.

Susan's reaction at the time was a knee-jerk defensive one, she now believes. "I'm always so tired, why are you blaming me? I'm already giving so much."

By a dozen years into the Hitchcock marriage, the wounds had festered until the couple was faced with a relationship-threatening crisis. Later we'll see how they and others get beyond such extreme plights.

## SOME ILLUSIONS ARE GOOD

> I can hear her saying, "I'm just being honest. I thought you admired my honesty. Don't you want me to be *honest?*"
>
> "No," I'd say. "I want you to *indulge* me. Say my efforts couldn't be improved upon—no matter how much it compromises your precious integrity. Lie, goddammit, lie! Tell me I'm the best. Tell me no one appreciates my true genius. JUST ONCE GIVE ME YOUR UNQUALIFIED APPROVAL!!" She couldn't. She was maddeningly sensible. That's why I fell in love with her. That's why, in the end, I couldn't stand being in the same room with her.
>
> —Patrick O'Leary, *Door Number Three*

You can't be disillusioned unless you harbor illusions in the first place. But good marital illusions exist too, and, as it turns out, they're commonplace. They serve a delightfully positive role in loving in flow.

Take Laurie, who, in real world terms, is quite unlike her mate. American-born, blonde, several years older than her Syrian-born husband Hamid, she pursued adventure as a journalist for six years in the Middle East. Laurie has a playful side. Hamid, dark, thin, and one of nineteen siblings, not only follows a different religion, but is nearly always serious. Yet here's how Laurie describes their total compatibility: "It's almost like we're one person, except we go to the bathroom differently."

To cite a recent study, nearly nine out of ten respondents felt that their marriages were better than average. Of course, that's a logical paradox (this was a study of nearly all the married students in a particular community college class—they hadn't been screened for happiness beforehand). Ask around: hardly anyone expects to get divorced, even with widespread media reporting of 40–50 percent divorce rates.

The truth is that we have some control over how we experience ourselves, our lovers, our world. Why not, then, choose a more positive version out of the many possibilities we can imagine? It's not as if you can perceive your partner's qualities directly—most human attributes are too subjective. You see behavior and you interpret it, guess at motives, and infer what your partner's personality characteristics are as a result. How we feel about someone is not an objective science.

Stephen A. Mitchell observed in *Can Love Last?* that it helps, in idealizing your lover, to do so in a "collaborative" fashion, in which the qualities you imagine your lover has match what he himself likes to think he has. Idealizing, however, is a delicate balance that may lean too far in the direction of fantasy. The narrator of the Nick Hornby novel *How to Be Good*, unhappy with her husband, tells us, "When David's asleep, I can turn him back into the person I still love: I can impose my idea of what David should be, used to be, onto his sleeping form, and the seven hours I spend with that David just about gets me through the next day with the other David." Would any of us want our mates to feel this way about us? Do you only love what you project about your partner? Might there be a value in being fully seen—enlarged pores and all—especially for those realists among us who can't bear feeling like imposters when our partners over-idealize us (and I'm not talking about trifling cover-ups of the knee pillow kind, but more essential bits of ourselves)?

When I met my first husband, I had recently enjoyed Kahlil Gibran's pocket-sized classic, *The Prophet*, and my brain played tricks on me: since he was from Lebanon just like Gibran, I projected my favorite values and qualities, as they'd been so sweetly epitomized by Gibran, onto him. To my barely post-high-school sentimental self, it seemed a perfect match. In that case, my imaginings turned out to be an unsustainable illusion. Sometimes we do need to do the cold-eyed (if not cold-hearted) work of recognizing and toning down such delusional thinking about our partners. Only then will we be able to reconcile, accommodate, and adjust without being struck down by crushing disappointment.

Generally, though, it's been found that being (reasonably)

idealized by one's partner, being seen in a more positive light even than we see ourself, predicts the most satisfying marriages. It takes a certain wisdom to integrate the annoying with the delightful, totaling up to a big picture perspective that keeps the positive in the foreground. We like those who see us at our best. Bea, 61, provides an example. Her sixty-five-year-old gregarious husband Herb will be sitting across the aisle from her at breakfast and suddenly say, "God, you're so beautiful."

"I look like shit," responds Bea in her typical blunt fashion. Tilting between seeing Herb's hyperbole as a minor failing she's gotten used to and recognizing it as his way of loving her, Bea is nonetheless pleased to have her own best version of herself thus confirmed.

Letitia and Lenny, in their late thirties and married eleven years, are busy with their jobs and a three-year-old daughter. Letitia tells me that Lenny says something almost every day "really nice or deep or thoughtful about how amazing I am to him. I say, 'Stop telling me that!' Of course I don't want him to stop, and he knows it."

If the particular attribute we're talking about is a more or less observable one, say, hand-eye coordination, or cooking ability, then it's suitable for a partner's judgment to be close to objective reality (although even those two examples can be fraught with subjective biases). One study found that among those who perceive themselves negatively, intimacy increases as their partners evaluate them more negatively. We like to have our perceptions verified by the person we love most. We need our weaknesses as well as our strengths recognized. If the way they see us is beyond reasonable, we tend to withdraw. It's not intimate or real. Pedestals are for the birds.

Solid couples typically shift toward seeking out increasing reality as they move from courtship to marriage, but they do it unconsciously and gradually. We fill in the blanks as we go along, but we don't instantly begin seeing a generous partner as a tightwad or an affectionate one as a prickly one, unless our connection is going drastically wrong.

When author Sherry Suib Cohen (*Secrets of a Very Good Marriage*) says about her lawyer husband Larry that he is "the smartest and funniest man I know," who's going to argue with her description? Or when she says that he "always looks stunning, better than anyone else there," who would waste time debating how much of that glitter is in her love-filled eyes? Especially since he returns the idealizing favor by telling her repeatedly "how beautiful and wonderful and fabulous I am. I don't really believe it, I know what I look like," she says. "But I really do think he means it." And that's what counts.

If you're not in a relationship where you find a lot of idealizing going on, no need to fret. I had to search for the examples I've given here, since the preponderance of the couples in my sample seem to lean more toward what I'll call, for want of a more accurate word, realism. That is, they can name their partners' flaws as well as their good points, and they see those negatives and positives and their own as complementing each other for a harmonious balance. Marylis, a painter in the Midwest, who met her husband-to-be while they were in high school and has been with him for thirty years, observes, "Since we met young, we had years before we *could* get married, and by the time we got married, we knew each other thoroughly, so we were going into it with open eyes. We knew each other's flaws."

In the best marriages, you may discover your inadequacies flip-flopped by an adoring partner into assets. When George Seeds Sr. talks about his wife Norma, who passed away a few years ago, he claims that rather than idealizing her memory, he sees her even more realistically today. "She could be a little anxious at times, a little insecure," he says. "But it was almost like an attraction." And then he laughs and adds, "My cute little Norma...", his voice heartbreakingly turning sentimental.

## EXPECT LESS TO GET MORE

One way to flow through the disillusionment phase of your relationship with less torment is to lower your expectations. It's not a matter of giving in and accepting less than you deserve, but of carefully reflecting on your unstated "conditions." Sam Keen, in *To Love and Be Loved*, suggests couples fill in this blank: "I will continue to love you if—." Problems arise when your romantic expectations are dashed, and you mistakenly attribute this to the failings of your mate. Stephen once said to me in utter frustration, "I've never experienced this in a relationship before," and I had to remind him that he'd never stuck with anyone else beyond the honeymoon period of two years. The longer you're in a relationship, the more you'll encounter phases and experiences you've never dealt with previously.

Having known much misery due to a frustrating mismatch in my previous marriage, my own expectations were much more down-to-earth in the second. Still, I got accustomed to—and was thus spoiled by—an unsustainably high level of attentiveness during the year Stephen and I dated. And when it passed, I felt cheated. It wasn't until I learned to take on more of the responsibility for my own happiness, that I became happy. Why are the truest insights the kind you'd blush to wear on a T-shirt?

The far end of disillusionment for too many couples is that awful sense of being bereft of hope. Once the first tiny tectonic shift in perception occurs, it may not take years before, as a character in the Rick Moody short story "The Carnival Tradition" puts it, "What was attractive became repulsive, this particular habit, this particular inhibition in the beloved, you were married and your heart was in *the freezer in the basement.*" In upcoming chapters, we'll see how it is possible to slip from ordinary disillusionment to the lowest imaginable point of your life, and then recover to spend the rest of your lives loving in flow.

# *3*
# COPING WITH CONFLICT

So this was going to be one of those rows: the same positions, the same lines, same recriminations, same right hooks. Bare fists. The bell rings. Samad comes out of his corner.

—Zadie Smith, *White Teeth*

One of my aunts battled loudly with her husband. Not just occasionally; I mean more than fifty years of constant contention. Then he died and she plunged into a deep depression from which she never recovered, thus proving how resistant to change a system of two can become, and how some people can get used to anything.

Several of the couples I interviewed were familiar with similar marriages of unlike minds, often those of their own parents. While I don't know anyone who *chooses* to become addicted to a lifetime of flying spittle, it's natural to find ourselves involved in conflict with our partners from time to time. Frank Pittman, an Atlanta psychiatrist and author, describes his 37-year marriage this way: "Like anyone else who is totally, permanently married, we bicker, and, if we are lucky, run through the full range of human emotions toward one another on a daily basis."

Take any two individuals with differing hormonal make-up, diverse family backgrounds, dissimilar education and experiences, divergent values and goals, and set them a task of making a lifetime of decisions that affect them both—and keep in mind that *everything* involves decisions, from when you get up in the morning to how you make a living, plan for the future, or have fun. Certainly you're going to have disagreements. A deep-seated desire for a loving long-term relationship requires learning how to negotiate those disagreements, how to move from those separate corners toward a genuine embrace in the middle of the ring.

## WHY WE CLASH

The world is full of marriages incomprehensible to outsiders, but enduring: warder and prisoner, swinger and homebody, beauty and the beast. Love, in the conventional romantic sense, does not seem to come into the equation. They are held together by need, each silently colluding with the other's unacknowl-edged longings....It has less to do with Romeo and Juliet than with Lord and Lady Macbeth.

—A. Alvarez, *Life After Marriage: Love in an Age of Divorce*

Some professionals figure the root of all this conflict is that we're attempting to rewrite the stories we grew up with. We seek out partners who evoke in some way the roles our parents or siblings played in our early lives. Only now, as adults, we'd like things to turn out better. It's not that simple, of course. You might "marry your mother" one time, then try "marrying your father" the next, and in both cases, you might be attracted to mostly negative qualities and contrary interactions so that, after much struggle, you're left as pained as ever.

When we commit to an adult partner, we bring along some dynamics from our family of origin. We want some of what our parents had, whether that means a certain amount of together-ness, a meeting of minds, a convenient division of labor where whatever you don't like to do is exactly what your spouse loves to do, or perhaps a perception of power where "bossiness" is inter-preted as "caretaking."

There are other parts of our early family lives we don't want to replicate—but do anyway. Were you disappointed as a child? Did you feel unseen? Then you might seek out someone who doesn't see you authentically, or you might wise up and find someone who *does* perceive you as you would like. Eventually, you might align yourself with someone who evokes enough of the positive aspects of a member of your original family, along with the inevitable flaws, so that the balance shifts and the relationship is a nurturing one. Or, if you're stubborn enough about your commitment, you might learn enough during *any* (non-abusive) relationship to turn it into a mutually positive one—no matter who your mate sometimes reminds you of.

Marylis, the Midwestern painter in her mid-forties I mentioned earlier, has been married for thirty years to Conrad, a lawyer. She knows by now that when they have one of their rare scuffles, a lot of childhood material still gurgles out. "I have issues about my mother not paying attention to me when I was sad or emotional," she explains, "so if I don't feel like Conrad's meeting my needs correctly, something balloons in me and gets really angry. When we're yelling, we're not even discussing issues that well."

It happens only a couple times a year now: Conrad gets agitated, he snaps at Marylis, she cries. Then, instead of hugging her, which is what she's craving and didn't get from Mom, he begins firing questions at her: "What are you doing, what is this about?" "It feels abusive," Marylis admits, and that only makes her cry more, and then she starts getting angry while she's crying.

"So what should be a five-minute thing turns into hours of being angry at each other, and not getting back to the 'right' place," Marylis explains. Such repetitive flare-ups tamp back down by the end of the day as they begin to converse more calmly and express how sorry they are. "We finally realized our repetitive pattern is all based on impulse," says Marylis. "My private theory is he has some real fear when I'm crying, because I'm not usually that sort of person, so it's kind of a scary event. He says, 'I'm gonna try to just remember not to talk to you, just to hug you.' But in the heat of the moment, he never manages to do that."

In a way, such repetitive couple conflicts mirror what goes on between parents and kids, the daily hostilities over who does what, and when, and how. One woman said she labeled her family's arguments A, B, and C, so that when the same topic reappeared, all she had to do was say "Argument A." Recognizing the knee-jerkiness of your patterns is a step toward lessening their frequency and impact. Then you might jointly decide to cut short Argument 103B the next time it begins. Or equally useful, you can learn to laugh at yourselves. Either choice is an improvement on taking yourselves too seriously as you clash over the right way to load dishes into the dishwasher.

The way you think about those thistles in your private Garden of Eden is what makes all the difference to the quality of the relationship, whether the annoyed words blow away with the wind or linger and pollute the days and weeks to follow. It often seems to me that love is a process of moving from "Oh, how much alike we are!" to "Ohmigosh, how impossibly different we are," to "Wow, we're both so incredibly complex and yet we share so much." Getting from the first stage to the third requires some time spent in the second, and that's where conflict is unavoidable.

What makes it even more of a challenge is that most of the families we grew up in didn't model the best conflict resolution skills. While some ignored conflict, others handled it passive-aggressively, while still other families dealt with disagreement violently. Some parents bestow affirming messages on kids who "talk back." But if speaking up got you knocked down, even if only figuratively, then you're liable to hesitate to do so later. If "love" to you, means never having to say "I don't agree with you," then you'll have a harder time being married to someone who speaks his or her mind fearlessly.

Jim and Zhita Rea only have a few remaining conflicts. "Zhita grew up in a home in which being direct and outspoken and disagreeing was a routine occurrence," explains Jim. "But certainly not in my upbringing. One time, after we were married, we visited Zhita's parents over a period of time and there were lots of vigorous disagreements. I felt as if this was a terrible kind of interaction. And it never occurred to her to think of that as being anything negative at all."

In my own relationship, the ink was barely dry on the marriage certificate when we developed a misery-making pattern whereby Stephen would physically and emotionally withdraw. I pursued him into his corner with a vengeance, terrified that if I let him be, it—we—would be all over. From my journal: "Last night my feelings were hurt and I got quiet, so he withdrew and went to bed at eight o'clock and wouldn't respond to my touch or pleadings. We're both feeling inadequate and blaming the other. My heart feels heavy, like I don't have the energy to struggle through this. I'm worried. And he talks of giving up. What does that mean?!"

Less than a month later I recorded that we had a breakthrough: "After the last serious conflict, during which I reached fresh depths of despair about our chances for a happy life—only because Stephen seemed so unhappy with me—we worked out ways of dealing with our differences. Our problem-solving styles are not complementary, but it's not insurmountable."

## HOW TO STOP

> Marriage is a fight to the death.
> —Elizabeth King

"Communication" has become such a buzz word for what couples need to do that it's lost meaning. What you say and how you say it certainly matters, and I'll focus on ways to talk more effectively later. First, though, I want to emphasize that you *can* cut down on headache-causing strife using any number of strategies, most of which don't involve struggling for the right words.

Might some conflicts remain insoluble? Certainly many persistently tricky situations will never be solved as one or both of you would have preferred or could have predicted. But if you're open to creative solutions, you *can* stop fighting the same battles interminably. Stephen half-teases me: "The most revelatory insight for me has been that you can actually *learn*." So can we all.

What you'll read next is an idiosyncratic blend of methods used by couples who have learned how to curtail their wrangling.

➤ **CONCENTRATE ON THE CONNECTION.** At the heart of many conflicts is the effort to control and change our partners, and that's because if they continue to act differently from us, we feel less connected to them. It can feel threatening to stretch that seemingly ephemeral thread that holds the two of us together. "The task for us is to learn to witness the flow," suggests psychologist Linda E. Olds. "We need to be able to be present at the whole array of feelings expressed by loved ones, including irritation and anger, without feeling responsible or guilty or even needing them to be different."

For an example of how this works in reality, consider Howard. At thirty-eight, he's been married just over ten years, with two preschoolers, and he says he and his wife have argued much less in the second five years of their marriage than in the first five.

"We're both very intense, in different ways," explains Howard, "and when we get wrapped up in an argument we both pursue it to illogical extremes. So whichever one of us realizes first that we're doing that, we'll back off and say something to the effect of, 'Hey, I'm on your side, we're making more out of this than there needs to be, there's a simple learning point here, let's focus on that and forget all this other stuff.' It's typically whoever consciously recognizes first that we're running down a rat hole, as we call it. We will go two weeks without any disharmony and then we'll have an intense argument that will last for forty-five minutes and then it's over."

↦ **REMEMBER YOUR PARTNER ISN'T YOUR PARENT.** Have you ever said to your spouse, "You're just like my father"? Without a doubt, your reaction to him is colored by your past experience with a parent. Harder to recognize are the more subtle ways we distort our partners. In *Couple Skills*, authors Matthew McKay, Patrick Fanning, and Kim Paleg suggest being on the lookout for certain indicators that distortion is going on. One of the most distinct is if you feel "a sudden rush of intense negative emotion in response to something your partner says or does." That emotion causes you to want to protect yourself out of proportion to the provocation. Or, when you experience a feeling in the present and it seems old and familiar, look for the possibility you're mixing up your partner with your parent, big brother, first wife, or other figure from your past.

Another time to be wary, suggest the authors, is when you assume you can read your partner's mind, because you may be assuming a reality that's based on a whole other person—your mother or father. Finally, if you fear you're going to be rejected by your partner every time you're in conflict, the fear could be a childhood echo from when you *were* rejected for speaking up.

↦ **DON'T AVOID CONFLICT.** One of the reasons some partners may not always do what they say they're going to do is that they've agreed only in order to avoid conflict. If you're with someone who constantly fails to deliver on what's been promised, recognize that it may be a form of passive aggression. Rather than labeling that behavior, though, see if you can make conflict safer for both of you. A "no" should not garner an angry response if you want your partner to feel he or she has the freedom to be honest with you about their intentions. If you're the one who often fails to keep your word, imagine how frustrating that is to the other person and how it frays the trust between you. Is it conflict you're trying to avoid? What's the fear underlying the avoidance? Deal directly with that issue.

→ **BE AN ANTHROPOLOGIST.** Search out the pattern of your struggles. Psychologist Andrew Christensen suggests you describe rather than reenact. In other words, try to behave like a scientist and analyze your emotions with some detachment. Beware, though, of falling into that familiar and stereotypical pattern where one of you is always very detached (often, but not necessarily, the male). There is a time and place for scientific detachment, which is not when one of you is weeping your heart out.

→ **BE A WEATHERPERSON.** Assess what else is going on in your lives that might be contributing to this particular clash. Do either of you feel emotionally exhausted at the start of a fight due to work pressures, children's demands, not enough sleep, or hormonal shifts? Trust each other's statements of your inner worlds. Deal with as many of those other stresses as possible first, rather than inflicting them on each other. Create ways to get the space you need so you don't say or do anything you'll regret later. One husband admitted to me that to calm himself, he repeats the mantra, "She's having a hard time right now."

It has been found that having good self-control makes it much more likely that you'll be able to react constructively—by brainstorming or trying to understand your partner's views—rather than by lashing out about past upsets. It's true, some folks are more self-controlled, but anyone's in-the-moment ability to self-regulate diminishes when inner resources are depleted by other stresses. It's the same process that makes it so infuriatingly difficult to stick to your eating or exercising resolutions when you're feeling overwhelmed in some area of your life: only so much self-control is available to you at one time.

Even in the best of partnerships, arguments are more likely when the stresses are multiple. One recent weekend, Susan Tyler Hitchcock was struggling with a lot of issues: "I was feeling a lot of grief over world events, and my son is in his senior year, which was making me really sad, and I had PMS. I started taking antidepressants and they haven't fully kicked in. When David sees me so upset about things, what I want him to do is say, 'Oh, Susan, I feel so bad to hear you say this and I'm going to change right away.' But he doesn't react that way." Nevertheless, even when she's most upset with him, herself, and the relationship, "what happens is I have such a down deep confidence that the relationship's going to last that I can say what I need to and I can go through the feelings."

Zoey and Josef, a Massachusetts couple married ten years with two school-aged daughters, both woke up snappish and grumpy one Saturday. In the past, those moods alone would have been ingredients, as Zoey puts it, "for a perfectly awful weekend of bickering and/or full-on fighting, all resulting in hurt feelings and lingering anger and resentment." Josef found a small ding on her car that she didn't remember caus-ing, the kids were fighting, Zoey spilled some paint on the garage floor, but all-out war didn't result this time. Josef went so far as to allow that perhaps he caused the ding, and that garage floors are meant to get messy.

"At one point in the afternoon, right after he had gotten up from his nap, he started to harp on me about something and then stopped and said, 'What's wrong with me? Let me go wake up and shake this off.'" Flexible couples reframe bad days as a normal part of the cyclical process of marriage.

Over-regulating yourself, on the other hand, can backfire: pressure will build so that you may explode the *next* time.

Although indulging in every impulse won't help your relationship, do learn to recognize when you're becoming depleted so you can put your irritability on hold.

➹ **REMEMBER THE CHILDREN.** Factor in the presence of children: it's been found that although marital spats take place twice as often when the kids aren't around, some of the most virulent, hostile, and destructive conflicts are carried on in front of the children. Psychologists guess that couples are least able to inhibit negative interactions when they're most distressed, with the unfortunate result that children don't often see adult problem-solving when it's being handled most constructively. This, then, is another good reason to become aware of your state of mind and not allow marital negativity to build to explosive levels.

➹ **TONE IT DOWN.** Those who are able to lower their emotional arousal levels during stressful interactions have happier marriages. To develop the knack, try this: begin paying attention to your state of emotional arousal and rate it on a scale of one to ten. It doesn't have to be when you're upset with each other—any stress will do for practice, and joy is emotionally arousing too.

During conflict, are you feeling overwhelmed by intense emotion? Does your partner's reaction feel unexpected and as though it's coming out of nowhere? Do you wish you could escape from the interaction? That's called flooding. When this happens, it's time to take a break and soothe yourself (if not your partner). Eventually, you'll be able to bring your arousal down to manageable levels whenever something upsetting is going on.

Studies have found that some men tend to do this more readily than many women. It is why they tend to withdraw from conflict: to make themselves feel better. Others, more typically (but not always) women, stick with the distressing conversation and get highly charged but don't necessarily feel negatively about it.

It's easy to see that hostile, sarcastic, or threatening language would be off-putting to your partner, but simply raising your voice can also be threatening. You can also work together to become aware of each other's level of emotional arousal, learn to say what's happening for you, then seek a compromise so you can both feel okay and continue to talk, perhaps after a brief break. Another way to tone it down is to try humor, but again without trivializing what's most important to either of you. In my previous marriage, my emotional outbursts were legendary: door slams that broke off chunks of plaster, screams I'm sure the neighbors heard. I find that Stephen and I see-saw in our emotional reactivity. He used to withdraw quickly from conflict in order to avoid the painful emotional charge. When I'd press and pursue—and raise my voice in frustration—he might erupt into a scary outburst. More recently, it's me who has to leave the room for a few minutes as I realize I've reached my emotional limit and I'm trying not to raise my voice.

➥ **TIMING MATTERS.** Timing is more important than many of us realize until it's too late and we've gotten embroiled in some snippy tête-á-tête that could have been avoided. Do some of your conflicts occur at transition points in the day, such as when you're awakening, are arriving home from work, or are exhausted? Sit in your car a few moments. Plan ahead for a refreshing drink, a quick reconnection-in-passing, *before* you fully transition, and plan to reconnect more thoroughly later. Learn not to take your partner's transitional needs as a personal affront.

When I was in grad school (admittedly during a strained part of the marriage), it used to be extra hard to mesh our separate rhythms when I'd return from a distant conference. Whatever I'd be thinking about the whole way home would clash with what Stephen was doing when I got there. One memorable time I spent the two-hour drive listening to stimulating music and imagining jumping directly into bed with him in a freshly-cleaned house (this last bit was the greater fantasy, to be sure), and he was in the midst of last-moment vacuuming and not at all ready to get sexy. Rather than adapting to his mood, I felt hurt and angry and disappointed, and it took us a couple of days to feel reconnected.

➻ **SPACE MATTERS.** Giving each other breathing room is a part of regulating your emotional arousal. Have the sense not to fight in the car, don't follow when your partner withdraws, *listen* when one of you says "I've about had it" (even if it's *you* who's saying it). Put your issues on hold, realizing that when one of you is about to expel steam from the nostrils and ears, this has to be respected. It's a primal thing and can't be talked away. Try choosing a phrase, something as simple as "time out," that indicates one of you needs some simmering-down time.

➻ **CHANGE THE ENVIRONMENT.** When Stephen and I need to talk, we often move to the living room, which has come to be known as "the talking room." It's a comfortable, undistracting place to sit. We may even end up leaning on one another on the sofa when we get to a point where we're ready for a renewed physical as well as emotional connection.

➻ **USE LISTS WITH CAUTION.** Some therapists suggest couples who feel distant from one another begin doing the loving behaviors their partners want, promising that the warm feelings will follow. One way to begin is for each of you to compile a list of specific caring behaviors you'd like your partner to try. Then don't miss small efforts made to please you. As is often suggested to parents about their children, catch 'em being good instead of always hollering when they're not. The problem is that, so often, one person makes a change that's barely noticed by the other partner, and then doesn't stick with it for long. If changes are made, they should *stay* made.

A long time ago, when we were mired in our most conflicted years, we came across a book by Doris Wild Helmering, called *Happily Ever After: A Therapist's Guide to Taking the Fight Out & Putting the Fun Back into Your Marriage.* Helmering lists lots of "Behaviors that make a difference," and at that time we each marked some. With hindsight, it's possible to tell which made a difference for us by examining those little marks and our memories. These are the few that Stephen marked: say thank you more often, give more compliments, be more affectionate, and approach him sexually. The items I marked included: tell her she's pretty, say "I love you," pick up after myself, make the time to do fun things together, cut down on drinking, bring her little surprises, do what I say I'm going to do.

Doing those things for each other, however, wasn't easy. Resentments kept getting in the way. What I'm saying here is that this type of list-making is a start to help you see what's upsetting each of you. But unless you get beneath the individual items to what they represent, you may end up no better than you started. And each time some self-help tip fails to work magic, you may get more discouraged.

➻ **IS IT ALREADY SOLVED?** Andrew Christensen and his co-author Neil S. Jacobson have observed that sometimes whatever you're doing about some problem, as weird as it might seem to another couple, *is* the solution, albeit imperfect. For example, the husband doesn't do enough parenting, the wife criticizes, and he tolerates her criticism. If he reacted nastily, the situation might escalate into a major fuss. The fact that she's able to relieve her frustration openly is a solution of sorts, so that the couple needn't constantly think of this as a problem. Is this a recommended attitude? Depends on the issue. Something as important as being an involved parent could be worth pursuing further, whereas if the conflict were over a less crucial matter, the non-solution solution could maintain the peace and allow good feelings to prevail regardless of the lack of full resolution.

→ **PAY ATTENTION TO YOUR INNER VOICE.** What we say to ourselves matters. If your self-talk is repetitively negative, you might succeed only in extending the hostilities. For instance, recently Stephen and I were taking a walk and found ourselves arguing with some vehemence. My flare of temper caused Stephen to claim I was getting scary, so I walked away to give both of us the space to calm down. As I walked, I spoke to myself, reiterating my case: "He's not fair, he just doesn't get it, he never thinks of my feelings," and so on. When you do this, you're not helping cool yourself down, and by not challenging such inaccurate and poisonous thoughts, you're allowing them to take a firmer hold. What's worse, I caught myself mumbling, "Hate, hate, hate." Which is not how I feel 99.999 percent of the time. I realized this wasn't productive, and that it would be best to think of something else until my boiling emotions could cool. Giving yourselves space away from each other is only helpful if you don't continue the emotional abuse in your head.

→ **WATCH YOUR OVERHEATED WORDS.** Some people spew very harsh words during fights. When the battle is over, they will say they didn't mean it, but the other party is convinced those words were indeed intended to hurt.

Marylis, who wished her husband Conrad would give her a hug instead of questioning her when she's hurt, admits that their angry emotions have mellowed as they've gotten older. "I can remember yelling fights on a monthly basis. Now, if it happens once a year, maybe twice, that would be more typical. It's true that we're both yellers, but we don't say things like, 'I'm out the door,' or something like that that we wouldn't be able to take back. I feel like when *I'm* emotional and can't control *myself* is when things go out of control. When one person's venting, it's so much fun to jump in there and vent yourself." Fun, perhaps, but certainly not helpful.

Think about the hot words you pronounce when you're angry. Calling someone a fat pig may never be forgiven or forgotten. Hurling accusatory judgments, such as "You're a loser," or "No one could love you," will leave indelible stains on your relationship. If such remarks do slip out, they often reflect some deep-seated resentment. *Before* the next rage overtakes either of you, face up to those hidden peeves.

If you say mean things in order *to* hurt, shame on you. Couples who've learned to love in flow do *not* fling statements intended to cause pain (which is not to say that no one ever gets hurt during conflict).

→ **PICK YOUR BATTLES.** "The biggest compromise I've made over the years is to learn how to choose my battles," says Mei-Ling, a thirty-seven year-old real estate agent who's been married twelve years. Although she says their conflicts are rarely about anything major, her husband Ramsey's critical tendencies bother her. The only time she makes an issue of it, though, is when he goes too far and pokes at her most sensitive emotional areas. Then she lets him know he's overstepped.

The "pick your battle" mantra can be misused, however. If too many petty annoyances seem to be accumulating, it's far better to confront them. They don't *have* to cause a battle. Be honest about why you're not going to continue hiding your discontentment. Perhaps you feel underappreciated or over-controlled. If you talk about those feelings as soon as you realize what's going on for you, you are more likely to get a fair hearing than if you let them build up until you're furious.

Harriet and Myron are a Florida couple in their sixties who have been married forty-five years. Harriet wishes she'd learned how to speak up many years earlier than she did. Her

husband, Myron, now a retired doctor, used to be highly sarcastic until a therapist helped her realize that she was allowing him to get away with too much.

"He wouldn't dare do that now," says Harriet. "The therapist told me, 'You didn't even ring the doorbell twice.'
Meaning: don't give up, be assertive, go after what you want,
voice what you are feeling and thinking. When I first let
Myron know my reaction to his sarcasm, he was stunned. If
you don't tell people things, how can they ever know?"

One of JoBeth's consistent irritations with her husband is
that he's only willing to help out around the house on his preferred time schedule. Recently a pair of eight-foot-long fluo-
rescent bulbs in the basement needed replacing, and she
asked for help a few times. Suddenly her husband decided
*now* was the time, regardless of the fact that JoBeth was
immersed in another task. You can fight these incompatible
styles endlessly, casting subtle accusations of insensitivity, or
else decide how important it is to get the job done—and join
in gracefully.

↬ **STICK TO THE POINT.** Try not to bring every other annoyance in your life to the table when you're embroiled over a
particular issue. And if your partner says, "That's another
subject, let's stick to this for now," accept that. Even if you
think what you're bringing up is related, leave it for another
time if it feels off-track to *one* of you. See if your partner will
agree to set a time to talk about the other issue, if that will
help you put it aside for now, but don't insist.

↬ **NEGOTIATE CREATIVELY.** One couple reports that
rather than ever compromising when there's a decision to be
made, such as whether or not to visit a relative, make a purchase, where to eat or what movie to see, they determine to
whom it is most important. For this to work, you have to
trust that the other person is telling the truth about what's

crucial and what isn't. And if you're with someone for whom *everything* is of number one importance, while anything you want is seen as not that important, this system might not be the best.

➼ **CHANGE THE MEDIUM.** Another way to avoid becoming entangled in a frustrating cycle is to write your partner an email message or a letter. That way you have a chance to plan your words before sending them, and there's time to reflect before responding. Fringe benefit: you can't interrupt each other.

➼ **BE FUTURE-ORIENTED.** It is pointless to spend a lot of time arguing over what one or both of you *ought* to have done, unless it's in the service of preventing the same alleged misbehavior in the future. Once you reach the point of irreconcilable views over what *did* happen, stop the bickering and ask each other, "What might we do to ensure this *type* of conflict doesn't happen again?"

➼ **SAVE FACE.** Consider when it might be sensible to let a conflict wind down without an overt apology on anyone's part and without necessarily agreeing on specific action for the future. At times, change will occur, restitution will be made, without anyone having to put their remorse into words. In the process of batting around your various disgruntlements, you will each have heard the other, even if neither of you wish to go on record. Or one of you might have a particularly hard time expressing apologies, no matter how bad you feel. If this describes your partner, be kind and allow him to save face. Perhaps his actions will speak up though his voice holds back.

➼ **PUT IT INTO PERSPECTIVE.** One simple exercise *always* works for me: when I'm exceptionally angry, I picture myself attempting to divide our commingled belongings so we can separate. It doesn't take long for me to realize what

I'd miss about him, what I'd regret, and how trivial this particular conflict is in the face of such dramatic (even melodramatic) thoughts.

↠ **REFRAME.** Practice not reacting in identical ways to the same old provocations. Your husband has once again misplaced a vital receipt, making your job of tax prep impossible to do efficiently. Can you still harbor warm or at least neutral feelings about him? Or as psychiatrist Peter D. Kramer describes it, "To be committed is to be able to find the receipts a mess and be perfectly fine—still aware of [your partner] in all her aspects. Or, when [he] asks where the tickets are, not to feel that all the air has been sucked out of the room. Though perhaps, as in skiing, it is better to begin somewhere less challenging, to 'drop back a level.' Could you look at an uncapped soda bottle, or cap one, without feeling violated?"

It is most healthy if you're able to accept that your partner is different from you, without taking it personally or catastrophically. But some couples make judgements of who's right and who's wrong all the time—a product of their families and their cultures that see things in only one way and can't grasp how we construct our realities depending on our unique experiences. As a character in the Patrick O'Leary novel *Door Number Three* says, "I watched her towel herself dry, thinking how myopic we are about the rituals we adopt. We think everyone does it our way. I would never rest my leg on the side of the tub to dry it, as Nancy did. But then, I would never make an issue of it, as if there *were* a right way."

↠ **REPAIR.** When in the midst of a battle, try to remember that it isn't conflict resolution at all that ensures marital success. Much more important is the way repairs are made when things fall temporarily apart, says psychologist John Gottman. If your marital friendship is strong, you'll be able to keep negative moments between you from growing into something larger and more damaging.

Liberating, isn't it? You can fight imperfectly so long as you patch up the relationship excellently. That seems to be what occurs most often in the relationships I studied, and in my own. We have dopey and trivial disagreements that sometimes turn into momentary alienations—though we're careful not to demean each other or say nasty things we'd never be able to take back. Then we calm down and reconnect.

# THE NO-FAULT APPROACH

We have to be careful not to be too sure of our perceptions. You might like to calligraph these three words and put them on your wall as a bell of mindfulness: "Are you sure?"

—Thich Nhat Hanh, "True Presence"

Imagine you're a stay-at-home mother caring for two young children. One night, your husband comes home later than usual, explaining he was stuck in a lengthy last-minute meeting with his boss. Choose which of the following you're more likely to think:

1. He finds his job more interesting than spending time with me and the kids.
2. He could have been having a drink with a female colleague.
3. He didn't consider us waiting for him—he takes me and the dinners I make for granted, the selfish SOB.
4. How stressful that must have been for him, knowing I was waiting but not wanting to let his boss feel slighted by rushing the meeting; it's hard to balance conflicting demands!

Does the fourth choice surprise you? It's the most empathetic reaction. It's often easier to find fault with your partner for some disappointment than to make the effort to see the situation as *he* might. Research has consistently found that attributions—the way you think about *why* people do what they do—directly relate to how satisfied you are in a relationship. The happiest couples habitually attribute good will toward one another, and that makes all the difference.

## BETTER OFF BLAMELESS

Any behavior seems changed when you remove the blame. For instance, Stephen never plans a fun outing for us in advance. I used to think that meant he didn't care enough to make the effort. Then I realized that he doesn't plan *anything* in advance. When he's very hungry, he eventually remembers to eat. When he's sleepy, he goes to sleep, no matter what time it is. When I take my clothes off, he starts thinking *those* thoughts. The moral is easy: if something requires planning, it's up to me. And no hard feelings.

Is your tendency to shout or to state your case, with teeth clenched, in chilling tones, when your partner behaves aggravatingly? All is not necessarily lost: you can go back later and try to enter into the other person's frame of mind. Even if you do this mind-meld imperfectly and with supreme effort, it will help reduce friction. For example, Alexander arrived home late one night and, after searching for some papers in the back seat of his car, left the overhead light on. The next time he wanted to use the car, it wouldn't start. Until his was fixed, Alexander used his wife Marcella's car.

Marcella didn't assume any malevolence on her mate's part. She accepted that Alexander, preoccupied, left the light on accidentally, and she didn't for a moment take his carelessness personally. If Marcella had berated him instead of dealing with the dead battery as a problem to solve, this could have turned into a fight, with Alexander feeling badly about himself and wanting to avoid the person who made him feel that way. Marcella intuited what psychologists studying newlyweds have found: this type of cooperative orientation, where you perceive and care about your partner's feelings, leads to greater stability in the marriage.

# WELCOME TO MY WORLD

Reality can be construed a vast number of ways, according to psychologists who adhere to constructivism. You perceive the world the way you tend to construct it. I like this idea, find it liberating—if you can construe an event one way, then you can learn to construe it other ways as well.

When freelance journalist Laurie's husband tells her, "You really should be working instead of watching TV," she doesn't jump to the conclusion that Hamid is trying to control her. Such a motive has never occurred to her, she says. "Comments like that don't bother me at all. He just doesn't want anything to waste too much of my time, since he wants more of my time for him." So instead of labeling his behavior as controlling, which could be pejorative and blaming, she views it more in the spirit he presumably intends it.

It's possible to train yourself to be more empathetic, to see things through your partner's eyes, according to psychologists Kim Paleg and Matthew McKay in their book *When Anger Hurts Your Relationship*. They suggest a somewhat structured format, wherein you interview each other and fill out a form. I believe many couples might benefit by asking a few of their suggested questions at an opportune moment during an escalating conflict. For instance, "If things could be exactly the way you want them, how would that be?" "What are you afraid will happen if this situation continues?" "What choices do you think you have in this situation?" "If I could read your mind when we're struggling with this issue, what would I see?" "What are you feeling physically when we're in the middle of this conflict and how strong is the feeling?"

If you can accept that each of you experiences the same event differently—and with an equally complex series of valid-seeming reasons—your hurt and irritation will dissipate.

An exercise you might try is to play at being a marriage therapist. Pretend that both of you are psychologically sophisticated but disinterested observers. Construct a version of events—some current disagreement, for example—the way outsiders might perceive it. What would they say to both of you?

Let's look at what follows when one partner misattributes the motives of the other. I've mentioned Mei-Ling before: she's the one who picks her battles. As you might expect, she tends to be more easygoing than her husband, Ramsey. She says she gives people the benefit of the doubt, "knowing they've also got these issues going on. I'm not the type that gets mad in traffic, for example."

Mei-Ling describes a recent difficulty: "We'd long had plans for me to have dinner with some clients, and Ramsey was going to go too. We were supposed to be there at six, but he came home from work at 5:45 and said, 'I don't feel very good.' Apparently he had a soreness in his chest and was worried. I said, 'Okay, what am I supposed to do? Can we just go there for a minute and then go to the doctor afterward to try to find out what it is? Because it's so late now.' We ended up going to the dinner, but then he wouldn't go to the doctor at all. His problem seemed to go away."

Mei-Ling says that Ramsey was upset with her because, by choosing to go to the dinner, it meant she was ignoring his problem. They fought on the way there, and they fought afterward. "He felt that I was not caring for his needs, that I was putting work first," she says. In other words, he attributed her efforts to find an in-between solution to her quandary, such as stopping by the meeting for a very short time, as a signal she didn't love him enough to take his potential illness seriously. She's still trying to figure out whether she ought to have called her clients to cancel the meeting, since her husband so rarely asks for "these types of things." All that weekend, they were distant and snipping at one another.

Mei-Ling's story is similar to what often goes on in intimate relationships: one partner acts a certain way and the other assumes it means she doesn't care very much about him. Much of marital conflict involves the fear that feelings have cooled on someone's part, though the threat comes from assigning motives that aren't there.

Take everyday teasing. Jane can tease her husband Bill about "being a bear, meaning a grump, especially when he wakes up, and he takes it good-naturedly because he understands that it's true." He doesn't misattribute her joking to being critical or malevolent.

Another example: when Letitia wanted her graphic artist husband to work fewer hours at an animation project, she said in exasperation, "It's just a cartoon!" Did Lenny feel as though his beloved occupation were being demeaned? No, he explains: "I took it in a good way because I felt, 'Wow, somebody cares about our relationship enough to give it that much importance over my job.'"

## EVERYONE MAKES THIS ERROR (BUT YOU?)

Many people are unaware of how common attribution errors are. For a flagrant but not so far-fetched example, consider what this character in Haruki Murakami's novel, *The Wind-Up Bird Chronicle*, says to her husband when he returns to the house with flowered toilet paper: "I absolutely *never* buy toilet paper with patterns on it. I'm just shocked that you could live with me all this time and not be aware of that....You've hardly paid any attention to me. The only one you ever think about is yourself."

What's known as the "fundamental attribution error" is the common tendency to explain an action as a result of the person's nature—"you only think about yourself"—even when there are clear situational reasons why the person acted a particular way. "He's just that way," we say, or "He's the kind of person who does that kind of thing," rather than bothering to explore causes in the environment or the situation—external factors—that might have been contributing factors. "Most situations are complex," asserts Jeffrey Kottler in *Beyond Blame*. "Everyone's actions are interdependent, playing off of and reacting in response to each other's behavior."

Most of us have a self-serving bias, giving ourselves plenty of leeway for having acted under the pressure of external events. If we make a mistake, we may take for granted that the cause was at least partially outside our control: bad luck, the difficulty of the task, the devil made me do it. At the same time, we manage to attribute the better things we do to our own nature and internal causes. In better relationships, we are as forgiving of our partners as we are of ourselves.

Assume good will. Always. That one bit of advice will save you numerous trips to the therapist. The person who has committed life and love to you isn't out to hurt you. He or she makes mistakes and is flawed and weak, as we all are, but none of it is done out of evil intent. "The true winner of a marital conflict might be the one who understands the other's point of view first," notes psychiatrist Frank Pittman.

If you blame a lot, perhaps you're feeling disenchanted and haven't yet found a way to mesh your current reality with the romantic fantasies of your past. In a *New Yorker* cartoon, one woman says to another, "I feel I'm losing touch with the unrealistic view I have of him."

Theo Park, a fifty-year-old gay Episcopal priest in Minneapolis, says about the challenges of the early years of his twenty-six-year relationship with his partner, Dennis Christian, "Those 101 things we had conflicts about felt so *personal* at the time. You have to learn to let go of expectations and stop projecting them onto the other person."

Our personalities have much to do with the way we make attributions: if you tend to be judgmental, to make impulsive decisions about what is right and wrong, or if you are only comfortable when in control or when imagining the world is a controllable entity, you'll have to work harder to give the person you love the benefit of the doubt.

It is possible, regardless, to separate causes from accountability, and accountability from outright blaming. What's crucial here is what you imagine was the intent of your partner. Was his intention to upset, annoy, or hurt you? If you understand that it wasn't, you have little to battle about.

And finally, there's a reverse to all this attribution business, one that can have positive results on a marriage. Some studies have found that spouses who are happy in their relationships tend to give their spouses more than half the credit for the good things that happen, and they blame themselves more for the negative events. It could be that happy marriages are based on just such mutual appreciation, as we saw when I explained positive illusions. But it might also be the case that some happy relationships are based on a reverse upside-down mirror-image version of that: I might sometimes point out your flaws and insufferable mannerisms and fail to say how amazing you are, but I'll put myself down even more tellingly and give you full credit for tolerating me.

Try putting into practice these additional ways of using the no-fault solution:

- Realize that when you try to figure out why your partner acted a certain way, what you're thinking is just a theory about what happened, an assumption, not a set of facts. Without knowing precisely what was in your mate's mind, you don't have the whole story.

- Find other words to describe what your partner did that vexed you. Could there be other reasons than the ones that come first to your mind? Did he intend for his actions to have the effect they had on you?

- Step back for a longer perspective to add detachment. Try "treating the problem as an 'it' rather than a 'you'," suggests Andrew Christensen.

- Take each other's part and role play the conflict. Verbalize throughout so you can each clarify how close you got to each other's mental state.

➻ Risk revealing what part you might have played in the origin of the conflict, going all the way back to childhood fears, if relevant. It's impossible to apportion percentage of responsibility, so don't try. But by acknowledging having played even a minor part, you go a long way toward defusing your partner's defensiveness.

➻ Although you may be loathe to over analyze a conflict, it can occasionally be helpful to process more thoroughly. What you learn from any one conflict will be useful in subsequent efforts to understand each other.

➻ Assume goodwill. This bears repeating. Dare to make yourself vulnerable with a comment along these lines: "My first thought was that you didn't care about how that would make me feel. But that can't be true, right?"

## WHAT REALLY CHANGES

> A decent marriage is neither sudden nor God-given. It has to be worked for like everything else worth having, and paid for in grinding small change, by compromise and growing older.
>
> —A. Alvarez, *Life After Marriage: Love in an Age of Divorce*

Your partner asked you to change, and you've tried. But some behavioral changes don't appear half as dramatic from the outside as they feel on the inside. Change that's too tiny and too fleeting may not be noticed.

If you believe you're doing what your partner asked you to do, and it doesn't seem to help, either try it more emphatically, or for a longer period, or try another tactic. Or do the obvious: ask your partner if he's noticed the change you made. Try not to allow sarcasm or frustration to creep into your voice: "Here's what I've been trying, and it doesn't feel like you've noticed. Am I way off-base?"

Can you entertain the possibility that, even when your mate accepts your efforts, he or she won't make similar attempts toward you? In the most loving marriages, one partner often acts independently of the other's reactions when making change, taking the first step regardless of whether a reciprocal second step is guaranteed. When you unconditionally give what your mate requests while putting your own needs on hold, your gesture will be accepted as more genuine.

It's always sad when you learn the hard way that your mate will not or cannot change in ways that will make the continuation of the marriage possible. Shauna told me only two months ago that she and her husband of eleven years, Claude, felt as though they were newly in love, only better: "I said he changed, he said I changed. I honestly think we both had a shift in perception around the same time. I started taking more responsibility for financial and household matters, and he took more interest in and became more supportive of my concerns and my friends. I decided to do something thoughtful for him every day, such as a foot massage at the end of the day, or ironing all his shirts in the afternoon (he usually irons one each morning), maybe buy him a surprise treat. I also planned some fun romantic rendezvous for us.

"He asked me why I was being so good to him and I told him I had made a deal with myself to do something nice for him every day, and the next day he gave me a foot massage and said he was very touched by my declaration and wanted to do the same. I think we discovered together how wonderful it feels to give and receive loving gestures."

It's never that uncomplicated, though, and in spite of Shauna's belief so recently that they had finally reached a place in their personal emotional development that made this happiness possible, the reality turned out to be more troubling. Her husband, in fact, soon resumed his contemptuous behavior toward her, arguments got more violent, and after a final ugly blow-up, they separated.

Not all requests for personal revision involve minor behavioral irritations. At times, one of you feels that the other is asking for a transformation of your essential immutable self. Friends of ours battled for years before finally divorcing over what he believed should have been achievable adaptation on her part. She didn't agree, insisting, "That's who I am," and the fact that he couldn't stretch his acceptance to cover who she was (or who she had become over a two-decade-long marriage), was fatal to their union.

For some couples, conflicts won't lessen until one or both of those involved are able to come to grips with their own backgrounds and vulnerabilities, perhaps via intensive personal therapy. Theo Park likes to say he and Dennis stayed together their first seven years out of a mutual fear of abandonment, and then they began to work through their issues.

"We both come from dysfunctional family backgrounds," relates Theo. "We have identified our particular issues as more what's been called a 'shame-based' identity, and we carry some pretty heavy residue from those patterns. Our whole task has been to get to the point of individuation where each partner is fully himself and yet part of the couple. Certainly in those early years it was bumpy and there was a lot of stomping out of the room, oh, it's all over, we don't agree, let's end it now. *Sturm und Drang* stuff. We always got past those things.

"Near the beginning of our relationship, we took a trip to Europe for several weeks, and in classic mode, when you're out of your normal routine for that long, stuff happens. There was a moment when we were in Rome at the top of the Spanish Steps and I wanted to fling myself down and he wanted to throw me down. Some of my caretaking, some of my anxiety for having to be responsible, came to the fore. When we came back I did some therapy, found the Adult Children's group, a twelve-step program, and began to look at the conditioning and patterning I'd had.

"It started out that Dennis felt if I just went to group and dealt with my issues, everything would be okay. But as I got a little healthier, it became clear that he had his own stuff. In a year or two, he also began to attend the same group and began doing his own therapy. Everything we did for our 'selves' was also good for the relationship."

The lives of Matthew and Georgia, married for four decades now, also illustrate the possibilities of change. Though both are psychologists at Ivy League universities, they didn't start out sophisticated about their own interaction. They admit that only in the last ten or so years have they gotten the hang of getting along beautifully. Matthew attributes this largely to subtle personality changes on his wife's part.

"Georgia's not the same person she was before. It used to be that, when we were young marrieds, she was very reactive, and if I were to register a complaint that I might feel rated a two or a three on a scale of one to ten, she would respond as if it were an eight or a nine. She had such a hard time being criticized, and so it was sometimes very difficult for me to be honest. I would always ask myself, is this worth upsetting her over?"

Thus, with Matthew and Georgia, they both changed: she became more secure, less sensitive to implied criticism, and he learned to be more honest as it felt safer to do so. And the more open he became, the less she suspected that every negative comment meant he'd fallen out of love with her. In other words, a positive cycle evolved over time, so that now they delight in each other's company and can barely recall how tentative they used to be together.

You may find that keeping a journal is a superb way of gaining insight into your individual and couple patterns and changes over time. What bothers you now will seem unbelievably petty in a decade—or in a month.

When you stop insisting that your partner change, some of those changes may occur naturally. Human nature is funny that way. But acceptance is not the same as "putting up with." According to Andrew Christensen and Neil S. Jacobson, co-authors of *Reconcilable Differences*, "'To accept' means to tolerate what you regard as an unpleasant behavior of your partner, probably to understand the deeper meaning of that behavior, certainly to see it in a larger context, and perhaps even to appreciate its value and importance in your relationship."

I like to think we learn to transcend the details of some specific behavior for the more "cosmic" essence of who each of us is. We all want to be loved as we are. But there's no reason you can't *combine* change with acceptance. In healthy marriages, each of you changes a bit and also becomes more accepting. Then the critic becomes less critical and the criticized one becomes more accepting of the remaining criticism. And sometimes, yes, acceptance does mean giving in and doing it the way your partner insists, whether it's being on time, avoiding conversation while watching videos, or any other formerly conflicted area.

In real-life couples, even satisfied ones, bits of leftover resentment may still escape. But the tiny steam hisses are so minor, and the good humor in the relationship is at such a high level overall, that it simply doesn't matter.

For instance, Jim Rea's preference for a second vehicle not long ago was a pickup, and Zhita found that incomprehensible. "She could hardly imagine there being a pickup in the family," he explains. "We discussed it quite a bit, and she really resisted it. This went on over a number of months before we actually shopped. Zhita finally grudgingly accepted the purchase of a sports utility vehicle, so we could carry grandchildren in it. She still hasn't fully made her peace with it, but occasionally she'll smile and remark that she sees that there's *some* advantage, and I kid her about it."

Or consider Elizabeth, married half a century, who has long since learned to at least tolerate the gruff well-intentioned comments her husband makes. "I once said to him, 'What do you think of this dress?' and he said 'I couldn't afford a new wife, so I had the old one slipcovered.' He's remarkable that way. And I can either cry and scream and get a lawyer, or send it to *Reader's Digest*." She did the latter and the magazine bought the joke.

# THE HOSE OF DEATH

Of *course* Stephen and I still have the occasional conflict. Here is a recent example: the difference between it and the hundreds of similar disagreements we had in the bad times (and all those fights couples have that never seem to get resolved and increase negative feelings between them) is that we were both able to let it go quickly.

This one revolved around "the hose of death." I didn't name it that; a friend did. Stephen wasn't pleased when I asked him, on Friday afternoon, to please coil up the lengthy hose that was splayed and tangled all over the backyard and across the top of the stone steps, since we were planning to have company on Saturday and would be traipsing up and down those steps. (Tripping on the hose, to me, involves more than a mere stumble: with osteoporosis in my family, I imagine being caught on the hose, tumbling down the rough unbanistered stairway, and breaking a crucial bone—a typing wrist, a hip—and from there it is a short anguished journey to terminal disability.)

This did not seem as reasonable a request to Stephen as it did to me—he said the hose was about as dangerous as a dead worm—but he finally agreed to humor me and coil it out of the way. Still, he continued to insist it was an unnecessary preparation for our guests, and I persisted in wanting him to accept that my request was a proper one, albeit based on my own deep-rooted and exaggerated fears.

"It won't be a big deal if you don't *make* a big deal out of it," he repeated, and I repeated my usual, "But it's not *about* the hose, it's about my feelings," and when he wouldn't relent, we stayed out of each other's way for a few hours. Maybe, I figured, his inexplicable reaction was mostly about saving face. Or maybe I'd attempted to get him to join me in delving into my own emotional nuttiness at the wrong time. And soon, even the minor emotion that had been lurking under all this talk had dissipated, and we were amiable toward each other and able to enjoy our company the next afternoon.

# TALKING ABOUT TALKING

It has been said also that silence is torture, capable of goading to madness the man who is condemned to it in a prison cell. But what an even greater torture than that of having to keep silence it is to have to endure the silence of the person one loves!

— Marcel Proust, *In Search of Lost Time*

Talk may be cheap, but it's not easy. Or, more accurately, speaking effectively in ways that advance a loving relationship is not everyone's natural forte. In this chapter, we'll explore how to talk both clearly and sensitively to one another, as well as how to talk about talking.

If one of you holds back from unfettered conversations, perhaps some past experience or lingering memories are warning you that openness usually leads to discomfort and hurt feelings. I tackled some of those circular-type fights and ways to circumvent them in the last chapter, and now I want to focus on the verbal component.

Despite the stereotype, it's not only men who have trouble talking about feelings. Even today, though, as in earlier generations, men are more often discouraged from expressing emotions that make them seem weak. If your mate has a tendency to see life as a poker game where showing his hand means he loses, don't assume he can't learn to relax and open up. Just be prepared to make it *very* safe.

## LANCE THE TALKING BOIL

Stephen and I like to walk in the hills around our home. On energetic days, we go all the way around the lake. These days, we walk peacefully, joking or chatting about plans for the weekend. Our talks weren't always so lighthearted. I used to save up all my complaints for this daily half hour when I'd have a captive audience. Stephen began telling our friends we were "lancing the talking boil."

I'd spill out every dissatisfaction: it bugged me that he said he doesn't mind house cleaning but he never does it until the last possible moment; he hadn't taken my strong hints about wanting to leave some party earlier; and so on. Ironically, I'd feel relieved by the time we arrived puffing back at our front door, while Stephen would feel overwhelmed and miserable. Even while I was spewing forth my grumbles, he wasn't yet sure he could reciprocate with his own. At least he was listening and not seeking shelter under the blankets. We were beginning the process of learning how to fix what was wrong with us. Our friends Candace and Jim weren't so lucky.

I once clipped a *New York Times* article about John Gottman's marriage research and underlined this sentence: "In examining the couples' approach to problem-solving, the researchers found the husband's actions—specifically a tendency to withdraw from the argument—were most predictive of divorce." At the time, Candace and Jim were always arguing, and Jim would withdraw into cold silence. I stuck the article on my bulletin board with the notation, "This predicts Jim and Candace's split."

They separated five years later, when their son was four.

And meanwhile, Stephen and I broke through the talking boil impasse. Although we had to hit bottom first, eventually we learned how to make it safe for each other to leak out our tiny dissatisfactions while they're still harmless. It's amazing how relaxed you feel when you harbor no secret grudges—even for a day.

Here are a few phrases to add to your repertoire next time you have a complaint, however niggling it seems. In solid relationships, these usually get positive results:

➻ I have something I really want to talk with you about, so let me know when you might be able to listen.

➻ I just need to talk about this. I don't need you to try to solve it for me, but it would be great if I could just think it through out loud.

➻ Would you help me think this through? Maybe one of us can come up with a solution.

You might be wondering whether your partner is always the right person with whom to talk over sensitive issues. Psychologist Ayala M. Pines claims that by confiding in a friend, you won't gain much insight into your partner's behavior, though you'll get validation for the idea that it's rotten behavior—which might only distress you more. I found that there are certain circumstances where this may not be true. I used to walk every morning with a female friend, venting my marital frustrations. She was able to help me grasp why Stephen behaved in certain previously inexplicable ways. What seemed to me like selfishness, for example, was reframed by my friend as autonomy-seeking. I could hear her explanations without resistance, then go home and face my own circumstances with fresh understanding.

## I LIKE I-MESSAGES

You've no doubt heard the common advice to use "I-messages" when you talk to intimates. Maybe you've tried it, perhaps consistently, but you haven't managed to avoid antagonizing your mate anyway. That's because it's possible to feel pummeled by even the most innocently intended I-message. Doing it correctly isn't obvious. You need to get behind the words to see what your I-message is actually saying.

"I think you're a slob" might follow the letter of the law, but not its spirit. The idea behind limiting yourself to I-messages is to focus on how your partner's actions are affecting you, how you feel hurt, irritated, or saddened by what the other person did or does. As Christensen and Jacobson note, if both of you—or even one of you who is most willing to take the risk—can break the pattern by disclosing aspects of yourselves that are deeply personal, this can be very bonding, and thus may get you over the hump of anger and withdrawal.

To go a bit deeper, psychologist Robert Kegan has observed that when you use I-messages, in effect you're addressing something about an injury to the way you want to feel in this relationship. Kegan gives the example of saying, "I don't like it when you leave your dirty clothes all over the house." You are expressing your viewpoint about what's wrong, acknowledging that your perception of your partner's behavior may not be identical to the way he or she sees it. You're not coming right out and saying it's wrong to behave this way, just that you don't like it.

At the same time, an effective I-message conveys that you are staying in this relationship, but nevertheless you want to talk about your unhappy experience of some aspect of it. While you can suffer negative feelings when your partner behaves a certain way, you're not saying he's responsible for those feelings. He's responsible for what he's done or not done, and you're responsible for the feelings you have as a result. And you don't have to feel less close to your partner just because you wish he'd behave differently. It's a sophisticated way of viewing relationships that is not easy to achieve.

Related to I-messages is the matter of direct communication. Natural to some, anathema to others, it's about being forthright in asking for what you want. How often have you said or heard your loved one say, "If I have to ask for it, I don't want it"? Yet well-adjusted couples figure out sooner or later that to get what you want, you may need to come out and ask for it, and that what you get isn't less valuable for having been requested.

A couple I know, not long after the start of their (now-defunct) relationship, were discussing how to meet their disparate needs. He's more needy, but she's willing to cooperate: "Just *ask* when you need some reassurance of my affection," she told him. His response? "Directness is one of *your* rules. When do we ever get to play by *my* rules?" His rules involve having his mind read as the epitome of romance.

Remember how we frequently make attribution errors? It isn't accurate to insist that your partner "should know by now" what you want—if he loved you. He can most certainly love you and *not* know a particular bit of what's going on in your psyche at any one time. It may be that one of you can better read the emotions of the other. Some people are more interpersonally intuitive. That's one form of intelligence, much like the ability to do calculus or find your way through a maze or repeat a melody you've heard once. Loving partners accept that the strengths of one aren't necessarily the strong points of the other, even when that means you must say, "I would love you to hug me now."

Another explanation for why your mate may hear a "you" message underneath the clearest of your I-statements is that he constructs the world differently than you do. If so, he might feel blamed, defensive, or guilty when you don't intend to sound accusatory. During our most contentious times, no matter how I phrased my dissatisfactions, using by-the-book I-messages ("I feel uncomfortable when you leave your papers all over the living room floor"), Stephen nevertheless interpreted this as my placing blame.

My I-messages were, I realize now, incomplete. Matthew McKay, Patrick Fanning, and Kim Paleg, authors of *Couple Skills*, clarify what it means to use "whole messages," one of the hallmarks of what they call "clean communication." A whole message is one that contains both your thoughts and feelings about an issue, along with a description of what you want or need from your partner. The former are your own version of reality, and the latter are what you're asking your partner to do about the former. So that you wouldn't say, "You work too much," but rather, "It seems as though you've been getting home late much more often than you used to, and I miss eating dinner with you. Is it possible for you to come home earlier some days like you used to?" That's direct, clear, and less likely to inspire defensiveness.

Another option is to express what you *feel* like doing instead of doing it: "I just want to weep when you say that to me because it raises my anxiety level so much." By expressing soft emotions like hurt and fear, your partner may respond with caring and concern. But it all depends on how you're able to say it. That is, if you come across as angry, and not as though you're in pain, you may not get a compassionate response. I'm not saying it's easy to do this all the time. It feels like you're leaving yourself vulnerable when you express loneliness or hurt or disappointment in a gentle way. Try it though, and you'll usually be met with a gentle compassionate response in return, at least to the limit of your partner's ability to show such tender feelings himself.

To ensure that you and your mate develop that total sense of safety, certain words can't be allowed, even when they're I-messages. I cringe when I recall that I once shrieked "I hate you!" at Stephen in the midst of one of our worst arguments, during a period of weeks-long non-stop reciprocal torment. He brings it up every now and then. Did I mean it at the time? I think I did—but what does it mean to hate momentarily? To me, it means you have run out of words to express how upset you are. It means you can't bear for things to go on as they are. It means you blame the other person in a thousand ways for your pain. But it also means that, for the moment, you've forgotten the connection between the two of you. Threats to leave or saying you don't love the other person are among the most damaging and hurtful words, and they are very hard to take back later, no matter how much you apologize.

That's not to imply that some couples don't work out their own quirky compromises. A couple who have been married for more than two decades, and who get along smoothly and seem satisfied (though I didn't interview them for this book), nonetheless had to learn to accommodate one another. During the first few years, whenever she was furious, Merrill would pack her suitcase, head for the door, and say, "I'm leaving!" Her husband Ron would always come get her at the door.

One day she decided to leave the suitcase empty, since she knew he'd stop her before she left and she'd only end up with wrinkled clothes. So she grabbed the empty suitcase and charged toward the front door as usual. When Ron lifted the suitcase out of her hands, as usual, saying, "C'mon Merrill, you're not going anywhere," it felt surprisingly light. They both had a huge laugh then, and they share a laugh now, retelling the story. She adds that she no longer threatened to leave after that, now that it had become a worthless bluff. Merrill admits that as a child she would sometimes threaten to run away from home. It must have gotten her the attention she wanted then, and later, in her marriage, the same ploy worked for a while. Not every husband would have laughed, though, and it goes against every rule for ensuring your partner feels safe to express himself during conflict.

Problems arise for some couples when one member's hot buttons are pushed inadvertently. But how many times can you say the same thing and insist you didn't mean to press those buttons, or blame your partner for having such buttons altogether? By changing a few words, your conversations could go much more pleasantly.

Some individuals, for instance, respond negatively if you say, "Do such-and-such," without the added "please." If it sounds like a command, they'll feel a sharp annoyance, no matter how long you've been with them and no matter how reasonable your request. Much better to say: "Would you mind doing this?" "I'd love you to do this." "Do you think you could find time to do this?" (And be sure to avoid any hint of sarcasm. It may not look like your partner is productively engaged, but we all have the right to spend our time as we see fit.)

## FOUR HORSEMEN, PASS ON BY

Certain kinds of talk enhance connection better than others. I've previously mentioned the work of psychologist John Gottman when I spoke of Candace and Jim, the couple who split because, among other problems, they couldn't communicate well.

Gottman and his colleagues watched a great many couples interacting in the lab and determined that the most successful ones avoid what he calls the Four Horsemen of the Apocalypse: criticism, contempt, defensiveness, and stonewalling.

Criticism, the way it's described by Gottman, is when you say, "You never take me anywhere." Complaint, the better option, is when you say, "We don't go out as much as I'd like to." Criticisms can usually be expressed with a "you" at the start, while most complaints might begin with an "I," though as we've seen with I-messages, it isn't that distinct. A common form of criticism is to list a batch of vexations in a row: "You don't listen to me. I feel neglected. You never do the chores I ask. I'm not having any fun." Even if part of this is legitimate complaining, the full barrage causes your partner to feel criticized, and that's bound to cause defensiveness.

Criticism tends to trigger an argument, if not utter silence. Of course, the behavior that preceded the criticism could as readily be called the trigger, and typically *is* considered the culprit by the criticizing spouse. Try not to get into arguments over what started a particular dispute. There is no way to go back to the beginning—causes precede other causes, and besides, looking for the first cause is usually about distributing blame. That neither resolves the problem nor contributes to loving feelings.

Like many, you may not recognize the signs of contempt—the Second Horseman—in your own words and body language. Contempt includes name-calling, mocking (imitating the way your mate waves her hands when she gets excited), insults, hostile humor (saying, "Oh, what a cute little wimp you are," when your partner says he's reluctant to ask for a raise), and body language that expresses a lack of respect, such as rolling your eyes or pointing a finger aggressively. If you don't have any respect for your partner's point of view when you disagree, that's going to come out in contemptuous language or behavior. If your partner says you come across as contemptuous, pay closer attention to your own comments and mannerisms.

The Third Horseman, defensiveness, can turn a conversation into a spat, and a minor tussle into an ugly situation. Every time you make an excuse for a behavior your partner has complained about, or put forth your own complaint in response to your mate's, you're acting defensively. The conversation cannot move forward. Also, it's likely to cause steam to come out your partner's ears if you repeat your point without attending to what he or she has been saying.

Here's an illustration of defensiveness in action. In Howard and Jane's marriage, she handles all the paperwork for his lucrative business, including figuring out his expense reports. Their styles are so different, though, that a miscalculation of $50 or so won't bother him, whereas, for detail-conscious Jane, it's well worth sorting out and getting credit for every last receipt. Jane used to spend hours searching through batches of messy bills to locate items Howard had forgotten to claim. When she'd tell him what she'd found—once coming up with a savings of thousands of dollars—Howard would get defensive and say, "Get off my back!" Now, explains Howard, "I've learned that it's not a criticism. It's just that Jane wants to know where our missing $6,234 is!"

When you get the urge to launch an attack on your partner because you're sure *you've* just been attacked, stop. You might be misattributing your partner's motives, and getting defensive will only confuse the situation. Even if, on some level, your partner *has* spoken in a way that can be legitimately construed as unfriendly, aggressive, or critical, you won't accomplish much by firing back.

Remind yourself that this is love, not war: your goals are far different. Put away that Uzi and tell the truth: "I'm feeling attacked. Can you please say that some other way?" Not only is that a fine and complete I-message, but it's likely to bring about the end of hostilities much sooner.

The fourth and final Horseman is stonewalling. It's when one partner withdraws, tunes out, disengages from the conversation. He or she may go silent and brooding, or go about his business as though nothing is wrong when the other partner is anxious to continue a hotly contested discussion. The mate who is always busy reading the newspaper or sitting at the computer may be stonewalling to avoid the complications and emotional convolutions of a frank talk. It's a protective device. All the more reason to make the conversational environment feel safe and loving for both of you. When confronted by a stonewaller, being gently persistent may not work, and if your timing is off, pushing will make your partner back off farther.

Wait until feelings between you are at their coziest before bringing up how you talk to each other. Try something like: "Sometimes when I want to discuss something that's important to me, you pull back—like the other day, when we were talking about our budget, it felt like I was being stonewalled, and that frustrates me. Are you worried that things will get nasty between us if we keep talking, or that I'll get too mad, or what?" Don't accuse. Ask.

All this talk of conversational apocalypse may seem surprising in a book about how the happiest couples get and stay that way. It shouldn't be. Among even the best couples, a great deal of negative communication goes on. Psychologists suggest that this is a sign that the couple are constructively engaged and willing to confront problems. In other words, the husbands, typical stonewallers in many marriages, are hanging in there and talking, and this increases the ultimate satisfaction of both partners.

In the next chapter, we'll delve further into the use, misuse, and styles of talking.

# CRACKING THE CODE

How much easier it would be to make a list for Nick. His non-committal attitude would be No. 1 under liabilities, his reluctance to give advice even when asked for it. He'd probably place it under assets and label it tolerance.

—Ursula Hegi, *Intrusions*

Say what you mean and mean what you say. Sounds simple enough, but what if the way you see the world, and thus the way you talk about it, feels overwhelmingly negative to your intimate partner? Is it a communication misfit or evocative of a larger disjunction? I believe it is both.

When I said earlier that my problem-solving style and Stephen's were different, as are many couples', I meant that I tend to enumerate all possible obstacles to a solution in order to overcome them one by one. This preferred style emerges from my realist core. Rather than be disappointed by failure, I lay out all potential routes and consider them one by one until I zero in on the best. It sounds like a lot of effort, but I do it intuitively. It works beautifully for me. Stephen, however, more vulnerable to a sense of helplessness, found my style exhausting and overwhelming. All those obstacles! Why bother trying at all?

He didn't realize then that when I brought up drawbacks to a prospective plan it didn't imply that I thought it would stop us from succeeding. Interestingly, a theory has been recently espoused giving credence to my style as a workable coping mechanism. Julie K. Norem, a psychologist at Wellesley College, writes about "the positive power of negative thinking." She explains that for some types of individuals, attempting to maintain an upbeat attitude at all times creates anxiety. The preference for confronting all possible obstacles and negative outcomes is called defensive pessimism. Those types who must remain upbeat in order to have the psychic energy to confront challenges are driven mad by defensive pessimists.

## NO, I'M NOT NEGATIVE

Even as we courted, I wrote in my journal: "Stephen is disconcerted, he says, by my habit of thinking and expressing everything in negative terms. He's making me aware of my dark bias in even my smallest comments. Can I change? I think I can, though a change like this would revolutionize my personality."

Months later, still before we got married, he elaborated in a letter: "The more I'm criticized, the more shaky my ego becomes, throwing me back in time to older defensive techniques, such as my withdrawal. I think one of my major fears in our relationship is duplicating a milieu of Inescapable Belittling. A prison, not only of mediocrity, but more essentially of hurt and humiliation, which as a child I could do nothing about and which seems to have damaged my immunological system—psychically, as well as physically I suppose. This probably accounts for my sensitivity to negativity . . . of any sort." For Stephen, a hint of criticism by me created fears he'd be emotionally abused, and his shorthand for the feeling was to call it—albeit broadly—negativity.

Andrew Christensen observed that it's easier to act positively than to do less of something negative. Using an example remarkably like ours (and I've heard this from numerous other couples over the years), he writes, "Luke complains that Caitlin is 'too negative,' and he would feel better if she were not so critical of him. She could change more easily by doing something active for Luke, such as being more complimentary of him, than by holding back her criticism. Yet this would not satisfy Luke." The change he specifically wants is less criticism, not more praise.

The clincher in Christensen's argument is that sometimes we are so fundamentally dissimilar that our partner's requests for change are very difficult to satisfy. We want attitude changes as much as we want behavioral changes. But—and I didn't figure this out for many years—both partners *can* adapt sufficiently to one another so that the original issue becomes moot.

At one point Stephen must have thought our marriage was like the big sign posted at the corner entrance to nearby Echo Park Lake, which begins with Welcome! and then lists about twenty Nos, including no boating, no ice skating, no shooting, and so on. It wasn't that he couldn't do whatever he wanted to do, but more a matter of the negative *words* surrounding him.

One of the ways we tried to get at this negativity construct was to play a game I called Positive Week. We only managed to keep it up for the length of one long walk during an afternoon. Yet that was sufficient to provide insight to both of us. The rule was to make optimistic comments only, to turn all sentences around so that they were upbeat.

I struggled mightily against my own instincts, but succeeded thus: "My, that wind blowing into my face is invigorating. I do hope it rains—the farmers and flowers will love it, and so will I, since rain reminds me the awesome beauty of nature. My legs are achy, which is great since it shows I'm working my muscles. It feels so great to have my work waiting for me when we get back— it's a million times better than being bored and having nothing to do. So many choices for dinner tonight! How lucky we are to live in this time and place and be able to choose whatever we want." And so on.

Over the course of a single walk, my efforts became more natural and less stiff. I even learned, for that short space, to change all my "buts" to "ands," as some positive types prefer. Such a minute difference can make a noticeable change in your conversation, and yes, in your attitude. Of course, it's easy to make fun of such simplistic positivity, and we did. And still, the effects of that one day's effort were lasting.

The irony is that I legitimately feel all those goody-goody sentiments and at the same time I feel their opposite. But by only expressing the downsides of every situation, I'd been exhausting my partner—partly because he was vulnerable to a depressed mood and partly because we were so enmeshed that he felt, on some level, that he had to fix things for me. When he'd try to change my views or point out more positive ways of perceiving reality, I'd argue. All in all, it wasn't that much fun for either of us back then.

I highly recommend another exercise: switch roles. When we each pretended to be the other, we were only able to sustain the effort for a couple of hours as we went about our business one afternoon. In fact, I never did get the hang of being Stephen—but he had a grand time playing me. Though he didn't deny that he might be exaggerating, what he did was "yes, but" me until I couldn't stand it. No matter what I said, he'd name an exception to it. Instead of being his naturally easy-going self, he found objections to everything I suggested. It became exhausting very quickly. "Is that how you see me?" Yup.

Illuminating, yes, but it's only half the solution to the puzzle of what negative means.

## SUBTLE ABUSE

Garden-variety verbal abuse—true emotional abuse—is easy to recognize. For example, Penelope, a hardworking waitress and mother of two preschoolers, once told me about an awful day she had. In the morning, she had assured her husband Tony that there was macaroni and cheese in the house for the girls' dinner. That evening in the middle of her shift, Tony telephoned to complain that there wasn't any macaroni and cheese in the house after all. Yelling at her so loudly she had to hold the phone away from her ear, he berated her for being "irresponsible" and "hopeless." She admits that a couple of years of being called worthless and lazy left her feeling just that. Emotional abusers are particularly expert at poking at your weakest spot.

But verbal abuse takes many forms, from obvious, intended-to-wound name-calling such as Tony's to comments that are much harder to detect as crossing the line. Such words deplete the hearer's sense of self and damage the relationship. A magazine article about subtle abuse by Julius Rosen clarified this issue for me at last. Subtle abuse is a form of verbal interaction that feels negative to the receiver even when it wasn't intended to hurt.

For instance, Rosen offers examples that range from saying, "Don't go out without your umbrella," and "Are you sure you made that reservation?" to "You'll feel better when you get a hair-cut." These might not engender annoyance on the part of some hearers, but for others, a constant litany of such reminders and instructions and veiled requests can feel belittling and become enraging. The subtle abuser thinks she's just "expressing her feel-ings," explains Rosen, but in reality, she's assaulting the other person's integrity with a manipulative evaluation. Even when the subtle abuse stays *quite* subtle, and doesn't slurp over into con-temptuous language, the recipient is disconcerted, in all proba-bility made anxious on some level.

After I read the article, I ran to Stephen asking, "Is this it? Is this what you've been meaning when you say I'm 'negative'?" I read him some examples and he agreed that, yes, this is precisely what he'd been meaning but hadn't been able to articulate. I'm not saying it was easy for me to accept that my everyday way of speaking to the man I love was considered abusive to him, but when I allowed that perhaps "subtle abuse" was a fair way to talk about this behavior, we were finally on our way toward the pos-sibility of improvement.

Admittedly, Stephen is sensitive to comments I hadn't before thought of as critical or belittling, while other individuals learn to let such remarks slip away without a quiver of tension. But I could finally grasp that the way I spoke to him was uncomfortably close to the way my ex-husband had regularly spoken to me. Ouch.

Unwanted feedback is one of the hardest areas to recognize as subtle abuse. Even solicited feedback, as when your partner asks you for your opinion, tells more about you than about him. This is because you only perceive certain aspects of any situation, and you do so in ways that are meaningful to *you*. So if you say, when asked whether your partner's shorter haircut is attractive, "It's nice, but long hair is sexier," you're telling about your own preferences. But at least you're answering a question that was asked. Many of us constantly give feedback where none is wanted at all. "Your best use of feedback is to note your impulse to give, then reflect on what is going on inside you," observe authors Charles N. Seashore, Edith Whitfield Seashore, and Gerald M. Weinberg in *What Did You Say? The Art of Giving and Receiving Feedback.* That urge to tell your loved one what's wrong with him won't improve your connection, change his behavior, or satisfy whichever deeper needs you might be working out this way.

A lot of subtle abuse falls under the category of nagging. In fact, when I mentioned that Stephen used to call me negative, a male friend immediately assumed he meant I nagged. Each person might apply his or her own meaning to the words "nagging" or "negative," with my friend never perceiving his own eye-rolling, or his saying, "Just get over it," as contemptuous and subtly abusive.

After I made the effort to feel what it must be like to live in my partner's internal world, we moved much closer to harmony. Now I try to take responsibility for my preferred way of doing things, so that instead of saying, "You're so messy," which is outright criticism, or "Why can't you keep the dining room in better shape?" which he hears as subtle abuse, I might now say, "We're having company and it's really important to me that the dining room be cleared out. Could you please help with that on Friday?" I'm being specific, telling him why this matters to me, and I'm not demanding that he do it or even agree that it's necessary.

Now when I speak in a way that Stephen considers sarcastic, demeaning, or subtly abusive, he reacts, not with anger, resentment, or withdrawal, as previously, but with one of our "training" methods. (As you can see, we mix humor into virtually everything.) A typical one: an arm slowly slips around my shoulder while we're walking past a patch of nettles, indicating a gentle mock threat to make me take a "weed walk." I always get the message: uh-oh, I've done it again.

If, in your own relationship, the subtle abuser is your partner, your best option for reforming him is to state what's going on for you clearly and gently. And don't forget to assume goodwill on his part. That will show in your voice and manner and help him face his own verbal habits less defensively.

Sometimes, however, you need to allow your partner to use words that might seem abusive because they're the only way he knows to get his message across. If you can hear such distressing words neutrally, as vibrant clues to his state of mind about how he perceives you, even if he isn't yet able to turn them into proper I-messages, then you can take it from there and have a genuine discussion about what's happening between you. Stephen has at times exaggerated his descriptions of me, and not only for humorous impact. He has called me a shrew, and when things were rotten between us, he'd say I was "eviscerating" him. The first time I heard that word, I was astonished. Who the heck could he be talking about? After all, I see myself as much gentler than that, timid and tentative even.

Now I'm no longer offended by such disjunctions, realizing they're emotional, not objective, descriptions of how my behavior makes him feel. It's all valuable information for me. It's the same as when our Sunday brunch buddies bicker and she says he yelled at her over some minor "error," and he denies that he yelled. But it felt like yelling to her, i.e., it was criticism (he does not deny that), and for some people, all criticism feels *loud*, intrusive, painful, makes them want to cry, hide child-like under the table, or strike back. Many cycles of conflict begin this way: I perceive what you said in a certain way and respond in kind, but you find it incredible to be perceived any such way.

Yes, it would be ideal if we could express ourselves in perfect I-messages. How mature and superhuman if, instead of making jokes, my beloved could say, "When you make remarks about any tiny aspect of my behavior that displeases you, they feel cutting to my sense of self. I know I'm super-sensitive due to impaired self-esteem, but could you reconsider before making critical comments and be a bit more easygoing about what's essentially no big deal?" Funny thing, though: that's what I learned to *hear* him saying.

## MY STYLE OR YOURS?

Harriet gives her relationship with Myron a ninety-six out of 100. He's more analytical and reserved and gives it a ninety. She resents that when she wants to talk things over, she's met with taciturnity. She's learned, she says, to keep repeating herself, "until he says, 'You're repeating yourself over and over.' 'That's because you're not getting my message,' I tell him. Then he gets it."

Harriet further explains that when she needs to feel she can count on Myron, such as during extended family crises, that's when she tends to repeat herself. "But then, finally, all of a sudden, after all of these years, he really understands me, and will say something like, 'You know, this is getting between us. I love you more than anything and it's bothering me because you're so hurt by it.'" This is what I mean by focusing on the connection.

Now that Myron has learned how important emotional conversation is to his wife, their ways of talking still remain different. "Even when he does understand what I'm trying to tell him," explains Harriet, "he has his own way of dealing with the situation. He's systematic, organized, and methodical. He can't switch to another way when I'd like him to, and I understand that."

Harriet has learned to value her husband's ways of showing he loves and cares for her, but it most certainly was not an instant or one-time recognition. "So he was not the handholder when we were young, or the man who kissed his wife in public," she says, "but he was the one who got up and gave the baby the bottle and changed the diaper." Whereas some men and women harbor years of resentment because their mates show love differently, others—the ones who have learned to love in flow—are more adaptable. But because it can take a bit of mental gymnastics to do all that translating, it's reasonable to hope that both mates will exert their share of the effort.

Other interviewees told me similar tales that evoked the stereotypical male/female difference in conversational style. For example, Letitia, whose husband constantly tells her how amazing she is, describes their varying styles: "He a really sweet guy, and he keeps me in check. I tend to have a little feistier personality. He would probably use a different word." She laughs here, imagining what words Lenny might indeed use to describe her. "He's on an even keel, he never raises his voice, and it's rare that my voice rises. If it does, he probably gets more quiet, or says we should discuss this at another time. Or he might say, maybe I should record you so you hear what you sound like. That makes me think, 'Oh my gosh, that's terrible.'"

When Letitia reads about a neighborhood shooting (they live in an urban enclave of the Los Angeles region), her typical reaction is to panic. Or she'll read about the smog and feel that they should get their child away from it before she gets asthma. "I get a little edgy," she says, and then it spills over into anger toward Lenny. "How could you come home late at night? I want you to be more careful," she'll tell him.

If Lenny's initial response is so preternaturally calm and cool that, instead of relaxing her, it seems uncaring, she'll make a point of explaining what she needs more directly: "I would like it if you were just a little bit more upset that this is happening and that the world seems a little scary to me these days." What he does then is search the Internet for statistics to show she is being more fearful than reality warrants. And this does the trick.

Some women would prefer a warm hug along with a "Now, now, everything's going to be all right, honey," or a hug and a commiserating validation, such as, "I can't blame you for worrying.

It sure can be scary out there," with, in some instances, an added note, "but we'll do what we can to stay safe."

Letitia laughs ruefully as she adds, "The truth of it is that unless we're willing to go to some small town, and even then bad things can happen...." Seems she's not so far from being a realist herself and just needs reminding sometimes.

Letitia also understands that the same quality in her husband that periodically drives her mad is what draws her to him. "For him, the glass is *always* half full," she explains. "It only irritates me when I'm particularly worried. Most of the time, it's his greatest attribute."

Here's another example: when Elizabeth reacts emotionally, Dan yells at her. "I was very upset over the national election [that was contested in Florida] and had a crying jag over it. Almost any woman would pat me on the back and say, 'Gee, I know how you feel, how about we'll have a cup of tea?' But my husband starts yelling, 'There's nothing you can do about it. Get over it!' Which makes me cry more." She tolerates this because she's come to recognize that her extreme reactions *scare* her husband, so that what once seemed an alien response on his part no longer disrupted their connection.

"It's always a good idea to know somebody's parents, if possible," she adds. "I understand where it comes from, because he's very much like his father. He'll scrub up the pots and pans, and then he'll get in your face like he's the boss."

One woman told me that when she and her husband get into a discussion focused on her emotions, he says it's "bunk" and tells her "we ought to just be talking about behavior." She recognizes—after some years of fighting it—that his take on emotional realities is deeply influenced by his involvement in a physical science field.

One long-married man told me that neither he nor his wife discuss intimate issues very much, which is fine with him. His wife "has some sort of wiring that works out things inside and resists articulating them in words, and when she's forced to, the result is harmful. Words can be of limited use in matters of intimacy and philosophy. Actions count more than talk, and many kinds of talk aggravate and distort issues."

For a typical example of talk that aggravated (but that *more effective* talk might have alleviated), consider this story told by Jeanette, a retired dancer: "I'm worried about aging. My mother has gotten very wrinkled, so I expect to also. And Bob said one day, 'You know, I think you'll be really upset if you get wrinkled like your mother. You should probably start realizing that you're going to want to do something.' I didn't like that this came out of nowhere."

Bob, who works at a university hospital, takes his turn: "We'd just visited her mom and Jeanette was commenting about the way her mother wrinkled. So when we came home, I said, 'If you think you're going to look like your mother and you don't want to be like that, look into it.' I'm much more blunt and factual, and part of Jeanette's contribution to my personality has been to make me softer. She's much more sensitive to criticism. It seemed to me that she needed to hear somebody say it was okay to consider cosmetic surgery. When she asked if I thought she needed it, I told her no. But I knew she took it wrong."

In an attempt to get at the core of these sorts of stylistic differences in the way people talk, I spoke with Washington, D.C.-based sociolinguist Deborah Tannen, who wrote *You Just Don't Understand: Women and Men in Conversation*. Tannen believes that women and men tend to have different conversational styles and have to make an effort to understand each other. Such disjunctions may develop because boys and girls grow up in different worlds (hanging out with same-sex kids, being treated differently by parents and teachers), and thus learn to speak what amounts almost to different languages. Here's some of our conversation:

**Q:** How come I often try to "fix" things for my husband when all he wants is comforting, and at other times, when I want empathy, I get practical solutions instead. For instance, one day my fingers bumbled onto the wrong computer keys, throwing me and my file into some alternate universe. I wailed, "I hate computers!" and within a millisecond, my husband had pushed me aside and taken my place at the keyboard. "Here, let me teach you something," he said, helpfully, when what I mainly wanted was to vent.

**Tannen:** People are not consistent in their conversational style, not even throughout the day. The differences *tend* to apportion a certain way among women and men, but that does not mean that any individual is going to fit a pattern. In fact, many of the differences I've researched are associated with different parts of the country, different ethnic and class backgrounds, and different family backgrounds.

**Q:** I often ask my husband to do things for me indirectly, because I hate the thought of hearing a "no." You've written that this is a typical female style of asking. He either doesn't get it or he ignores requests that are not specifically requests. Yet if I come out and ask directly, he often won't do it either. So I ask again. Then I'm accused of nagging. Any solution?

**Tannen:** Isn't it ironic that women are called nags when men often tell women what to do? I suggest it's because men are inclined to put off doing what they're told because they feel that puts them in a subordinate role. So the woman asks once more, and she becomes a nag! She could wait longer before asking again. I run into this with my husband too. He says, "Make it clear to me how important it is, and if it's *really* important, I'll do it." Or compromise: give him a deadline after which you hire help.

**Q:** A friend of mine recently told me that whenever she says to her husband, "Honey, we need to talk," he responds with, "How long is it going to take?" Then, before long, he tells her, "Get to the point." What's going on there?

**Tannen:** I think both women and men feel that the other goes on and on, but about different things. Men complain that women go on about what took place in their friend's life, or the ins and out of making a decision, or the relationship, as in this example. And women say that men give them lectures when they wanted a brief answer—or just a sympathetic one. They have to agree on how much each gets to talk—or listen.

**Q:** You've said that men and women often behave the same for different reasons. Why does that matter?

**Tannen:** It can lead to misunderstandings if we don't understand *why* people do things. For example, I once visited my family and brought along a camera I'd been trying without success to get fixed. My brother-in-law just took it and disappeared. Now, I might easily have thought he was being anti-social; he doesn't care about me. I came all this way to visit and he spends two hours in his workshop. But he showed his caring by fixing the camera.

I think there are definitely men for whom one of the major ways they show caring is to do things like that. That doesn't mean you can't say to your husband, "I'd rather you spend time with me and we'll hire someone to fix things." But it would be good to understand that his motives may not be to get away from you.

**Q:** Do you have any advice on living with someone who has a different conversational style from you?

**Tannen:** Understand that there is no one right way to talk or listen. Don't be too quick to assume negative motives. It helps if your partner is open to discussing ways of talking. Just by understanding what style differences are, you have a better chance of keeping your disagreements from getting out of control.

Sometimes disagreements will have deeper roots than mere style. People take philosophic stances based on their own sense of right and wrong. For instance, Frieda, one of the wives I spoke with, described a recent exchange. When Frieda's girlfriend, who was single, found out she was pregnant, the father of the baby didn't want her to have it, but she decided she was going to go ahead anyway, and she later sued him for child support.

"My husband didn't agree with her decision," relates Frieda. "He doesn't feel women should make a man pay child support if the man didn't want to have the child. I told him that's true, but the child is here, so what's next?" For Frieda, the immediate human need takes precedence over what seems to her a more remote general principle of justice, and an argument ensued.

Psychologists and those who study ethics have long debated which way of making moral decisions is more highly evolved. Perhaps some of your own debates will be less distressing if you keep in mind the various ways in which equally well-meaning individuals can think about such questions.

## LISTEN CAREFULLY

Good listeners are hard to find. They're easy to recognize, though: they give you their full attention, head cocked, eyes on yours, forehead slightly wrinkling to demonstrate that you're being taken seriously.

When you listen nondefensively, you put your own emotions on hold and pay full attention to those of another. Attentive listening has been termed a gift by some. It's also the wisest and fairest way to act. It's the only way to get inside your partner's mind, validate his feelings, find commonalities, work on relationship problem areas, and achieve deep intimacy.

"An empathic response is restrained," writes Michael P. Nichols in *The Lost Art of Listening*, "largely silent; following, not leading, it encourages the speaker to go deeper into his or her experience." Most times we jump in too soon, sympathize too much, reveal our own similar experiences. Or we're busily judging instead of listening, although the process is subtle: we think we're trying to get the facts straight. Even an "Oh?" said in a certain tone may be judgmental. By saying "I can't believe you said that," or "How could you possibly believe something like that?" we're judging without admitting it.

If you're sure of what your partner is going to say before he or she says it, that's another form of judgment. By assuming you know already, you're not letting yourself find out in reality. This reminds me of that scene in the film *My Dinner with André* in which one character so articulately speaks about his deepening relationship with his wife, of how there's always more to learn and understand.

Nevertheless, one of Deborah Tannen's liberating insights relates to differences in interrupting style. Some people were raised to believe that any form of interrupting is rude. But others do it all the time—it's called "talking along"—as a way to show interest, without meaning to derail or dominate the conversation.

Tannen's explanation helped Stephen understand why no one ever gets to finish a sentence in the family I come from, and why none of us cares. We listen impatiently, itching to jump in, make comments, get clarification of some earlier bit. Stephen doesn't mind my overlapping talking style, he insists, except when he warns me, "I need to finish my thought."

When a weighty issue is at stake we'll try our "talking pillow." One of my sons had given me a tiny pillow, about six inches by six inches, with a bunny on one side and a weasel on the other, but any small soft object will do as well—soft because you might toss it robustly across the room at times. Here's how it works: one of you holds it and says his piece. The other person listens attentively without interrupting. When the one holding the pillow finishes, he gives it to the other person. I can attest that it takes an extraordinary amount of effort and concentration (and lip-biting and sitting on hands) for a habitual interrupter to wait her turn. I often toss the pillow to Stephen, but as he begins speaking, I remember some vital additional tidbit, and there I am interjecting. "I have the pillow," he reminds me, and I simmer down.

Another therapy technique that's gotten popular press coverage lately is "active listening," which used to be prescribed by many therapists. This is a technique wherein you say to your partner, "This is what I hear you saying," repeating what you think you heard your mate say, so as to clarify points of view during any potential conflict.

Exponents of a well-known approach called Prevention and Relationship Enhancement Program (PREP) believe that active listening is one useful method couples should have in their arsenals. According to Howard J. Markman, Scott M. Stanley, and Susan L. Blumberg, authors of *Fighting FOR Your Marriage*, by agreeing on the strategies you're going to use to structure your sensitive conversations, you achieve some predictability, which helps keep the more negative emotions under control. They suggest what they call the "Speaker-Listener" technique, which is a lot like our talking pillow sessions, with this crucial addition: you must paraphrase what you hear, and you may not rebut. It takes practice, but those who try it and make the effort to perfect the technique (the listener keeps paraphrasing until the speaker feels he's got it right) may feel safer to engage in conversations about touchy topics.

Not long ago, however, marital researcher John Gottman announced that in his extensive research with distressed couples, he and his colleagues found that active listening isn't effective after all. The main difficulty with the technique, per Gottman, is that it's asking couples in the midst of very troublesome conversations to apply superhuman restraint. Your partner is complaining about you and you're supposed to remain nondefensive and repeat everything back. Accurately.

Andrew Christensen, too, focuses on the difficulty of paraphrasing what your partner has said without injecting your own bias into it, distorting the message and leading to even more complex arguments. The words you use to paraphrase may turn evaluative. Suppose you say, "When you eat the last banana and don't add bananas to the grocery list, I find it irritating." Here's a possible paraphrase: "So you're saying you can't handle my casual approach toward food." You expressed your distress at what you saw as inconsiderate behavior, and all you got back was that the lack is in you, that you can't "handle" something as innocuous as "casualness"? No wonder this is such a difficult technique for the unwary.

## WHAT WORDS MEAN

> Perhaps she was only laughing at my words.... To her, words were useless for getting close to reality, in her opinion they were rather an impediment. She admired my rhetorical skills, but not so much for what I said, more as one admires someone who is good at waterskiing or flipping pancakes.
>
> —Jens Christian Grondahl, *Silence in October*

An attentive listener also realizes that words don't always mean exactly what they say, even when spoken by someone who intends to be straightforward. As we get to know one another over many years, we learn to interpret meanings that may have been hidden to us before. Seventy-three-year-old Sam, for instance, told me that he and Ida still argue after a decade of marriage (her fourth, his second), "because I'm literal and mean exactly what I say, and I take what she says literally and she doesn't always mean it that way. There's another level that I haven't quite understood how to interpret." He keeps trying.

Stephen and I once visited a long-married couple we like and found ourselves in conversation about the abundant miscommunications in our respective marriages. Roland and I were cheerleaders for the necessity of getting the facts straight, but Jocelyn insisted that facts don't matter, that what she *says* isn't what's important. Roland explained that, for him, when Jocelyn changes her mind about what she's said, he becomes frustrated. I began to realize that what Jocelyn wasn't able to explain to her husband was that it was her feelings that mattered, not her actual words. As articulate as she seemed, at times she was unable to convey the *emotional* facts to Roland.

Suddenly, Jocelyn interrupted Roland's gentle yet logical diatribe to say, with an endearingly broad smile, that her husband looked like a cute little chipmunk. Luckily for our evening and their relationship, Roland seemed not to mind the potentially demeaning remark. Figuring that neither of them was feeling heard, I said, "Jocelyn, you live in a less linear world than Roland. But instead of pirouetting away in the middle of a serious conversation with him, maybe you could try to enter the rational world of causes and effects, at least until Roland feels heard." I could see that Jocelyn was thinking about this, and that Roland liked the idea, because such a compromise would mean that his perception of reality would at least occasionally get a fair hearing. Love and commitment were obviously present, and, last I heard, they were still trying to get through to one another.

What's most astonishing to me, considering how sympathetic I was to Roland's plea for rationality that night, is that I've occasionally found myself on the other side of this debate.

Stephen: "But you *said*..."

Me: "But I *meant*..."

And on and on. I tell him I can't bear when he gets what I call *legalistic*. (I read somewhere that Tolstoy wrote you can tell a marriage is on the rocks when the spouses speak to each other rationally.) After all, what could be wrong with correcting a statement you made earlier, if you now decide on a more accurate way to express yourself? That's not lying. Perhaps it's a manipulation of words, but then, what are words for, if not to be *used* to make ourselves understood? And the best way to accomplish understanding, short of taking your case to the United Nations, is to keep struggling with those words until you both feel understood.

I realized this communication business wasn't going to be simple after only a few months of fledgling intimacy with Stephen. That was when I learned that he's not very hidden: what you see is what you get. I, on the other hand, presented more of a challenge. Yet Stephen enjoyed playing around with the subtexts that are a part of my own style, as can be seen in these excerpts from a very early letter he wrote me:

Dearest Susan, I must be developing a flinch reaction. Last night, after I mailed a letter to you, I ruminated (slightly hypnogogic) on all the ways my words might be misinterpreted. Even now, I picture you in a fainting fit rivaling Snow White's. Some potential indiscretions and implications fermented by my imagination, hopefully:

A. You reacted to my mention of E. [a female friend of his of whom I was very jealous] by mailing away for *Cosmopolitan*'s "Assassinate your Date's Female Friends" kit. This includes a French perfume bottle filled with gopher barf; a personalized letter with the "c's" especially designed by Pac-Man (a way to involve the kids, also); and an exploding dildo, decorated with Jewish runes to throw her off.

D. You were disconcerted by my writing to my friend Bob *first*, thus exhibiting suppressed homosexual tendencies.

E. Even though I mentioned E. in that letter disparagingly, my loving references to you were smaller numerically—thus demonstrating that my subliminal area of interest *really* lies with the trollop-bitch.

F. E.'s angular and mannish features correlate with point D.

G. My writing to you now—with complete Love and devotion—is simply proof of gratuitous placation. After all, what modern woman could admire such obvious and uxorious simpering— clearly a product of retroactive guilt.

H. My love is an attempt to drown your individuality.

J. No pelicans were mentioned in the letter, but I was probably *thinking* about them.

K. The letter could have been *much* more romantic.

M. The intent of that letter—as well as this one, come to think about it—was to camouflage with light humor and affection a basic hostility.

N. I didn't mention my wonderful sex life with you.

0. And, if I had, I only would be reducing you to a body.

P. My being able to enumerate points up to "P" in this letter PROVES that there must have been *something* pernicious in the first; better do some careful rereading tonight.

Yours, with lots of love, Stephen

A few of his facetiously-phrased subtexts did point toward my insecurities, and I was delighted that he was trying to unlock my thought processes. After all, as Alice says to Humpty Dumpty in *Through the Looking Glass*, "That's a great deal to make one word mean." Humpty responds, "When I make a word do a lot of work like that, I always pay it extra."

Why is it imperative to learn both to speak clearly and to read between and under your mate's words? One reason is because hidden expectations can get in the way of intimacy and complicate negotiations over the plainest matters.

An example: I used to scour the free tabloids for author events that would interest Stephen, whether or not I wanted to attend, knowing I'd ordinarily go with him. I felt I was making a generous offering to him, but without a hint that I didn't much feel like going. Since he'd doubtlessly say yes, I'd be annoyed that he didn't realize he owes me equal nurturing. Finally I stopped notifying him of events I didn't want to attend, unless I figured it would be of particular interest to him, in which case I'd mention my lack of interest. Then he could decide whether he wanted to attend without me. The directness dissolved my resentment.

I also stopped asking, "Do you want pizza?" when *I* didn't. Stephen would always say yes, with never an inkling of my unspoken sacrifice (I preferred more healthful food). If you're only making one of these internal compromises in hopes of obtaining more appreciation from someone who tends to be oblivious, you're going to be disappointed and eventually resentful.

One distressed couple was seeing a therapist for years. At one point, frustrated from her attempts to help them, the therapist told them they each made a convincing case when they spoke, as if both sets of facts could as easily sway a jury. Their marriage didn't improve until they were able to get beyond facts to care what the other was feeling.

Similarly, a friend recently complained to us, in front of her husband, that he'd just been critical of her. He insisted he hadn't been. It seemed to me he *had* been, but he insisted "the facts would show otherwise." But what matters most weren't the facts, but how his words had felt to his wife.

That my mind only retains a murky impression of the above incident is unsurprising. A study reported in *Cognition in Close Relationships* found that women are more likely to store conversations as relationship memories, while men tend more to store them in terms of the issue discussed. So that what's recalled by the wife is the husband's efforts at nurturing, even when solid practical help may have been lacking. Or it's the feeling of being criticized that's recalled, when the words offered were meant in a benevolent spirit of "here's what you should have done."

A viable rule of thumb, then, is that when your efforts to communicate deteriorate into back-and-forth argument, focus on what you more often neglect, either the emotions underneath the words or the content. If your partner is using angry words, trust the connection and ask if hurt lurks under the surface of those words. Sometimes when we are hurt, we speak angrily to make the other person feel what we're feeling.

So many of us get stuck at the level of bickering over trivial details of our lives, when what's underneath are more essential conflicts over sex, money, or fairness, or even deeper issues: caring, control, integrity, commitment, and so on. We all want our partner to fully accept us. Strive as a team to discover, explore, and handle the hidden issues in your relationship. Stop before you ask your partner what he's feeling, and instead ask yourself what *you* are actually feeling. Only then can you begin to use words that say what you mean.

# 7
# HOW DO YOU DRIVE ME CRAZY? LET ME COUNT THE WAYS

Humming a song on a Saturday morning was not the kind of aggressive act that could easily be explained in a court of law as an understandable reason for murder, but it struck Ervin Neal that he might finally have to kill his wife, or get rid of her in some way.

—Lawrence Naumoff, *The Night of the Weeping Women*

Six weeks into my relationship with Stephen, I wrote in my journal: "I ought to *try* to be at least slightly more rational and consider what some of his traits might feel like to me in the long run. Not that I envision any of them ever being bothersome to me."

Such naiveté! I had no excuse either, since with my first husband I'd already learned, for example, that what seemed initially to be unstinting integrity could later morph into ramrod rigidity. Alas, while we're busy examining the front porch for the faintest clues of negative personality traits, new ones clamber in the back window waving huge warning signs we manage to miss.

This chapter is about those slight behaviors that get on your nerves. I share my own detailed list, and later I explore what some of my interviewees reported as straining their equanimity. Most people I interviewed were able to come up with only one or two examples of partner behaviors that chronically bother them. I think this tells us that most of the happiest couples don't keep such lists boiling on the front burner, waiting to splash their spouses (or an interviewer) at the earliest opportunity. What gets some folks through many days is blissful forgetfulness.

To say such habits drive a partner insane, of course, is to exaggerate—unless the wrong hormones are in the ascendant, or one child is battering another with sticky hands while you're getting ready to go to the doctor, or three or more appliances have broken down at once. In such instances, what might be a minor annoyance can flare into a maddening provocation.

In this and the following chapter, we'll learn a lot more about what it means to loosen up and let go and how that can make loving in flow so much easier.

## AN EASY LIST

> Maybe it wasn't charming after all, the way he bit into an apple, as if he were rabid, as if he were attacking it, going to get the better of it. Would she, for the long haul, be able to lovingly wash his stack of crusted dishes, and scrape the burned oatmeal, the burned noodles, the burned SpaghettiOs off the bottom of his three pots? When she considered his failures and a few of his slovenly habits, she'd have to shake herself. She'd have to remember that it was his boyishness, his wide-ranging curiosity, and his hungry-dog appetite that had been appealing in the first place.
>
> —Jane Hamilton, *Disobedience*

Over a one-week period, I compiled the following not-at-all-comprehensive list. Some of these behaviors I've never mentioned to Stephen because they're embarrassingly trivial. My beloved:

- ↦ Takes several paper towels when one would do and doesn't replace the empty roll.
- ↦ Uses the auto air conditioner in winter, sometimes while wearing a sweater.
- ↦ Removes pots from the stove without turning off the burner first.
- ↦ Leaves lights on everywhere.

- Leaves his soda cans everywhere instead of placing them in the recycling bag below the sink.
- Leaves the stereo on all day, with nothing playing, when he's in another room.
- Puts recyclable plastics in the regular trash bag.
- Throws his laundry into the hamper twisted, rolled in a ball, inside out, coins in pockets.
- Drinks a soda while we're walking, with his other hand in his pocket.
- Lets rose bush branches with thick thorns grow out over the front sidewalk, endangering passersby.
- Leaves garden hoses kinked so they crack and have to be replaced.
- Leaves cutting tools on the front porch (tempting amateur thieves to cut our alarm wires).
- Takes my stapler from my desk and leaves it elsewhere.
- Lies back on the sofa while eating, like a reclining Roman emperor.
- Pours buckets of oily dressing on dinners I make for him that would otherwise be healthful.
- Leaves cabinet doors and dresser drawers open, often with the tongue of a sock showing to taunt me.
- Jiggles his glass full of ice cubes repeatedly.
- Rounds down when quoting prices, even when the number is $11.98.
- Lets the dishwasher door drop sharply when he opens it so that it bounces.
- Mixes big and little spoons in the drawer when he puts clean silverware away.
- Drops clothing he's worn only half an hour on the bedroom floor or chair.
- Keeps *all* email he's ever received in his computerized inbox, with no sorting system, and since he rarely responds to a piece of mail upon first encounter, items are forgotten in the huge pile.

➛ Leaves the back door open, even when the alarm is set.
➛ Forgets to remove tomatoes from their resting place on top of the broiler before turning the broiler on.


Nitpicky? Sure. But perhaps you can relate to at least a few of these habits. Maybe you have some of them yourself. If inspired, list your own partner's annoying behaviors. Then list your own, as he/she might describe them. If you can't think of many, dare to go ahead and ask. Don't make the mistake of presuming you're not as bothersome to others as they can be to you. But if you've been married a long time, you know this.

## SOMEWHERE UNDER THE RAINBOW

> "You are so wonderful," I said, lying back down and stretching my arm across his chest; "there's no one in the world like this. I'd follow you everywhere if I could. I've never leave you alone even for a second. And you have no faults! I wish you had some so I could show you how little they mattered to me!"
>
> —Susan Fromberg Schaeffer, *The Madness of a Seduced Woman*


When I told a friend of mine that I was compiling this list, she said, "But isn't that opening a can of worms?" But it's precisely *not* that. Most of the above have merely vestigial emotional content for me now, except when my psychic immune system is depleted due to other stresses, and other couples have told me similar stories. But a few years ago when my relationship with Stephen was struggling to regain its footing, any one of the items I listed might well have thrown me into a frenzy of reactivity. How, then, do I deal with such a long list of minor vexations that keeps them from becoming legally-actionable grievances?

"Lighten up" is the typical marriage manual advice. Getting used to "impossible" habits can be like living with a constant ringing in your ears. Remove the emotional component, by realizing there is no real threat or danger, and you can relax.

Theo Park, for example, tells how he deals with feeling irked by his partner: "Den is messier than I am. He doesn't clean countertops, he's not as interested in making sure that the bread board has the crumbs swept off. I could go down a whole little list, but I long ago let go of that. At one point, I would kind of passive-aggressively 'tease' him about how sloppy he was. And he finally said, 'You know, that gets really old. I am the way I am and I'm not going to change.' Now those things don't matter to me anymore. I've also relaxed a great deal about some of my need to control my environment. That's one of the ways *I've* changed."

Jeanette was slightly embarrassed to tell me about all the "silly things you don't even want to think about," such as: "He didn't put the milk in the refrigerator. The electricity thing: every room he walks into he turns the lights down to the absolute minimum. Even if he's in a room, he'll keep all the lights off except the one he's using. My attitude toward electricity is, okay, rooms I'm not in, turn the lights off, but if I'm in the room, I like it to be bright and comfortable. He might say, 'Do you have to have all the lights on?' Sometimes he leaves his shoes in the middle of the floor. But it's hard to even come up with little things because they're so meaningless," she concludes, laughing.

Yet how do you accomplish this lightening up if it's not in your nature to let what feel like transgressions slip away unnoticed? My own way of coming to terms with exasperating behavior may not suit everyone. As a character in Evelyn Waugh's *Brideshead Revisited* says, "I have to turn a thing round and round, like a piece of ivory in a Chinese puzzle, until—click!—it fits into place—but by that time it's upside down to everyone else."

Many couples never reach this point. People tell me all the time that they're stuck in the stage of "But how can I possibly live with such and such? Who does he think I am that I'd ever accept that?" "I threw boots at my first husband once," says Kat Meltzer, a San Francisco writer now happily married for a decade, "because he was eating raw carrots and even though his mouth was closed, the crunch echoed in his big Teutonic sinuses and drove me insane."

A recent study looked at a related question: do successful couples compartmentalize (keep all the negatives in one part of their mind and the positives in another), or do they integrate everything into a full picture of their mate? It was found that as a relationship continues, integrating the positive and the negative is necessary to maintain an overall positive view of your partner. What this means is that if the stress—the crazy-making behavior—is less prevalent than the pleasing aspects of your partnership, it's fine to ship it off to the Siberian corners of your psyche. Eventually you'll develop the ability to accept the whole person, one who drives you nuts sometimes but whom you love anyway.

## I AM A CULTURE

You may notice that a lot of the actions and inactions that disturb me have to do with recycling. A generation or so ago, daily acts by one spouse wouldn't have caused the other to grind her teeth because "they're bad for the planet." In this, I realize I'm a product of my times.

My parents fume over waste as though the Depression were still in full swing, and I picked up these habits. My in-laws, while delighting in sales and discounts, don't seem as consistent about conserving. When we go over there to open holiday presents and I collect the wrapping paper to take home and reuse, they tease me. It's no wonder that Stephen never picked up strong messages of saving every scrap.

Thus we have the "waste not, want not/save the planet" items on my list. Am I living in an inflexible past, neurotically attached to a Depression-era mentality when the world has irrevocably changed, when two cents worth of electricity is basically meaningless, when saving half a paper towel may be more bother than it's worth in the larger scheme of things? Or, as I prefer to think, am I being most ethical by doing what everyone ought to do?

When I notice I'm equating waste with sin, I see that this subject is largely an emotional one. Then I use mental reframing: just as I don't harangue my neighbors about their habits, I must let go of my sense of responsibility—and my judgmental tendencies—toward Stephen's. I continue to attempt to mold certain habits, though, even if he only recycles to please me. One of our private rituals, indicating you can teach an old dog new tricks: whenever Stephen places his soda can in the recycling bag, he emits a short bark. I hear this wherever I am in the house and am pleased.

## THE ONLY THING YOU HAVE TO FEAR

Back to the list: another set of acts are those that signal DANGER! to me. These include not wiping slippery bathroom floors, leaving shoes at the top of the stairs (not on my current list because he stopped, as likely due to some random mutation of behavior as to my shrieks), allowing rose thorns to endanger passing children (whose parents could sue and take our house), leaving cutting tools outside within reach of would-be thieves, and worst of all, leaving his keys in the front door overnight (the few times he did this, my dramatic reaction shuttled an "uh-oh" into his longer-term memory).

When we were dating, the lock on Stephen's apartment door wouldn't lock from the inside, and he hadn't bothered to pester his landlady about it. When I slept there, I felt protected by him—our love was new, after all!—but just barely. He's not frightened by the thought of strangers apt to pillage and rape, partly because he just doesn't think about such risks. He's more of an "it's a random universe" kind of guy anyway.

Even so, there is less emotion in all this for me than there used to be. I check the front door locks myself, bring in the sharp garden tools, remind him to prune the promiscuous roses, look more carefully where I step.

When Stephen showers in a rush, a water blotch the shape and size of Atlantis may appear on the floor. One day I asked him to wipe this up, which he argued was unnecessary. I explained that I was afraid the water would seep into the cracks between the floor tiles and harm the wooden floor beneath, or worse, that I might slip on the wetness and come crashing down. He insisted the water wasn't there—I showed him how to bend so the light reflected on it—but then he insisted the splot was puny, not huge, and that it would evaporate by itself. Still, most of the time, I grab a towel and wipe it up, taking responsibility for protecting myself. Sometimes, when we are both in an especially agreeable mood, I might spy a fresh puddle and point to it. He wipes it up, which convinces me more than ever that the silly things we insist on have more to do with momentary moods than with logic.

## WHOSE LIFE IS IT ANYWAY?

Another category: what he does that seems to me to endanger *his* health, which equals danger to me too, of course. (We once joked about what I call the "marital medical system," where an extra Prozac for me means one less needed by him, and vice versa.) I imagine spending vast amounts of time pursuing medical care for him, following up endlessly with our health insurance, visiting him at the hospital, and so on.

Some of the most innocuous-appearing acts fall into this broad category. Here's a minor one: when we are out taking a walk for our health, he might drink a soda at the same time. The casualness of drinking while walking annoys me, somehow reminds me of my ex-husband who only rarely would walk with me but smoked while he did. Then it reminds me of the fact that Stephen hardly ever drinks water, preferring to down at least half a dozen diet soft drinks every day, replete with suspicious chemical additives. Just one of my own peculiar cascading series of thoughts.

But I've learned that berating a lover about his eating habits is counterproductive. It's the prime example of what said lover calls nagging. Thus each instance of his helping himself to seconds on some sugary or white-floury foodstuff, each time he opts for fries over salad, each time he drenches his salad in cups of dressing ("But it's low-cal!" he tells me, feeling naïvely pleased with his choice), I feel a twist in my own abdomen.

If you want to help change someone's health habits, you first have to consider what motivates them and how prone they are to feeling controlled by others—by you, in particular. Does your partner like to be reminded of things? He knows, he hasn't forgotten. He has chosen to behave a certain way for short-term gratification. I surely don't like to be reminded of my own lapses. Once that cookie is on its way to my mouth, heaven help the person who speaks up for abstinence. It can feel insulting to be told what you obviously already know.

What about the jiggling ice cubes, which I've mentioned to him, and the big and little spoon confusion, which I never have? It's not worth delving into my own deepest neuroses to figure them out. Here's where it's got to be a case of live and let live. I recently mentioned to him that his ice-cube clinks were on my list of crazy-making behaviors. He looked up, then continued jiggling the damn glass. He insists it cools the drink quicker.

A lot of the trifling matters may evoke laziness to me, or lack of consideration, but they may only be a lack of detail consciousness. Stephen is compassionate and wouldn't add to someone's burden purposely. He has a one-track mind, though, which comes in handy when he's in hours-long flow during any project. I'd love to be so intensely focused, but the tradeoff—being unaware of details in the real world—is a higher price than I want to pay. I don't think you can have it both ways, except by marrying your opposite.

In my more benevolent moments, it's easy for me to appreciate how easygoing Stephen is. Luckily for both of us, he neither harbors a list like I do nor worries about mine.

I had an adult student who said he and his live-in girlfriend had to vacuum the bathroom floor daily or the fallen hair would show. A female student chimed in that her husband regularly berated her for hair he found in the sink or on the floor, so that she had to be on the lookout constantly for strays. I feel fortunate that Stephen doesn't care about such lapses. If you were to gather the hair that falls to the bathroom floor in our house every twenty-four hours, you could process enough to fill a pygmy pillow, nest a platoon of unfussy rats, or cushion a minor neutron explosion. He doesn't care, so I don't have to feel shame over my hair's natural tendency to toss itself into corners (and my belief that I have better things to do than fret about it). The least I can do, I remind myself, is offer him the same freedom from stewing over trivialities.

## MY WAY AND THE WRONG WAY

I asked all my interviewees what bothers them about their partners. Nearly all of them seemed amused as they catalogued their few vexations. For instance, Tina Tessina's husband Richard is meticulous, she says, whereas she's a "get it done now" person. Because of his perfectionism (her term), he procrastinates. "I will get it done, though it may be slapdash, and then I'll worry about cleaning it up later," she explains. And that causes antagonism between this otherwise serene duo. She recognizes how deep such seemingly superficial differences can go: "When I get going fast, I literally frighten him, and he digs his feet in."

Another well-matched couple divides up this way: Jim is a worrier, and Joyce is a glosser, to use their words for each other. "He can see a crack in the foundation of the house and picture it all the way to the whole house falling down," Joyce explains (which endears him to me). She admits she may be a bit too far the other way, so that unless a piece of plaster hits her on the head, it's not yet time to call anybody to deal with the (non-)problem. He may hear a barely perceptible rattle in the car and want her to listen to it too, to touch parts of the car to see if the noise will stop. Yet not only will she not hear it, but she won't even want to turn off the radio long enough to pay attention.

Is Jim overdoing it, as Joyce believes, or is she in deep denial over the reality of physics and entropy, as he might say? "I've learned over the years not to do something I don't want to do and then get angry over it," says Joyce, "but to just refuse in the first place. Now we negotiate it pretty well because we trust that somewhere down the middle is the truth." It's not so much compromise as believing that each of them is most comfortable on the extreme end of some continuum of worry and being willing to hear the other's side and move toward the center so that disaster is both averted and no one has to spend too much time preparing for the improbable.

For the past forty-five years of their married life, Harriet has been telling the same story about her husband's denial of his own vulnerability, which is in reality about how *she* feels her own vulnerability is not tended to with compassion. It's become a story to laugh at, to share with others, and in that way, adds to their bond: "This is who we are: aren't we something?"

As Harriet tells it: "This is many years ago, when our kids were still only one, four, and six years old. I'm afraid to fly, but I fly. So we're on our way to Puerto Rico, and the first two planes have had electrical failures, and on this third one, while we're in the air, the pilot gets on a la Bob Newhart and says, 'Ladies and gentlemen, I regret to inform you that the hydraulic system has failed,' or something. I say to Myron, 'What does that mean?' And I look down and the runway is covered with foam, and there's an ambulance and a fire engine, and I'm thinking of my small children and of my father and my sisters, that we're going to die. And Myron just says, 'I don't know what you're so worried about. They'll get it down, whatever.' The way I explain to Myron what I dislike is that if we were in Germany, we would be the last Jews left."

When I ask Myron, he tells me the following: "I think her interpretation of that flight has become much worse over the years. I think they had problems with the hydraulic gear and they manually put it down. She used to have a tremendous fear of flying, and she assumed it was a life/death situation and I don't think it *ever* was. I would say my stance was based on objective reality rather than denial."

Their recitations of what happened don't differ, except that Myron was confident at all times and Harriet was petrified. So she keeps telling the story, hoping that her listeners will sympathize in a way that Myron doesn't. Who knows what would happen to her social repertoire if Myron surprised her by saying what she's longed to hear all along, such as, "That must have been so scary for you. I should have held you tight and murmured reassurances."

Sorry, Myron, but that's all it might take to nip off that story. (Though now it's such a habit that Harriet might still tell it and add, "And can you imagine, it took him forty-five years to get it!")

Beyond that, Harriet says only "little things" annoy her these days. "For example," she says, warming to the subject, "I'll start to talk about what I believe about politics. Oh! We almost got divorced over the last election! After all these years, oh my God. Philosophically we were miles apart. We have similar values, but we are the absolute opposites in so many ways. He likes the tax cuts to go to the wealthy, and I want them to go to everybody."

But they both believe their essential values are the same, especially their belief in each other. "We value one another more than anything in the world, and I know that," Harriet says. "That's number one. He would give up anything for me if it were really important to me, and I would for him. That's what makes our marriage work."

When I asked decades-married Sherry Suib Cohen about her marital pet peeves, she mentioned her husband's sloppiness, which conflicts with her own craving for organization. Yet, if she knows where an item is that he's looking for, she helps him. Why not make him search for it himself? "I do whatever I can to take any stress off him," she says, not entirely altruistically. After all, her goal in life, she explains, "is to make him live another fifty years."

Amusement—ours and his own—is the main goal of the quirky English writer Mil Millington, who maintains a very funny website, "Things My Girlfriend and I Have Argued About." Yet there's a core of truth in the arguments he describes having with his partner of more than a dozen years. Here's a single example:

We have differing goals, y'see. She's an 'Mmmm, has it got character?' kind of gal, while I'm a 'Will the roof last out the week?' kind of guy. Once she tried to persuade me to go for a house (really) that had no floor. It had collapsed—the carpet just sort of dropped away into an abyss. "No!" said the bloke from the Estate Agent's, jumping in front of us in panic, "I wouldn't go in there if I were you—just look in from the doorway." Yet Margret had got that 'I can just see where I'd put dresser' look in her eyes. She beams. "It has wonderful light."
    "What?"
    "The light. Can you see the light?"
    "No. But I can see the Earth's core."

Curious as to how Millington manages to remain with someone he unfailingly describes as irrational, I contacted him. He responded with uncommon candor: "I'm harder work than Margret, certainly. I try to indicate my sloth, insufferable anality, wearying pedantry and so on on the page." When I asked how stable this relationship is, he told me, "Splitting up is never just a few vowels away. We, both of us, fully expect to be together until one of us dies. Though we're aware one of us might die before the day's out if something isn't done about that situation in the bathroom. (I jest.) Seriously, we do expect to be together forever. I *know* that *everyone* expects that, but we don't think 'Everything will be great and music will play heart-warmingly over a montage of images of us laughing as we grow old together.' We are both fully aware of our shortcomings and absolutely expect there to be lots of tense silences in cars coming back from parties."

Millington and his partner face the truth of what relationships are, rather than being swept away by impossible ideals and then bogging down in the day-to-day of living together. They have plenty of conflict, and yet they can laugh at their incompatibilities.

Asked his advice for others, Millington demurs, hesitates, then makes a brave attempt: "I think that why we've survived so long is simply down to the kind of people we are. Which is very realistic and unflighty to the point of dullness. Yes, we complement each other very well and, yes, we do love each other, but one could have those things and the relationship would still fall apart if one or both the people were inherently 'dreamy'."

Take a moment to discuss with your partner whether certain of his behaviors that used to be annoying have become more cozily reassuring over the years. If there remain grating behaviors resistant to accommodation, consider whether some of them are more your province than your partner's, as I've shown in this chapter. Also, with your partner, consider how each other's behaviors may be complementary, helping you be a satisfying fit for each other. So that, if your partner became a tidy freak without any warning, your own level of neatness might not seem up to par, or if he stopped eating sandwiches out to save money, he might then begin to question your own purchases of gourmet coffee.

Another issue that can halt a marriage's progress toward peak satisfaction is the mundane topic of who does what around the house. Let's move to the next chapter, where we discuss the chore wars.

# 8
# BEYOND THE CHORE WARS

> It takes ages, years and years, to train a man to be even moder-
> ately sensitive and to equip him with the expertise to carry out
> ordinary household tasks. By the time all the information has
> been dispensed and processed, the trainer is worn out.
>
> —Jane Hamilton, *Disobedience*

I grow weary of doing Stephen's laundry. He wears multiple T-
shirts some days: one when he gets out of bed, a fresh one after
his shower, sometimes a third later in the day after a walk, and
yet another if he's teaching or we're going out. Eventually all
these wrinkly balled-up shirts find their way to the laundry
hamper.

I tried separating his clothes when I do the wash, handling
only my own, but I tended to run out of my favorite underwear
long before I'd accumulated enough for a full load, so I eventually went back to washing his clothes with mine. It seemed petty
and uneconomical to do half loads on purpose.

I used to figure the least I could do was leave the clean clothes
for him to fold. And sometimes he does. More often he'll take
what he needs out of the clean laundry basket on the bedroom
floor, until, days later, it's empty again and the hamper is full.
Now I usually dump the laundry basket on the bed so one of us
is *sure* to fold the clothes before we go to bed at night (unless I'm
too tired to outlast Stephen and thus they end up scrunched, by
him, into a pile on his desk chair).

But once in a while he will try to fold them himself. I say "try," because he has trouble with socks. He mixes up mine with his and confuses similar ones of mine with each other, bundling unmatched pairs.

One day I ask, "If you're so good at detecting fine details in poems and paintings in order to analyze the symbols and hidden meanings, why do you have such a hard time matching socks correctly?"

"Socks are not my art form," he says with a grin.

I am about to say that perhaps he didn't play Lotto as a child, when I remember something. Standing in the doorway to the bathroom while he shaves, I venture, "I guess that explains, then, why I've noticed you on the Internet concentrating so fiercely on that game of 'Match the Boobs'?"

Lacking an alibi, he offers a mildly sheepish look. I finish folding the socks and put them away.

## WHO DOES MORE HOUSEWORK AND WHO CARES?

> And after I cooked there was always this stunning moment when the meal was done and the dirty plates and cups and saucers were teetering in a stack around us . . . there was this moment of arrest when he would feign a distracted expression, a scholarly absence, as if the life of the scholar were so profound that practicalities didn't enter into it, and it was then that I understood that I was supposed to do the dishes myself. . . .
>
> —Rick Moody, *Demonology*

While men today no doubt take a more active role at home than their great-grandfathers did, it isn't news that women, in general, still perform more of the household tasks and child care. Ken Dempsey, an Australian sociologist, reported that one husband he interviewed was proud that he regularly prepared Sunday night dinner. The wife, when asked about this, chuckled and said that what he did was buy a pizza on the way home. Some men would say, "So what? He handled dinner, didn't he? Why is *her* way the only right way?"

My husband appreciatively eats any meal I put on the table, so I've concentrated on learning how to make quick, easy, inexpensive, healthful lunches and dinners that satisfy all my own requirements (he has none). I have to do the work, but I get what I want. Where you run into difficulties is when the more controlling spouse insists the *other* do the work. In my first marriage, my then-husband demanded I add salt to food as I was cooking it, instead of letting the one who lusted after great gobs of it add it later. "It tastes better that way," he insisted.

What's key for purposes of a happy marriage is not so much who does what, but how each partner feels about the division. Resentment is not sexy.

Frank, a teacher, told me that when he and Margie, an actress, were both working a lot and had a child at home, "we had a big pow-wow to figure out what was fair." They designed a chore wheel, and each of them, including their son, was responsible for two nights of cooking and washing the dishes, with one night left for eating out. "The simple chart kept things running smoothly so we could all count on things getting done."

But which comes first: happiness or equity? Researchers looking directly at this question found that when you're unhappy in a relationship, you begin to analyze your own efforts, finding them much more voluminous than your partner's. Of course, the study notes, you're there when you stop at the market or take out the trash, but you're not necessarily aware of what your partner has done, so that when partners' efforts get totaled up, it's not a scientific accounting. I still have a copy of my own "chore division" list, made at the depth of Stephen's and my wretchedness. I can laugh at it now, except that it reminds me so forcefully of how a person tends to nitpick when larger matters are unresolved. According to Ayala M. Pines in *Couple Burnout,* if all else feels right, "the exact sharing of chores is seen as trivial in comparison." In fact, she says, chore dividing becomes the focus of jokes when sex and communication are good.

Sometimes, one person might scoff at what the other considers a valuable contribution. Some men might believe that having given up the option of having sex with all the other women in the world is a fair trade-off for the wife's doing the child care and laundry and shopping and cleaning forever and ever, amen. It could be argued, of course, that the wife, equally, is giving up sexual opportunities. Hardly anyone talks honestly about how they feel about such tradeoffs.

In some relationships, it's been found, when the husband spends a lot of time with the children, wives don't fuss so much over being left with the grungier aspects of housework. But a lot of men don't reach that level of involvement with their own kids. And admittedly, households with two working parents and needy young children have the toughest challenge when it comes to chore equity. Both partners are stretched thinner, and differing perceptions of the way things *should* be can lead to contention.

## OTHER COUPLES' LITTLE DIRTY SECRETS

Before their daughter was born three years ago and they lived in a smaller apartment, both Letitia and Lenny worked full-time, went to the gym, and still managed to have a couple of hours to themselves each day. Letitia says she had plenty of time to straighten up and do the laundry, so chore division was never an issue.

"Now that we have a child and the house is a little messier," she explains with a wry smile, "I have to remind Lenny, 'C'mon, I need your help, the room's a mess.' That occasionally bothers me a little bit, that I have to be the nag. I'm sure it's a negative for him too."

One contented husband tells me that he and his wife never apportion duties or keep track of who does what. In fact, "I insist that she actually does more work than I do, and she swears the opposite," he says, which sounds like a fantasy come true—a fantasy that several of my satisfied couples actually experience.

The way it works is this: she does what she likes to do, while he does the tasks she dislikes. He adds, "But there is a form of what might be called 'flow' to it: more the result of an overall viewpoint, values, preferences, the friendship. Our chore division is more the result of those sorts of underpinnings than of talk."

Be honest about what each of you likes most or loathes least, and when you're divvying up tasks, don't focus only on how long they take. This is strictly an emotional accounting system. It takes more energy to iron if you hate ironing than it does to pay the bills if that helps make the world feel more agreeably predictable.

Discuss frankly what sub or barely-conscious fantasies are buried within your ongoing chore conflicts. Does one of you come from an ultra-clean family where dirt represented sin? Or perhaps your childhood home was a disaster area, and that didn't feel right.

When I ask Ida to consider the question of chores, she takes a moment, then replies, "It's funny, thinking about who does what. Sam is handier, so he takes care of all things mechanical. This includes replacing light bulbs, turning on sprinklers, fixing my computer when I can't make it behave, which is frequent, and cooking on the grill. My jobs are more eclectic. I get the groceries, go to the cleaners, balance the check books (fourteen in all), send out cards and gifts for birthdays, anniversaries and the like, handle all social obligations *except* football (clearly Sam's responsibility), prepare breakfast and lunch, and try to keep things neat and tidy, which is impossible."

Both those couples fulfill what psychotherapist Gregory J. Popcak calls exceptional service. He writes that in the best marriages there's a "dance of competence" wherein chores and other tasks are passed back and forth gracefully. Such behavior is not a means to an end but rather "service is its own reward." Sure, both of you recognize that all this mundane work needs to get taken care of, but you personally don't *have* to do it. You do it out of love—yet you appreciate being appreciated for it. More on this in the next chapter.

Frieda told me: "Over the years we've established the fact that I take care of the inside of the house, and Rodney takes care of the outside," but sometimes it doesn't feel fair to her, she admits. She can, however, ask him to do more, such as vacuuming, and he'll do it. "He doesn't have a problem with helping me, and I don't have a problem with asking," she adds. They take turns grocery shopping, or she'll ask him to pick up a few items. "We kind of work it out," explains Frieda, with a vagueness as to the specifics that's not unusual in world-class marriages.

Unless a particular aspect of the chore wars is particularly bothersome to a couple, then the details stick in the mind. Howard, for example, told me that he and his wife Jane no longer argue at all about who does what, although they used to disagree over time lines.

"Jane is a morning person," he says, "and I'm not. She'll jump out of bed on a Saturday morning and get dressed and make the bed and start doing things. She'll have given me a list of things that she wants me to do. And my Saturday routine used to be (before we had kids, of course), that I would get up and for two hours not do much of anything except wake up. I hit my stride in the afternoon. I like to do my honey-do list in the afternoon. And it used to aggravate her that she'd be up running around doing her chores and I'd be sitting there. And my response was, 'Look, I'll do my stuff, I'm just getting to it on my own schedule.' Which I would do."

Eventually, Howard explains, they found this solution: "We have a little white board on the fridge, and there's a piece of that white board where she writes things that she'd like me to do: put up a shelf or do this or do that. On Saturday or if I have a day off or whenever I have time, I will go and look at the list and I'll ask her if there are any particular priorities, and then I'll do them on my own schedule."

So what's different than in the early years? Not much, except now Jane is glad that jobs are getting done. "She finally realized that my way of attacking things is not bad, it's just different," he explains. By recognizing each other's autonomy needs, husbands and wives can avoid behaving like drill sergeants.

You might also consider dividing tasks by time sense, i.e., she who values daily dusting does it, he who must have bills paid on time writes the checks. One of you might take on single larger tasks, such as painting the balcony once a year during a specific month. Particular tasks can be marked on the calendar, such as having him make dinner every Tuesday night (or give you a back-rub whenever you want one, or commit to taking the car in for servicing at the slightest hint of trouble).

Lou Owensby told me that with a husband who was a doctor working long hours, getting outside help was both financially feasible and the only reasonable solution. Not long ago, after retirement and moving to an easier-to-maintain house, Norman said to Lou, "What would you think about us giving up the maid? And I won't get any more computer stuff." Lou says she thought about it, then replied, "I'll be happy to give up the maid, *if* we will solve the housekeeping problem."

"Well, that hit the money nerve," says Lou. "So I divided our responsibilities by room and swore to him that it wouldn't take an hour a day if we keep up with it. I gave him his list, and I have my list, and they're pretty even. He's doing *great* with this chore stuff. There are days he misses, and there are days that I miss a few tasks, but we can catch up the next day."

When I asked Elizabeth about chores, she insisted there's no problem. "Dan's always been very considerate about the real stuff. 'You're probably too tired so I'll take the two o'clock feed-ing.' He's not the type who'll stand at the door with flowers, which by the way was my father's shtick, but Dan is there for you. When we were married, I realized that there is an innate consid-eration gene which I valued immediately. It's lovely to get sur-prise gifts and flowers, but it's even lovelier when somebody takes the two o'clock feeding."

Those helpful infant feedings, by the way, took place several decades ago, but apparently added enough to the husband's emotional bank account that he's still drawing on them. So although she speaks with a minute sigh of the more romantic symbols that her own dad favored, Elizabeth is deeply appreciative of her husband's more practical consideration. For instance, when she has to go out and meet a client late in the evening, he knows how absent-minded and distracted she tends to be, so he offers to fill her car with gas.

Some husbands *do* see what needs to be done. When I interviewed Sherry Suib Cohen, author of *Hot Buttons: How to Resolve Conflict and Cool Everyone Down,* she told me that her husband "does whatever has to be done." When dinner is over, for instance, he takes the dishes and they start dealing with them together.

"He's just a person who sees that there should be an equity in marriage," she says. "He loves me as I love him. He just wants to save me from doing the work. And I him." As in many other functioning partnerships, each of them does what the other can't bear to do: for instance, his realm includes the dog's vomit and doo-doo. As a boating enthusiast and veteran fish-cleaner, "he just doesn't mind doing stuff like that. When the kids were little, and the diapers were particularly repellant, if he was there, he would *always* do that."

It's not exactly equity, though, she explains further, "it's loving generosity. He says, and it's true, 'When we do it together, it's fast and easy.' After a dinner party, we close the door on the last guest and we fall into each other's arms. We're so happy everybody's gone and we hug each other. It could be three in the morning and he could be exhausted or I might be, but we clean up together. How could one go into the bedroom and put on TV or read, and the other one's in the kitchen? It can't happen. It's always been that way."

If, in your home, one partner thinks it's *de rigueur* to sit and read while the other picks up after a party, point out graciously that it would be so much more *affectionate* an ending to the event if you both tidied together.

Another husband whose mother "did a good job of raising him," according to his wife Marylis, could run the house if he needed to. Conrad cleans the bathroom, does all the yardwork and more, though he has a full-time job and she's free to pursue her not-always-lucrative art. She feels extraordinarily lucky to have such flexibility. "I'm home taking naps, taking showers in the middle of the day, I truly have a lovely schedule. So I feel some of my payback is taking two-thirds of the housework."

## THE CLUTTER FACTOR

One of the most resolution-resistant skirmishes of the chore wars may well be clutter. Most of us are familiar with the battle-field: my piles of paper are a carefully organized system, your piles are junk to which you're abnormally attached.

Elizabeth has two persistent—albeit minor—complaints about her husband Dan. "We fight over the fact that he keeps too many newspapers for too long," she says. "He doesn't see it as a problem." They also fight over plastic bags, she tells me, laughing. "He wants to keep more and more and I say we've got enough. It's very trite and very silly."

Similarly, only one element keeps Lou Owensby from perfect satisfaction with her married life. The 5 percent she deducts "has to do with clutter," she explains, chuckling. "Norman used to get irritated with me for telling him what to do. It was pretty much that I'd put up with his clutter for a while until it really bugged me, *if* he'd agree that when I'd say it's bothering me, that not only would he do it, but he'd do it without hating my guts."

How long did that solution take to evolve? I ask Lou. "Oh! My Lord," she responds, laughing uproariously for half a minute, "we're talking years, not days! It's been ongoing for forty-three years." Since the Owensbys have moved, their space situation is better, so there's less conflict than there used to be. She leaves him certain areas that are his turf, and that helps.

Why can't couples get out of gridlock over "stuff"? Two indi-viduals might have a warring set of urges: order vs. freedom.

One partner may feel much freer with fewer possessions crowding his psychic (and physical) space. One of our bachelor friends winnowed his kitchen implements down to a single cutlery serving for four. He augments that with plastic when necessary. To him, this means valuable freedom from being swallowed by a mass of junk.

Clutter can cause some people to feel out of control, as though universal entropy were closing in. It goes well beyond not being able to find things, or the *fear* of not being able to find things. In my own admittedly more neurotic moments, I've imagined my descendants sorting my junk after I'm gone, and perhaps coming across items I would prefer were lost to the historical record.

Some so-called pack rats (not obsessive-compulsive hoarders who may need professional help) might be creative thinkers who make more than the usual number of mental connections. A thing discarded represents a loss of possibility. A travel brochure hints at the tantalizing promise of a future trip, a clipping about an odd physical disorder means having that knowledge instantly available should the symptoms occur. Of course, the more clutter accumulates, the less available any specific item is in reality.

It's even possible for the same person to have warring sides within herself. I love the richness of my own environment: books by the thousands, music of all kinds, magazines, file folders full of every subject I've ever written about or might want to explore someday, souvenirs of every period of my life and my kids' lives, old kitchen implements that I might use someday (or my kids might need, or perhaps, someday, my future grandchildren, who might also play with the tiny toys crammed in a drawer which take up hardly any space but which may come in handy on some imagined babysitting afternoon.) Ah, the rationalizations for keeping things are as limitless as the exasperation felt by the partner less tied to scraps. But as an easily distracted person, and a supposed nonmaterialist to boot, I also wish, sometimes, for the clean spare environment of a hotel or a forest, a veritable monk's cell with nothing extraneous at all. How refreshing! But what it would take to achieve that would require too high a cost for me. So I spend my time begging my family to help me declutter *their* stuff, just so long as they don't touch *mine*.

Typical advice for clutterers is to focus on the gain, i.e., order, instead of on the imagined losses and missed opportunities. But fear of loss might be too powerful a motivator for the average accumulator. Understand this if your partner is one. One compromise might be to help organize the obstreperous objects so they don't interfere with daily life.

Feelings over clutter and how space is organized can stir up enormous emotion. Some friends of ours were once discussing their own form of this battle after dinner. The wife complained that her new husband, with whom she shared a desk in their small condo, would never go through his mail, just left it piled all over the desk, so that she had no room to do her own work. She admitted, in front of him, that she sometimes went through his papers and tossed what was obviously worthless. I jokingly called her a tyrant, and she became furious. He, on the other hand, didn't seem particularly concerned over her admission. They hadn't yet learned to laugh about their incompatibilities.

When Ida married widower Sam, she moved into the home he'd shared for thirty years with his previous wife. Ida expected clutter, but she was surprised by how much of it she found. She insisted on a garage clean-up day, and Sam, a world-class procrastinator about tossing things out, agreed to get involved one Saturday. She describes the result:

> We put on our grungies, we ate a hearty breakfast, and I led the condemned man out to tackle the garage. Two hours into the project I realized we had a major problem. Sam was painstakingly checking each carton, examining every plug, each nail, all the wires, the rope, every broken tile, before he would make a decision. I was becoming exasperated. It was now eleven o'clock, and not one shelf had been emptied or even straightened. Instead, there were more piles scattered on the floor. I could see

that proceeding in this fashion would result in several months of tedium.

"Sam," I said in my kindest voice, "how about our setting up a chair for you outside the garage in the shade? The boys will bring you all the boxes. You can sort through them, and we'll put away what you decide should be saved."

He seemed relieved. All he had to do was say yes or no in a timely fashion. He started to act rashly—things were flying into the trash pile. Five hours later, we were done.

When Stephen and I last did one of our series of garage declutterings, it was even more complicated. I'm the one who can't throw out anything without being sure that someone can't use it. This meant asking my handyperson son Kevin (who wasn't present at this time) whether this miniature wrench set, albeit extremely rusty, might still be of use, or whether that old pipe or piece of rubber or tube of adhesive or piece of a sound system might someday come in handy. It meant deliberating over each piece of carefully saved cloth: should these be added to the piles for "use under cars" or "miscellaneous rags," or should they be tossed or put in the thrift shop pile because they have some use left in them? Some piles, when upended, turned up little boy shirts from twenty years ago, already beginning to dissolve into mulch.

What we finally did was this: when I became exhausted (physically and emotionally), I went back inside the house, and Stephen spent a couple of additional hours adding masses of the obviously (to him) useless and/or ruined bits of detritus to a huge pile to be hauled away later. He managed to sneak some items into the center of the pile where I couldn't see them, and then made the mistake of telling me this (so that to this day I wonder what vital bit of antique fluff is missing). I did manage to investigate in time to riffle through one supposedly empty tossed box which contained some photos of him from high school, which I managed to save.

Why was this entire process so fraught with meaning and trauma for me, and so easy for Stephen (analogous to what Ida and Sam went through)? It's not only that I've lived here much longer and that most of the junk is part of my past and not part of his. It's more that I live in one continuous burst of time, where past and present and future are all entangled in my mind. So that when I come upon some wire contraption stuck up in the garage rafters, unseen for more than twenty-five years, it brings back memories of my own was-I-ever-that-innocent youth, making a stimulating baby mobile contraption to place over my firstborn's crib. But it also brings back a filmy past time when his father and I still shared the same goals, and it reminds me of when making things (the mobile) and painting things (one stubby set of drawers) and even growing things (one tiny can of tomato plants bought at the supermarket, a market that has changed names four times since then) seemed like great fun to me.

No wonder I couldn't merely throw away what was no longer useful. Who doesn't need memories?

## HISTORY OF A BATTLE

In spite of the laundry anecdote at the start of this chapter, I didn't always grin at my partner's pathetically feeble efforts. Oh, no! I gnashed my teeth at his refusal to do his share and wasted precious energy fighting what might as well have been the heat death of the universe for all the effect my protests had on reality. Looking back at my journal, I see the battle began quite early in our relationship. The first recording of it took place just under three years after the wedding, and this and succeeding entries show how big a bite this discord was already taking out of our pleasure in each other's company:

"In the afternoon we discussed cleaning and household tasks yet again. I *know* that my irritation at his avoidance of taking responsibility only grows to furious proportions when other areas of our life are unsatisfying for me. But I finally realized on an emotional level that Stephen's perception of what neat, clean, and in good repair mean are totally different from mine. He thinks he's been doing 'the cleaning' as he promised, while all I see is that he vacuums most of the house and dusts every two or three weeks. Which of course leaves a *lot* undone."

What I needed, I informed my journal in those bad old days, was for Stephen to *only* say "yes" when he could commit to following through. But he said I would punish him interminably if he ever said "no." And I responded that, of course, I would be unhappy if he said "no" without an explanation or an offer to help figure out alternative ways to get the job done.

Then I reassured him that I would cheerfully accept a "no" answer if he would say it only when he had to. And that I would take on the cleaning and house repair and stop nagging him about them. Then there came a day during which I vacuumed the spider webs from the whole house and the front porch, a big job. Unfortunately, I resented that he was lying in bed reading while I was cleaning. But I reminded myself of all the times I take it easy when he's working, especially before I got my procrastinatory monster under control.

Nevertheless, I complained to my journal, "I do need to work out ways of asking for help. I carry a lot more responsibility than he does. It's incredible how problems can get swept under the (wrinkled) carpet and resurface repeatedly. The garage door broke this weekend. I was furious that I had to deal with this, after months of knowing it needed to be taken care of and making it clear that I didn't want to be in charge of this task. I don't hate having to do the banking or some of the other things I've taken on that I never had to do before. But this repair stuff, the decisions, the calls, the supervising of workmen, being around when everything is disrupted—I absolutely loathe it!"

In retrospect, I can see the problem much more clearly: the way I felt taken care of was the way I was used to being taken care of, by the men in my life doing certain tasks. I hadn't yet recognized what Stephen does to care for me, things no one has ever done before and without which I can barely imagine functioning now.

We solved the garage door problem this way: from then on, anything that had to be done within a certain period of time (*any* amount of time, whether that week or that year), would fall within my purview. All tasks that could without harm await Stephen's more casual approach would be his. Admittedly, many more household maintenance tasks now became mine officially. The reality, of course, was that they had been mine anyway, only now they would get done in a timely fashion.

More than one so-called expert still brings up the old saw that if you become *less* competent around the house, your partner will become *more* competent. I've not found this to be true. At issue are the incompatible ways two people perceive what is in front of them. Seems to me you'd have to turn a blind eye to dishes piling up in the sink long beyond when the odor was noticeable to visitors, or you'd have to allow the laundry, as I've said, to pile up until you'd be doing constant undersized loads of just your own undies, or you'd have to wait until the dust exacerbated your allergies to the point of misery.

Once I let the tub mold grow to the point where there was a large ugly patch around the spout and drain, and then brought it up in couples therapy. Stephen had agreed to take on tub cleaning duties, since, for one thing, when he showers he throws off more vile contaminants than I do because of his gardening, and for another thing, because tub cleaning requires hard rubbing—when you let it go as long as he does—and that level of pressure while leaning over tends to give me hand- and backaches. Stephen argued, however, that I was exaggerating, so I said I'd bring a photograph into the next therapy session. When we got home, he *finally* looked at the blotch and then cleaned it.

## HOW WE SOLVED THE CHORE WARS

I reached my wit's end soon after I began grad school. I felt overwhelmed with multiple responsibilities, and Stephen had recently lost his main money-earning job so it seemed to me that he should take on more of the routine housework. Yet the best he ever did on a regular basis was to wash the dishes once a day. And I was *very* careful never to downplay that effort.

One Sunday morning, I attended what was meant to be a meeting of my grad school colleagues. But as only two others showed up, we talked casually instead. And these two people solved the chore wars for me, or at least provided the cognitive key I had been lacking. It might help you, too. Here's a reconstruction of that life-changing dialogue:

**Susan:** My husband won't help with the housework. I can't do it all.

**Response:** Even if you ask him to?

**Susan:** Sure, if I ask him, he will "help," but he never sees what needs doing on his own, and he never takes on any of the responsibility himself. It's making me furious with him all the time.

**Response:** Why is it so important to you that he sees what needs doing by himself, if you're always aware of it first anyway?

**Susan:** If he shared the responsibility, then I could let that amount of responsibility go. I could relax more, knowing my partner was handling it.

**Response:** What does he say about what you want from him?

**Susan:** He says, just tell me what you want and I'll do it.

**Response:** And that's not enough?

**Susan:** No, because that feels like I'm being asked to be a parent to his child. I hate that feeling!

**Response:** But he's telling you how he prefers to operate in this one realm of behavior, around housework. He's not like this in other areas, right?

**Susan:** True. I mean, he's certainly independent about the things that matter to him. In fact, he strenuously resists my attempts to tell him what to do in other areas. When it comes to sex, he takes much more initiative than I do. With our computers, he's the one who tells me when it's time for a virus check. He makes all the garden decisions and does all the grunt work without a peep out of me. I won't ever lift a finger there.

**Response:** Then maybe you could try to turn this around: accept his preference for a way to behave about housekeeping chores. This is one very adult decision that you can agree to allow him to make. By not letting him make that decision, you're in fact infantilizing him.

**Susan:** You mean, I tell him what I see that needs to be done, and he does it? He doesn't share the responsibility for noticing?

**Response:** What "needs" to be done is, in reality, subjective.

**Susan:** That's true, now that you mention it. In my first marriage, I was so busy with the two small kids and doing what was important in the long run, that I would sometimes let the dishes pile in the sink for three days. Then my husband would do them, but angrily, slamming them around and calling me lazy, and worse, for not doing them on *his* schedule. I've never forgotten how that felt. I wondered why he couldn't have just pitched in gracefully if it was so vital to him, trusting that I was doing what was more meaningful to *me*, instead of trying to force me to change my order of priorities.

**Response:** Hmm. So maybe Stephen feels that way sometimes?

**Susan:** I bet he does. How awful! I *should* let him tell me how he can best pitch in. Then everything will go smoothly forevermore.

And that's the end of the fairy tale.

In fact, the worst part of our marriage was yet to come, which proves what I've said earlier, that the battle for chore equity is often a reflection of larger issues. But truthfully, flipping that internal switch made a huge difference. Once I was ready to act, all I had to do was keep this conversation in mind. It was a lot like a geometry theorem: by memorizing it, I could put it to good use.

## TODAY: THE REALITY

> What does a marriage look like? Ours looks like this: a side plate smeared with mango chutney. That's how we tell it apart from all the others. That mango chutney is the white smudge on the cheek of your black cat, or the registration number of a new car, or the name tag in a child's school sweatshirt; without it we'd be lost. Without that side plate and its orange smear, I might one day come back from the toilet and sit down at a completely different marriage.
>
> —Nick Hornby, *How to Be Good*

These days, when the tub accumulates grime and I want to take a long soak in hygienic safety, I clean it myself, scrubbing only as hard as my wrist permits. If I can wait, I add it to Stephen's list, or I catch him when he's not otherwise occupied and ask him to do it right then and there. And he usually does.

We expected company recently, a bachelor friend. Rather than bother Stephen this time—it had been a busy week for him—I waited until fifteen minutes before our friend was expected and then used the child's broom that I keep in the corner of the bathroom behind the hamper to sweep up the accumulation of hair from the floor. Then I did the same in the kitchen, where our toes have a habit of shoving all errant foodstuffs under the counters, where they're barely noticed when company is *not* expected (multi-colored linoleum has been a great labor-saver over the years). I also went downstairs to set the VCR and stooped to the carpeted floor around the couch to gather the larger chunks of organic matter that could well have turned sentient given one more night.

Today, when Stephen was hip-deep in plant trimmings, laboring in the hot sun to keep the Garden of Dorian Gray the showplace that it is, I stopped waiting for him to empty the dishwasher and deal with the dirty dishes (another of his jobs—which goes against our rule of only assigning him non-timely tasks). I knew he'd be exhausted when he finally came in. Later, I told him I'd taken care of the dishes. "Oh, bless you!" he said.

Some would say I contributed to his erratic doing of the dishes by stepping in like that. I suggest, rather, that this is what flow is all about. I wouldn't want to mislead: even when we first concocted this reasonable solution to the chore wars, a more elemental lack of good feelings still prevented us from following through. After I'd written the above section, I asked Stephen what *he* thought had solved the puzzle for us.

"It's not an issue now. When the feelings are good between us, I just do what needs to be done," he said, which I found enlightening. After all, I inscribe tasks I'd like Stephen to do on a list that keeps getting lost in his piles of paper, so that I am constantly recovering it and putting it in plain sight. It takes a long, long time for most of the items to get accomplished.

In other words, nothing has changed, yet everything has changed.

# 9
# THE COUPLE'S MANIFESTO OF LOVE

To love...is a redefinition of the self itself, as a shared self.
—Robert C. Solomon, *Love: Emotion, Myth & Metaphor*

No matter how hard it is to agree on what an equitable society would look like, most people—at least those reading this book—value some form of fairness in their intimate relationships. The familiar Golden Rule—Do unto others as you would have them do unto you—has analogues throughout the world's cultures. But when we succeed in observing such a credo with our dearest loved ones, we're merely offering what we want for ourselves, not what the other person wants. A better version of the Golden Rule for couples—and one of the secrets to loving in flow—is to do unto your partner as your partner would like, not as *you* would like or as you *wish* he or she would like.

And that brings us to what I call the Couple's Manifesto of Love: "From each according to his ability, to each according to his needs." For our purposes, "needs" equals "wants" (and "his" obviously equals "her"). In following such a manifesto, we forego a tit-for-tat mentality, what psychologists call an exchange orientation, to a focus on what's good for both of us, known as a communal orientation. Research has shown that such a cooperative attitude is far more likely to contribute to sustained satisfaction for both partners.

So: you scratch my back, I scratch yours? Not necessarily. Rather, when tonight's scratcher has a need, whatever it is, his or her partner will be pleased to acquiesce. And this is precisely the attitude I found prevalent in the most satisfied couples I interviewed.

## WHAT'S FAIR IN LOVE AND WAR?

It was true that Al had asked her to move the jars and magazines, and there was probably a word for the way she'd stepped around those jars and magazines for the last eleven days, often nearly stumbling on them;...maybe a simple word like "spite."...He'd also asked her to make the boys three meals a day, and clothe them and read to them and nurse them in sickness, and scrub the kitchen floor and wash the sheets and iron his shirts .... If she tried to get credit for these labors of hers, however, Al simply asked her whose labors had *paid* for the house and food and linens? Never mind that his work so satisfied him that he didn't need her love, while her chores so bored her that she needed his love doubly. In any rational accounting, his work canceled her work.

—Jonathan Franzen, *The Corrections*

The dividing of household tasks, covered in detail in the previous chapter, is only the beginning of the subject of fairness. Now we move beyond who does what, to more intangible matters.

In struggling relationships, both partners often believe they've compromised, considered the other first when making decisions, put their own needs on hold for the sake of pleasing the other. And each may believe the other has *not* done so with equal consistency. It's easy to slip into such unconsciously biased thinking, especially under stress.

Here's an example from the life of Jorge, thirty-seven, who directs educational and career development for a medium-sized Southern California firm, and his Filipino-born wife Rosalisa, thirty-eight, a nurse. They've been married sixteen years and have two young children. He's an involved dad, but the majority of the child care falls to Rosalisa. He admits that he finds himself "keeping score" occasionally, particularly when tired. For instance, he says, "Sometimes she'll be in the kitchen and I'll be upstairs and she'll ask me to get her a glass of water. I'll get the water, but it bugs me at the time. Then it just fades away." While Rosalisa might feel entitled to this minor bit of caretaking, Jorge feels he's done more than half the work by putting in those long hours, and thus briefly resents being asked to do anything extra.

It comes out most evenly if the two of you accept each other's subjective analyses of how much is being contributed. It took me a while to trust, for example, that the many hours Stephen spends maintaining our garden is as valid a use of his time as is my reading of two newspapers daily. Actively supporting your partner's view of the world is a way of showing love.

Consider speaking to your mate about how various activities exact a different amount of psychic energy from each of you. You may be surprised to learn that one of you would prefer to give a half-hour massage than untangle one garden hose. Psychologist Andrew Christensen told me in an interview that his wife hates making business phone calls, so he makes them. "If I can do a thing easily," he explains, "then I do it. I think that's the best system because it's individualized. You can't just take a template and apply it."

If you both adhere to the Couple's Manifesto, you'll feel secure that you'll have your turn too. What psychologists call reciprocation wariness, in fact, inhibits strong interpersonal relationships. If each of you holds back from giving what might at any one moment seem like more than your half, that might lead to further wariness and less trust on the other's part, the very behavior that keeps you from getting what you most want.

Laurie, for instance, expends much effort to cook what her husband likes and never thinks of complaining that most household tasks fall on her, even though she also works hard. She says it's because she believes Hamid tries equally hard to please her: "Anything I want, he'd give me."

When I recently judged a parenting book contest, I discarded one that promoted this motto: "Never give away the ice cream." This author's distressing suggestion is manipulative: be sure every pleasant activity is connected to desirable behavior preceding it. But the opposite is true: you *should* frequently give away the ice cream. If you espouse a philosophy of "only give when you have already gotten," it's as though you're standing there with your arms crossed, waiting for the other person to show goodwill. In the best relationships, goodwill must be taken for granted.

But say you've started taking out the garbage almost regularly without being nagged, and you're beginning to wonder when your spouse will start initiating hot impromptu sex, as you've been wanting? In distressed marriages, we feel "it's your turn to change," as though we're owed recompense *because* of the efforts we've made.

Some therapists go so far as to suggest that the partner who makes any small change should get a payoff of some sort. So, in an example given by psychologist Ayala M. Pines, if you talk to your mate for a half-hour as she's been asking you to do, you get to choose a movie that week. From my own experiences and those of others, I can tell you that such tit-for-tat efforts are ineffective at creating long-term change. Fairness ought never become a battle cry. If you're too busy tabulating every penny spent, every minute of effort, every compromise made regarding what to eat or watch, it's liable to slip your mind that you're on the same side in this relationship.

Peter D. Kramer points out in his insightful book *Should You Leave?* that men whose wives complain they aren't doing enough characteristically argue that the wife's standards are unfair and that he doesn't have a say in establishing them. And what if he does what she wants (i.e., becomes an ideal husband from her standpoint), is she willing to do the same from his standpoint? And what might this mean? Only in the best relationships are wives willing to look at themselves from a mate's point of view:

maybe I'm *not* giving up as much as he is, maybe I don't often play fantasy sex kitten, maybe I do carp on matters that are trivial to him. Or it might be the husband who is locked too tightly inside his own perceptions and unable, for a moment, to see through his wife's eyes.

Talk openly about what "fair" means to each of you, sharing incidents that exemplify or contradict the word. When my children were small and I spent a lot of time reading to them, taking them on enriching outings, playing with them and keeping them from maiming each other, my then-husband would have preferred that I get a paying job. He said, and I'll never forget this, "Anyone can do what you're doing with the kids." Our perceptions of the value of my mothering were at such loggerheads that we couldn't resolve this issue amicably.

## MY MONEY, OUR MONEY

Christensen cites an old Ben Franklin story: a rooster wanted to make a deal with a horse—"If you don't step on my feet, I won't step on yours." In actuality, some couples take such thinking to mean that if your husband spends $600 of joint funds on a pre-amp, then you get to buy several expensive pairs of shoes you hadn't planned on. But what if that leads to a more depleted bank account, which isn't pleasing to you?

Or what if one spouse works more hours than the other? Is it equitable, then, for the one who labors longer to get more of the benefits? What if the one who puts in more hours earns less? Or one spouse may make more money than the other for about the same number of hours of labor. Does that one then get more say in how the money is spent? In some traditional couples, that's the way it's done, but they've obviously eschewed the Couple's Manifesto altogether.

Pepper Schwartz, after analyzing thousands of couples, dubbed some of them peers, about whom she concluded, "Each partner can and should give in different coin." True peers agree that money isn't the only coin that counts. Still, money does matter, and couples choose a medley of accommodations in the pursuit of fairness.

In my own marriage, as in the marriages of many of the couples I interviewed, we commingle all our funds. Back when Stephen worked two jobs and earned a lot more than I did from my freelance writing, he never hesitated to turn over his paychecks to me, knowing that a large chunk of them would go to pay for private school for my son that lived with us. Now that I'm making more, it's fine with me that Stephen spends less of his time producing income. We believe that each of us has the inalienable right to pursue our own goals and that the unit has to create a way to make that possible.

Still, when one of us acquires "extra" money, we have very different thoughts on where it should be used. I add mine to our joint funds, whereas if it's fallen into *his* hands, Stephen considers it bonus money with which to buy flowering plants (his passion) or to add to his computer equipment. We communicate, we struggle, we make deals.

There is no one right way to handle money. A few of the couples I interviewed separate their financial affairs in the interests of their own notion of fairness, with some switching systems over the decades.

Bea told me, "For years, it was my business that supported everything. And now it's Herb's. At one point, I kept my money separate. But it was also my money we used to remodel this house. Every time it would come up and feel negative to me, I'd push it aside. And then you'd have the fleeting thought, 'If we were ever to split up, I'd never get that back.' You have to override that: you can't handle every situation like that, as though the worst thing that could happen is going to happen."

Tina Tessina told me she and her husband each have their own money, and they divide expenses in half. She pays for all the food, he pays all the utilities. They tracked it for the first couple of years, finding it came out sufficiently even. But if they go out to dinner, they split it fifty/fifty.

Why such a strict division? Not only does Tina remember her mother standing with her hand out asking for money to buy Tina's clothes for school, but Tina and Richard relate to money very differently. "We wind up in the same place, approximately, but he balances his checkbook to the penny, and I'm slapdash. This way we're not struggling with each other all the time."

Laurie also insisted on separate bank accounts when she married Hamid. "We split the rent, because I wasn't young when we got married, and I thought, my God, I'm not going to support him. If one of us can't pay our bills, though, which just happened a couple of months ago, I paid the whole rent for three months, but he paid me back."

## BUT YOU *OWE* ME

> Even in sweet moments, she was calculating debt, *I don't honestly believe that you have given back a proportionate amount and even if money is irrelevant and I have enough money to a pay a larger portion of the rent it doesn't mean that I can forgive in perpetuity the fact that I have spent more than you even if I say I love you.*
>
> —Rick Moody, *Demonology*

In the working world, you put forth effort with the expectation of getting paid—that's where exchange relationships are the most prevalent. It's different at home. In communal relationships, the kind between family members, we not only don't expect repayment for favors, but it might dilute our warm feelings if we *are* treated on a tit-for-tat basis. Of course, this makes perfect sense when you consider all that is now known about rewards and intrinsic motivation. In a loving relationship, you're not expecting some additional reward beyond the love itself; the more you move that relationship to a reward-based footing, the less likely that flow will prevail.

Even so, playful point systems aren't unknown among intimates. Naomi, in her late forties, has been with her partner

Janice, in her mid-fifties, for eighteen years. They have evolved an informal routine in which, when one mock-grudgingly accommodates to the other, she gets points.

"Janice has a very high need for order and routine," explains Naomi, "so that if I leave my mail out for more than one day, it starts to bug her. I tell her, 'That's too bad, I live here too, and I get to do this.'" Here Naomi laughs at the silliness of such an interaction, then continues: "She'll get to a point where she says it's getting to her, and I don't think it's worth having World War Three over, so I just bitch back a little bit and then I'll say, 'Well, sure, I'll go take care of that, but I just want you to know how much I hate it.' And while we're being mad at each other, we joke about a scorecard.

"Or, every now and then when one of us does something really good for the other one, like cleaning up sooner than I want to, or leaving sooner to go out than I think is necessary, those kinds of things, I'll just say, 'Okay, but I get points for this.'"

Naomi explains that what's most important about such interactions is that the partners are communicating to one another that they know themselves and each other, that they're willing to do some compromising, but that they also want to make sure that each respects the other's independence. "When we were younger and hadn't had as much therapy, et cetera," concludes Naomi with another laugh, "those were bigger battles. And now they're not battles at all. They're almost like scripted exchanges."

Some couples even play around with outright barter: I'll have sex with you later if you wash the windows now. So long as your bond is a healthy one and you both see the humor in such play, occasional stylized deals will do no harm.

"What we call love," suggests author Phyllis Rose, "may inhibit the process of power negotiation. If the impulse to abjure measurement and negotiation comes from within, unbidden, it is one of life's graces and blessings."

If you find yourselves scorekeeping seriously, then it means that something's already amiss. Let it serve as a warning that, uh-oh, somebody's going to start withholding, and then severe conflict is sure to follow. If you deal constructively with dissatisfactions as soon as they appear, there's no need for the relationship to tilt toward a tit-for-tat, and less caring, direction.

Frank's resentments, for example, would be over trivial things, such as when the couple had a garage sale and he felt he had to sell his favorite popcorn popper. He didn't have to, insists Margie, but at the time he *felt* obligated, and that stuck in his mind. When such feelings would eventually emerge, Margie would tell Frank, "You have a resentment book."

Couples design their own ways to achieve a feeling of ultimate fairness, whether they use the word or not. For instance, Teresa told me that when Derek raises his voice at her, she feels attacked. Then, a couple days later, "to get back at him, I won't fix him something to eat that he wants for supper. He'll just look at me and go, 'Okay.' It's a kind of teasing that says you're over the anger, but you want to press the point and say, 'You hurt me, see?' It feels more like we're even then." If such minor vengeance served cold two days later were to become a substitute for communicating frankly in the moment, only then would it be time to have qualms.

One woman told me she'd figured out a way to even things out when she gets disappointed. Say her husband isn't able, at the last moment, to take her somewhere she'd planned on going due to the demands of his job. "Then I tell him to go buy me a candy bar to make up for it. Or this chocolate cake from the bakery. I think it's just that I want to feel like he's done something for me. It's like buying my friendship," she says, laughing. "Then he'll rub my back."

## ME, MYSELF, AND I...OH, AND YOU

Buying into the Couple's Manifesto does *not* mean that each partner gives up a "self" in the interests of the union. A marriage needn't be oppressive to your personal growth. I can't forget my former husband telling me when I wanted to go back to school,

"I don't want *you* to grow, I want my children to grow." What a contrast it was, then, when Stephen said to me, "Be who you want to be."

Yet sometimes sacrifices are necessary. Not every marriage will permit each partner to have everything each of them desires, whether due to time or money constraints, or some environmental consideration (he wants to live in the city and she prefers suburban life). What do you do when your goals aren't the same, when you and your partner are competing for free time, use of funds, sympathy, or some other scarce resource? In the most long-lasting and satisfying marriages, a Dutch social psychologist and his American colleagues found, both partners are willing to sacrifice for each other. Address what you're each willing to give up for each other or for the unit. See if you agree upon when an action feels like sacrifice and when it doesn't. Among the couples I talked to, I found that some of them endured stages where an exchange mentality was later replaced with one that was more communal and more contented. Mei-Ling says, "The one thing I did come up with when we were going through therapy was that marriage is never equal. What's important is that with the two of us together, the life we create is more than just the sum of us."

Eric J. Cohen and Gregory Sterling suggest in *"You Owe Me"* that when you let go of an artificial effort to make things equal at every moment, "the spontaneous flow of giving and receiving can take place with both parties maintaining an internal sense of everything being fair." The authors explain that what you end up with is a whole wide base of evenness. So that when your interaction moves too far outside what feels fair to one partner, threatening the balance of the relationship (leading one of you, no matter how generous you are, to feel taken advantage of), it must be dealt with to restore the sense of flow. When you're feeling even again, you can start anew, if need be, without counting. I might liken it to changing your accounting method mid-year, and then when the accounts are balanced, throw away the books and don't look back. (Better yet, burn them so you can't dig them out later for a big argument.)

We all prefer when we get what feels like "enough." Make a point of telling your partner what essential needs are met by your relationship, needs that are not based on actions but on who the other person *is*. For example, I've often told Stephen that he makes me laugh, and that's enough. But what I mean by that is so much more than finding his jokes ha-ha funny. It's about his sharing my existential aloneness, joining me mentally and emotionally in the ideas that dominate my life. It's about being part of a family—in the deepest sense of the word—a family that crosses all the usual borders of birth and background.

# SEX (MORE OR LESS)

To feel nothing, not the feeblest pulse in the dead mouse from which his urine issued, for three weeks, to believe that she would never again need him and that he would never again want her, and then, on a moment's notice, to become light-headed with lust: this was marriage as he knew it.

–Jonathan Franzen, *The Corrections*

Some of what the happiest couples reported about their sex lives was predictable, even mundane: they do it regularly, if somewhat less frequently than they used to, and it's just fine, thank you. Yet, I did learn something surprising: as pleased as couples are with one another, many of them nevertheless have ongoing sexual quandaries that may never get resolved. Some mates expect their circumstances to improve, wish intensely that their sex lives would—soon!—change for the better. Others, though, are satisfied in spite of no longer believing that much will ever be different. It's amazing what you can learn to live with (or without)—and still be unswervingly committed.

In this chapter, I'll share what I was told and what those revelations mean for any long-term relationship—in and out of the bedroom. In the context of a vital relationship, what matters most, it turns out, isn't how often you engage sexually or in what techniques you and your partner are proficient. Frequency in the couples I spoke with ranges from daily to hardly ever, without an obvious correlation to the satisfaction score each partner gives the relationship. What counts much more is what sex means to both of you, how it meshes with your daily lives, and how you deal with differences and change over time. A major share involves personal development: who you are learning to be, in and out of the relationship.

Then, in the next chapter, we'll see how sex with a long-time partner can become more lively, and how such vibrancy can be one route to loving in flow.

## FIVE (OTHER) REASONS TO DO IT

Sex feels good, and it can make babies. It's a fine way to express love. Beyond those reasons, have you considered why you're motivated at any one moment to initiate a lovemaking session? Reflecting on those other, sometimes more hidden, reasons may clarify your or your partner's sexual motivations and lead to greater mutual understanding. Here, then, are a few more reasons to make love:

1. **Sex is a form of play, and play can be a form of lovemaking.**
Where, in fact, do you draw the line between play and sex? Why bother? A man in his seventies tells me he had a hard time keeping his hands off his wife. "Lustful or playful?" I ask. "Both. One faded into the other." And a thirtysomething woman in a very sexually active marriage says, "We're always making offers to each other—real and for fun. I might say, 'Hey, you want to go make out in the car?' It's not just sex in the bedroom. It's a sexuality that exists between us constantly."

Play—having fun together all the time, not only in bed—is perfect foreplay. And sometimes playing's what we want, and *all* we want. Play—including the bedroom kind—is also the epitome of flow. The best sex in the best long-term relationships contains features of play: nonjudgmental and lacking any goal other than enjoyment for both partners.

For example, based on her husband Bob's constant stream of sexual innuendo, Jeanette sometimes suspects he would like to have sex as frequently as humanly possible. Still, she's not sure he would follow through if she took him up on his teasing that she's "not putting out enough." She realizes on some level that he's not complaining. "It's just this gauntlet that he's always throwing at my feet. But on the other hand, I like that he wants me that much. And when I feel that he's not after me, I start to get upset about it, am I losing it? Why doesn't he have the hots for me?"

Bob confirms that he's not seriously complaining about infrequency, but teases to keep sexuality in the air between them. I can relate to Jeanette's feelings because Stephen and I play the same games: he teases a lot about wanting it. In our homegrown system, I figure he's bluffing (as Jeanette suggests her husband does), but I suspect I'd better not take him up on it unless I intend to follow through. So we keep the system as it is, with him teasingly asking and me playing mock "hard-to-get" just enough so it stays a game. Our interaction, like Jeanette's, is slightly off-balance so that no one is sure at any one time what might happen. That's what keeps such playful systems going: that fine line between unease and titillation, keeping the possibility of sex afloat on a current between the two of us, keeping *us* feeling desirable and keeping our partners' seduction techniques honed. Is it play or is it sex? No one knows for sure, nor do we want to.

2. **Sex is an excellent way to share concentrated time.** When a couple spends time together, they reach a shared rhythm, and "sex is the ultimate coming together of rhythms," writes Stephan Rechtschaffen, M.D., in *Time Shifting: Creating More Time to Enjoy Your Life*. That's surely one of the main reasons we continue to crave sex long past the enraptured first years. To reiterate the obvious, it connects us. And that shared rhythm of unselfconscious sexual activity leads to flow.

3. **Sex is a way to get the physical contact you need, the bodily manifestation of affection.** One woman told me, "I feel closest to my husband when I'm making love, when I feel

physically as well as emotionally loved. Loved in every sense of the word. I crave physical contact. My husband's not a toucher. He doesn't like to be kissed or hugged. It's wholly different when we're making love. Then he loves it."

4. **Sex fulfills intensely personal emotional needs.** Some couples run into trouble when there's a disjunction between *her* needs and *his* needs. Susan Tyler Hitchcock told me that their early problems related to the fact that her husband didn't feel his best about himself unless they had frequent sex. He'd become grumpy when he missed that connection, when she turned him down due to her lack of erotic interest. They were finally able to turn the problem around on their first months-long boat trip together, when the atmosphere was relaxed, bedtime arrived early, and they talked a lot. "We became more emotionally intimate, so it felt like there was more to the physical intimacy," explains Susan. And that combination of emotional and physical met the needs, for the first time, of both partners.

One woman I spoke with gives her husband and marriage an overall high score, yet is vexed about their sex life. His interest is much less than hers, though she's told him that she makes her emotional connection with him bodily. "And when we aren't connecting physically, oh my gosh," she says, "it's like, you might as well be my brother or my roommate." Whereas being loving roommates is sufficient for some, this woman continues to push for a resolution.

In my own marriage, this same issue surfaced after the first year, as I'll discuss in more depth in the next chapter. Stephen, at that time, only felt fully loved by me when I accepted him sexually. When I began to ease off my earlier constant availability, figuring it didn't much matter so why bother, I found out how much it did matter. A "yes" meant "yes" to him as a person, and a "no" was tantamount to "I don't care about you enough to make love with you."

If you can learn to talk about what sex means to each of you and create ways to compromise with goodwill and grace, neither of you will feel cheated of what you need to feel close.

5. **Exploring the (safe) dark side of yourself.** This reason for having sex overlaps the others, since it involves deep emotional needs, physical desires, focused time together, and play.

I wrote to Stephen early in our relationship: "I loved what you said about the joys of doing unspeakably nasty things to someone you really care about. I haven't mined the depths of you or your depravity yet. Your goodness and your badness excite me equally." More recently, whenever I apply scented body powder after a post-sex shower, he teases, "Getting civilized again?" It's a way of acknowledging that I am more comfortable leaving my vixenish self (such as it is) in the bedroom. In the daylight world, you can be a good girl (or boy), and at other times you can choose to be whatever and whoever you want to be.

Of course, not everyone has the urge to safely let out their so-called badness, and not everyone enjoys a naughty partner. Howard, for example, thought the suede mini-skirts Jane used to wear looked trashy. She stopped wearing them when he asked her to. When she asked him if he wished she were "vampier," he responded, "Honey, you couldn't be vampy if you wanted to be." He doesn't see her as "that type of girl," even though I suspect she might recognize a bit of "that type of girl" lurking somewhere inside herself. Or she might be influenced by the larger media culture that keeps insisting that men are turned on by over-the-top sexual displays. But here's what Howard prefers: "When she runs around the house wearing one of my shirts with the top three buttons unbuttoned, I can think of nothing that turns me on quicker. I'd rather see her in an ankle-length skirt than with a skirt with a big slit up the side. That to me is more sexy. And she dresses that way because she knows it pleases me."

# HAPPY COUPLES, IMPERFECT SEX

> It occurred to me that a guy who is really, really good at making
> love to a woman, the same woman, and who is inventively and
> exceptionally good at it time after time, who is carefully brutal
> at some moments and solicitous at others, who knows her sweet
> spots and concentrates on them and seems to be worshiping her
> body and is keen on driving her to a sweet distraction every time,
> is not someone to be ignored or otherwise taken for granted or
> dismissed on minor charges.
>
> —Charles Baxter, *The Feast of Love*

Let's get more earthy now and discuss how various of these
best-of-all-possible relationships handle differing expectations
and sexual styles:

↔ **WHOSE TURN TO RISK REJECTION?** When one partner
is the frequent—or constant—initiator, the other is regularly
the gatekeeper. The initiator is the one who risks getting a
negative response, and, depending on the couple's dynamics
and each partner's ego strength, this can be a ho-hum experience or a crushing blow. It's natural that the partner with the
higher sex drive would be the initiator, though in reality it's
not automatic. We all want evidence that our partners desire
us, and some people feel less attractive when it hasn't
occurred to their mates to make an occasional overture.

Marylis explains how this plays out in her marriage: "I
think he has the ultimate yes or no in the sexual arena, like I
have the ultimate yes or no about money. I have a higher sex
drive than he does. But if he doesn't feel like it, he'll often
accommodate me." Marylis relates how in her early forties,
she felt especially negative about her body, having gained
weight, developed a thyroid disorder and a skin condition. "It
was like everything was falling apart, and I'm sure I was less
sexual at that time. When Conrad was thirty, he had a sort of

existential crisis about death and religion, and he was off *his* game at that time."

When Marylis talks about their sex life now, it sounds so resolved, so congruent. But it wasn't always that way, she admits. Negotiating their two different drives has been the toughest compromise they faced. "I had to learn to be assertive and learn that he's happy to take care of me, and that he's comfortable with it. And I think he had to learn that I don't judge him because he's *not* where I'm at sexually. It took a while to adjust to that, because when we met, we were teenagers and hot like monkeys. We hadn't settled into any kind of adult pattern."

When Conrad is feeling stressed at work or is bothered or preoccupied, he isn't interested in sex. Even though he's been clear about that with Marylis, it wasn't a speedy adjustment: she had to learn that his sexuality is tied to his emotions. "I really had to realize that it's not about me," she explains, "that it doesn't mean I'm overweight."

Sherry Suib Cohen admits she rarely is the one to initiate sex, probably because her mother's wrong-headed lesson that "nice girls don't" still kicks in. But her husband Larry understands her so well that "he never gets insulted when I say no, he never gets angry, he never gets hurt. He just talks me into it. Then when I'm there, it's marvelous," Sherry says. By persisting and humoring her, he helps her surrender to the moment.

Check with your partner and see if he's feeling a bit neglected by your consistently waiting for him to take the initiative. Some do, and some don't care, so long as you don't often turn *him* down. Play fair, though, and take your turn risking rejection.

↪ **MESHING CLASHING SEXUAL STYLES.** The various ways you approach each other and how you act during lovemaking can cause difficulties. I knew a woman who fretted over her husband's passivity in bed. "He *has* no sexual style," she would complain, but of course he did. They eventually split up.

It helps to be with a partner who has a similar need for intimacy as you do, a compatible desire for privacy and separate time, and a matching urge for physical closeness. If you're someone for whom sex is necessary (if not always sufficient) for feeling close, and you're with someone who prefers feeling close via conversation and disclosing vulnerabilities *before* loosening up physically, that can lead to conflict.

Consider, too, the following plaint from the comic novel *Conjugal Bliss* by John Nichols: "To me, I suppose marriage was like a great big sanctified monogamous orgy—of bodies, words, emotions, intellects. It was a goofy happy carnival that I didn't want to analyze. I just wanted to have *fun*. To Zelda, marriage was a sacred trust. It was an opportunity to forge a downright mystical connection between us by boldly breaking apart old restraints, facing the issues, demanding accountability." This reflects the truth of more than a few marriages, and some of those manage to find their way to compatibility. The trick is in combining the two perspectives, not in winning over one's mate to the "right" way. For the open-minded, fun and a certain sacredness aren't impossible to reconcile, if not always in the same encounter.

Tina Tessina laughed intermittently as she shared how she and her husband Richard manage their intimate moments: "I'm even a 'get it done now' person sometimes in sex. I'll say, 'C'mon, let's get going with this, I've got a day to deal with.' We have this joke where I write down 'romance' and then on top of it I put a big red circle with a slash through it. His idea of romantic is he looks at me funny and I immediately feel pressured, like there's something he's expecting of me. So we've turned it into a joke. Now I say, 'Just ignore me and fuck me.' He can get into it. I think he wants connection and he wants it to be slow and there's no time for it to be slow today.

Of course, sometimes we do find time for that, especially on vacations." Jeanette shares that, for years, there's been one constant bit of sexual contention between them: "I require a certain level of personal interaction. Hel-*lo*... I need a transition. Bob will come home, and we'll have dinner together, and then he'll go up to his study and work all evening. A lot of times there's something on TV, a game or something, and I'll go up there and turn it on. He likes me in the room reading or with the TV on, but we hardly have a conversation. And then at ten o'clock we get into bed, and I'm tired, and he starts making moves, and I'm like, 'Hi!' when he's like, 'You're my wife, what do I have to do chit-chat for?'"

Laurie, another otherwise contented wife, told me that she feels, frankly, a sense of loss due to Hamid's never having been a cuddler. "I mean, you either do it or you don't. Sure, I would have liked that at one time. Now I just go along," she says with a barely perceptible sigh but no apparent resentment.

↝ **LAUGH, AND KNOW WHEN TO STOP.** It can be quite erotic to find the same ideas absurd, to share full-bodied laughter to the point of near-exhaustion. "Laughing can take you through sex," says Sherry Suib Cohen. "I never knew you could laugh in the middle. That's the most wonderful thing about being married a hundred years. Right in the middle of the greatest sex in the world, you can just become hysterical."

In my previous marriage, sex was deadly serious all the time. Which is why in my post-divorce singles ad, I sought a lover with whom I could "laugh in bed." I found that person, a hundred times over, in Stephen. The longer we've been together, the more relaxed we are in bed, and the more readily we laugh before we finally make ourselves settle down. Occasionally, I've wanted to cut the silliness sooner, especially if it feels like we're keeping intimacy at bay because we're feeling insecure. Still, a deep laugh can have as profound an effect on your sense of connectedness as a good orgasm. Luckily, it's not a choice of one or the other.

➦ **THE SOCKS-SEX CONNECTION.** I am married to a man who enjoys being taken care of in countless ways. I used to think his carelessness around the house was a demand that I do everything. I eventually learned that he didn't care if either of us did *anything* practical, but initially my hyper-efficient nature ("Ach-TUNG!") bumped up against his "I'll get to it *manana*" tendencies. I got annoyed, which translated into lessened desire to connect sexually. I had to learn to keep in mind that my husband's casualness had nothing to do with me personally, and that our sexuality was too valuable to let unrelated habits interfere with it. You can choose to be angry all the time, or you can decide to let many irritations go, for the time being. Socks and sex have no necessary correlation.

A bit of advice I once read for "unmommying" a man is for the wife to continue to "mother" him, if that's what he likes, but in a sexual way, to convert that caretaking energy into adult behavior, such as drawing him a bath and bringing him a martini while he soaks. Rather than thinking of being extra nice to your mate as equivalent to mommying, I see it as the essence of adult caring. And it helps if the tables are turned every now and then.

➦ **LOVING WHILE ANGRY.** There are two kinds of people, and the odds are you've found yourself hitched to your opposite. It's possible for one type to have sex and put all emotional friction aside for the duration of the act. As one woman told me, "Anger never got in the way of sex for me. By the time I'm done, I'm not angry anymore. Sex is important to him, so keeping that going has always been a positive thing."

And then you have the other kind of person: "I don't want to make love when I've been pissed off at him. At most, I'll be upset for maybe two or three days before I get over the worst of it. Then we'll talk about it and sex becomes possible."

I haven't found that this is a preference that can be changed at will. I remember reading advice by a counselor who said that if you believe you can't connect sexually when you're angry, you should make the effort anyway for the bonding that will follow. I don't agree that this is always valid. It seems to me that if you're angry and having trouble communicating *outside* the boudoir, your discontent may become exacerbated by what goes on *inside*. There are too many possibilities for extending your disconnection, rather than mitigating it.

## WHAT A DIFFERENCE A DECADE MAKES

The truth is that mature Celice would rather have her cigarettes returned and, yes, some undemanded tenderness in the shape of books, opera CDs and house plants, than her old appetites. Lust had abandoned her; she had despaired of it—and there were times when irritation was the only passion that she felt.

—Jim Crace, *Being Dead*

Sexuality is most overpowering when you're unfamiliar with one another. Although that stage morphs, it does so in ways you couldn't haven't foreseen. Consider: when you were a child and certain toys were your favorite possessions, you couldn't have imagined that someday they would merely be fond souvenirs. Similarly, when you've just fallen in love, and you're rearranging your life to grasp every possible moment with your beloved, you can't believe you'll ever be blasé about an extra five minutes in his presence. It's likely that not again until the final moments of life will you ever value each precious moment with your partner the same way you did at the start of your hotly eroticized connection.

Few would argue that passion—for your partner and altogether—changes over time. I recently heard about a woman who claims that she still, after many years, gets aroused seeing her husband across a room—but I'd suspect that tingle is not quite sexual arousal or passion. But as that instant-on kind of passion calms down, intimacy doesn't have to level off. It can get deeper and more complex over time as you share a life together. And a few goosebumps are never ruled out when you spy your beloved after some absence.

When I told one man the title of this chapter, "sex (more or less,)" he quickly said, "Isn't more always better?" Well, no, it isn't. Not for everyone, and not always.

The inevitable shift from lust to what follows can be quite a surprise. For some it's a surprise in *every* relationship because they don't understand that this is how we're wired. Jane Hamilton, in her novel *Disobedience*, writes this about a character: "She loved him so much that the sight of his shoes made her go soft...It's a terrible thing when a person's shoes do it to you, make you think you can pay any price to follow him." That's first-stage lust, when you can't have enough of what you desire.

I remember feeling that way back in college, when I fell in love with my Lebanese boyfriend. I'd stand entranced before the shelves of books on Lebanon in the U.C.L.A. bookstore. With Stephen, at first, I felt an excitement akin to that around whatever was connected to poetry, but now, after two decades together, I feel nothing tingly related to, for example, his shoes. Of course, I can imagine circumstances in which those empty shoes would take on a lot more emotional resonance.

Chemistry is, of course, part of that melting feeling. Intense infatuation and craving for the loved one is caused by an amphetamine like gush of PEA (phenylethylamine). On the other hand, for long-term lovers, there's an "attachment chemical": endorphins. According to Diane Ackerman, "Separated even for a short while, the partners crave the cradle of the other's embrace. Is it a chemical craving? Possibly so, a hunger for the soothing endorphins that flow when they're together. It is a deep, sweet river, just right for dangling one's feet in while the world waits."

Of course, as Yale psychologist Robert J. Sternberg points out, passion is based on both psychological and bodily arousal. When you meet, there's a jolt of arousal, and then, at the peak, to keep your equilibrium, it starts to cool down until you reach a state of habituation. If you lose the person, you'll be depressed and feel worse than before you met.

Along those lines, a calligraphed quote from Emily Dickinson hangs in our hall: "Had I not seen the sun / I could have borne the shade / But light a newer Wilderness / My Wilderness has made—." (This was one of the first objects I smashed during our troubled time, because I suddenly felt how terribly, painfully true it was.) Love is like an addiction; lovers need the same amount of stimulation or more to continue to feel merely okay, or arousal starts to ebb.

We all think we know by now that comfort and romantic fantasy are at odds—popular culture tells us constantly, in cartoons, prime-time sitcoms, pop fiction bestsellers that portray affairs as more to be sought after than sticking around with old-faithful-and-steady-but-dull. Not long ago, however, a poll of one thousand married adults in Britain reported that by the time a couple were middle-aged, five times as many husbands and wives would rather own a dog than have an affair. No matter how excited we are at the start of a relationship, the intensity *will* dim, and that dimming is widely derided and feared. So many of our stories are about people torn between what they see as the twin poles of grand passion and dishwater ordinariness.

Occasionally I have a chance to see these principles in action. A couple divorced after a two-decade marriage, and one of the explanations Harry gave to those who knew him was that his wife Jolene was no longer affectionate toward him. He would come up behind her in the kitchen to cuddle and she'd push him away, justifying her distance by saying she knew it would turn into sex if she let it, and she wasn't in the mood. Marital driftings are incredibly complicated, of course. Jolene had her complaints too: Harry was too critical of her response during sex, urging her to be a tigress after decades of marriage.

Later, I spoke with Jolene's new boyfriend, Nat, who told me about his first marriage and divorce. "My wife would always push me away. How long is a man supposed to wait while his wife is unavailable?" Then he shared what a pleasure it was to be with Jolene, how affectionate and accepting and relaxed she was.

Here we have the same woman who no longer desired her husband's intimate advances, inspiring confidence in a man whose own wife had turned him down repeatedly. He is under the illusion that this new woman, Jolene, is qualitatively different from the old one. Is she? Or is it just a matter of time?

## SEX ON THE TO-DO LIST

> They were down to the occasional poke, and even those were corrupted by their singularity: sex, if it is not regular, becomes a little ludicrous; your sexuality becomes a special guest star on some long-running sitcom, your very sex organ becomes some old, safe, vaguely revered has-been, trotted out in a tux on Oscar night to receive his Lifetime Achievement Award.
>
> —Scott Spencer, *Men in Black*

Checking on sexual frequency among long-marrieds, I was told about a wide range of interferences, from kids to careers to cancer. Fatigue, naturally, is mentioned by many couples.

When the children are young and careers are on the ascendant, making time for sex is sometimes a priority in name only. That can be by mutual consent (or mutual neglect and inaction), as some of the younger couples I spoke to explained. But when it's a unilateral decision to place the couple's erotic life at the bottom of the list, trouble might follow. I'll go into this in the chapter on crises, since several of my interviewees spoke of those post-baby years as the hardest they'd overcome in their entire marriages. For now, when I ask Letitia, working mother of a preschooler, "Is there time for sex?" her response is telling: "It's not like it used to be. It's a cyclical problem, but there are times when he's working six days a week until four in the morning. When a few weeks go by that we haven't gotten together, I think, 'Oh gosh, that's sort of weird.' More like wondering if something is wrong, though nobody's complaining. I worry because I want to keep that bond strong. We talk about that, and then we both say, 'We need to have a date.'"

Ironically, Letitia's and Lenny's date nights often turn out not to be an occasion for sex, but merely a chance to get out of the house and be an unencumbered couple. They've considered checking into a hotel, but haven't done so yet. When they do set aside time for one another, they have to give up some other option, and they want to do it *all*, according to Letitia, from reading every book, to pursuing each of the many interests they both have, to maintaining contact with their many friends. Letitia admits they've realized that if they hadn't had those friends over until eleven at night, they wouldn't have become too tired for sex. Then they'll say, "Tomorrow night let's just rent a movie, and hang in, and have dinner, and put her [their daughter] to bed, and have a date and be together." Instead they'll fall asleep on the couch while watching the video. Letitia adds, laughing, "And we'll say, 'Next time let's skip the movie.'"

Howard also blames lifestyle constraints—especially their young kids—for why he and Jane don't have the more leisurely lovemaking sessions they both prefer. "Sometimes we're relegated to the quickie, and that is exciting, it has its own appeal, but I much prefer, and I think she does too, making love when we can relax and it just happens." He travels a lot, too, and when he's home and the children are in bed, they may have planned a date for making love, "but also often one or both of us is just too damn tired." But they love to read next to each other on the couch or watch TV together. "I like to think of myself as a normal virile guy with normal sexual appetite," adds Howard, "but quite often the coziness is more important than sex." Howard and Jane, by the way, are only in their mid-thirties.

A New York couple, Rose Arem, a school counselor (and my cousin), and Morty Richberg, an insurance agent, had what they both agreed was a fine sex life, with matching appetites. But she sometimes wondered if maybe they weren't having "enough." She says that although they'd be tired, she was determined to make sure they did it three or four times a week by keeping track on a calendar. Otherwise, she feared they might stop altogether.

Marylis believes her ideal frequency would be every couple of days, and she thinks her husband's ideal might be as seldom as every other week. "Maybe I *really* would only want it once a week at this point," she admits. "I'm definitely not like I used to be as a kid. I was much, much hornier. Incendiary."

Jeanette tells me that the first couple of years—more than a quarter of a century ago—she and Bob made love nearly every day. With children around, their pattern changed. When their daughters were older teenagers whose room was just on the other side of the connubial bedroom wall, it was especially challenging to relax into the mood. "I couldn't get their being on the other side of the door out of my mind. My ability to really enjoy it was less," she explains. Besides that, as she and Bob got busier and busier with their jobs, they fell into a routine of leaving sex for the end of the evening when they were tired—or certainly *she* was. "I'm good at like four o'clock in the afternoon," she concedes.

What's going on for many of these couples is most likely a combination of a natural drop-off from the heady days of intense sexual intimacy and an additional factor. According to psychologist Karen J. Prager, it's possible that couples merely take their intimacy (sexual and otherwise) for granted and don't realize how crucial it still is. But if the intimacy is disrupted or dissolved, the couple may be shocked by how much it meant to them.

Jeanette brings up another factor—health considerations—that can play havoc with a couple's sex life. She is currently perimenopausal and gets hot flashes. "Interestingly," she relates, "there are about three days when I'm ovulating that I'm like a cat in heat. For those three days, I call to ask, 'Are you coming home?' I'm probably giving off a scent." Her husband particularly enjoys it when she's feeling that way, and she frets briefly about the future, post-menopause.

Several women coping with hormonal changes mentioned their flagging libido and how that stresses both partners. Laurie, for instance, doesn't take estrogen due to her fear of breast cancer. She adds that Hamid's drive has also dropped off of late, so that they only make love about once a week. When I suggest this isn't an unusual frequency, she tells me wistfully that it's not only how *often*, "but it's no longer hearts and flowers and sirens..."

"Do you miss that?"

"No," she says, and adds candidly, "but I think probably that if I met another man and I was attracted to him, that would probably happen."

Of course, medical conditions that affect sexual interest and ability may occur at any age. Some couples struggle with the side effects of antidepressants such as Prozac and Paxil, which frequently diminish libido and the ability to maintain an erection or to have an orgasm. Harriet, who says she has a high sex drive, reports that when her Myron retired, he was initially depressed. The medication he took made him very tired and affected their sex life. "And now he got off that and, boy, sexually, things just went right back to normal," says Harriet. "Luckily, he's adjusted to retirement and is over the depression for the most part."

A woman in a later-life marriage that's more joyful than she ever expected describes the changes wrought by getting older: "Aging is all about readjustment. No, the sex isn't steamy and exotic and fun and wild, which were characteristics up to over sixty for me. At this point I'm happy for lots of cuddles, occasional sexual encounters which take all forms, some satisfying and some good only because we tried. Women can go on forever, but their partners can't. So what? He tries to satisfy me, and I do my best for him, but there's lots of respect and feeling. It's plenty good enough."

Finally, although exceptions don't prove any rules, I'd like to share the story of a thoroughly well-adjusted and sexually active twosome: Christine and Jed. He's the gentlest, most patient police sergeant you could ever hope to meet, with a genuine smile and a softening physique at forty-one that implies he hasn't turned down *all* donut offers. He's also got a logical streak with just enough assertiveness to keep you from messing with him. She's a thirty-seven-year-old housewife who's attending school to get her business degree. They have been married for thirteen years, live in a suburban community in Southern California, with two school-aged children. And they have sex daily.

I suppose it helps that he's on duty most nights and is available days for hanky-panky, and that she's there, too, when the urges hit. But it's more than availability. Christine attributes their busier-than-average sex life to her belief that sex brings you closer. "We're pretty open as to what we'll do sexually, what we'll try with each other. If I think it looks interesting, sounds interesting, we'll try it. I have my faith and I believe in it and practice it, go to church and raise my children Catholic, but the Church doesn't live my life."

Having kids in the house doesn't slow down this couple. They lock the door, turn up the television, and keep their voices down. They each initiate, but most telling, Christine has never said no. "It's been important to him, and I won't deny him that. If I'm tired, sometimes I'll say, 'If you're willing to do all the work, I'll go along for the ride.' You don't feel like it all the time, but that doesn't mean the other person doesn't. He can rub my back at the same time." Here she laughed, I assume, at the amusing image she had just painted. "I can orgasm very easily."

Jed appreciates his luck in this department. "I don't think of myself as being a stud, but we have a very active sex life and I enjoy it a lot, and in talking to others, I find that's unusual. My dad and mom were the same way. I can remember as I became a teenager, thinking, 'Oh, that's what they've been doing all those years, locking the doors.' It's kind of funny, because I always think that that brings a closeness to you and maybe if more people did that more often, they would have less time to fight."

Are these all hurried interludes? No, claims Jed, they take as long as an hour or so at times, but less so as they get older, and they joke about a half-an-hour session being a quickie. "We're told we act like newlyweds. We're seldom more than a couple feet away from each other, anyplace we go. We're always holding hands, or she sits on my lap." A close couple, indeed.

Does Christine and Jed's robust sex life make you envious? The next chapter begins with some ideas that might help you act on those loving feelings.

# SEX REDUX (KEEPING IT FRESH)

*11*

"Turning love into marriage is like having the Unicorn Tapestry and using it as a tablecloth."

"But that sounds wonderful. That sounds exactly how a Unicorn Tapestry ought to be used."

—Scott Spencer, *Men in Black*

To remain in flow—a mental state that's refreshing and pleasurable in its own right—you've got to keep changing. That's because boredom is the antithesis of flow. It's also why marital sex stagnates. Too little challenge, and you risk boredom. Too much challenge? Anxiety is the result. When, as a couple, you ride the line between the two extremes, you're alert, stimulated, able to *feel*, and in flow together.

Possibly more than any other aspect of coupledom, as we've seen in the previous chapter, sexuality risks becoming monotonous if you don't pay enough attention to it. Sex may be a natural act, but keeping it fresh after the first year or two is not instinctive.

If you've shared genuine passion, beware of permanently downgrading sex to "comfy," warns Pepper Schwartz in *Peer Marriage*. "Having something to hope for," she writes, "whether during vacation time, intentionally special moments, or random heightened erotic occasions, may make the difference between being satisfied with a long-term sexual life together and being vulnerable to other passions with other people."

What many couples don't realize is that even a tiny change can have a powerful effect on retrieving a sense of flow. When you become accustomed to a particular behavior, no matter how thigh-shattering it felt at first, you begin to tune it out. You're no longer able to feel as intensely stimulated, physically or mentally, by the same action. It's no one's fault. It doesn't signal the need for a new partner. What it does indicate is the need to enliven your interaction.

## FLOW-ENHANCING IDEAS

Next time you think about making love, let one or more of the following suggestions lead you from humdrum to "hooo boy!"

→ **SEEK NOVELTY.** A minuscule change in your usual routine may suffice to reawaken your senses. Try changing where you make love. Stephen and I got a lot of laughter out of starting out at a slightly different angle on the bed. Intending to shift our way around the bed over a sequence of evenings, we placed our pillows at a one-eighth turn from the usual position. That offered an altered view of the room and made the mattress feel a bit firmer, the sex just novel enough to perk us up.

One couple decided, after a fresh home remodel, that they'd try making love in each room of the house. When that turned out to be such fun, they said, "Why not see if we can do it on—or up against—every possible item of furniture?"

Modify the time at which you ordinarily make love. Leaving it for bedtime is fine for night owls but can be counterproductive for those who are more alert in the morning. Noontime or mid-afternoon trysts can be remarkably rousing if you can squeeze them into your schedule. I don't mean to downplay how challenging this can be when you have children around. But do you really care if your babysitter suspects why you've hired her for two hours in the middle of a Saturday? Or you might arrange to trade turns with another couple to take everyone's kids to a park or enrichment class on Sundays for a couple of hours. If you typically spend that time grocery shopping, reconsider.

You might be familiar with magazine articles that recommend romantic dinners by candlelight or giving each other flowers or love notes in your lunch bags. Such tips seem to suggest that you're just not making the right efforts to revive romance and passion in your sex life. But you should also be aware that such pop culture prescriptions are designed by editorial committees who then may choose a writer to go out and unearth examples of people who fulfill certain specific requirements, i.e., a couple willing to say their sex life was recharged by exchanging helium balloons on all occasions. But bouquets and commercial greeting cards, even personalized love notes, may not impress some women to the point of instant arousal. One woman's romance is another's kitsch.

It can be fun to brainstorm erotic adventures. One journalist wrote of a wife who livened up the evening by applying three new colognes somewhere on her body and asking her lover to track down each one. Stephen and I have played one of those trivia games with this rule: the loser of each round had to do whatever the other wanted. The results were delightfully unexpected and adult. Almost any game could be similarly adapted.

↪ **GIVE SPONTANEITY A CHANCE.** When you're tempted to say, "Not tonight, honey, I have an email," consider how that makes your partner feel. Some of us (here's where my ears start burning) have a hard time relaxing into our more sensual selves until all the household chores are done. A friend complained that his wife insisted on folding the laundry before she'd agree to a sex date with him. Understandable on *some* level, if the clothes might then require ironing and she was feeling overworked as it was.

But as I've learned from my studies of writers with writer's block, there is no way to get "everything" done or fully "clear the decks." Give some thought (before you're next solicited for a sexy interlude) to how much deck-clearing is necessary before you let yourself relax with your partner. Distractions from sexuality are rampant and neverending, and they are often used to rationalize a reluctance to make love that is based on unacknowledged factors.

Now, to play devil's advocate—and to explain my personal perspective on this quandary—it doesn't seem unreasonable to wait good-naturedly while your partner completes one or two tasks so she can thoroughly relax and pay attention to you. No one likes to be interrupted and told they should move instantly into a sensual mode when they've been heretofore immersed in bill-paying or laundry or dishwashing. Best of all scenarios? The one who's in a hurry might offer, "Anything I can do to help you get this stuff off your mind more quickly? Or could I help you with it later? I'm really feeling in the mood to *be* with you..." Such an approach would be direct, realistic, sexy, and appreciated.

➤ **MAKE A DATE-PLUS.** Many couples plan nights out, especially when they have young children, specifically to spend time alone together. Which is fine, but turning those nights into sexual adventures takes an additional commitment.

Twenty-four years after lust first brought them together, Margie and Frank agree that their attraction toward each other is only slightly cooler than before. What they do is plan "intimate parties." Margie explains: "Either we set the scene—candlelight, champagne—or we'll go to our favorite margarita place, then come home and listen to a Barry White tape and have a little party and dance. Or we go out for dinner, or make a whole evening of it. We explore a lot of sexual things. We brainstorm, or I'll suggest some small thing, and we'll do it." Frank adds that they've made use of books like *The Joy of Sex*.

One woman gathered a batch of 3" x 5" cards and wrote down a few erotic activities she thought might be fun to try.

Then, whenever her mate was in a relaxed and experimental mood, they'd pull a card out and see if they felt like trying it, but without pressure on either of them. Here are a few she was willing to tell me: visit a sex shop to peruse the sex toys, use a blindfold, do it at night in the backyard, search for the G-spot, play doctor, play sex surrogate, shop for a naughty negligee and wear it, and brainstorm ten additional cards. Compile your own card file of erotic variations, including some you know you *would* do, and perhaps a few you'd *like* to be brave enough to try.

↝ **TRY QUICKIES.** When I told a friend I wanted to write about the joy of quickies, he said, "What can you do in one minute? Grab her ass? I thought women wanted the opposite of a one-minute lover. 'Slow hands' and all that." And many of us do. When I suggest quickies, I'm thinking of brief, romantic, sensual, or bawdy interactions to keep love exciting in even the busiest lives. Pleasure often increases when gratification is slightly delayed, whether on purpose or due to the press of life. Examples: Leave your partner a sexy note, offer a foot massage, shower together, hint of later pleasures to be bestowed, play footsies at a restaurant or friend's home, engage in sophisticated double entendres while the kids or others are around.

↝ **REDISCOVER FOREPLAY.** It's not exactly the opposite of quickies, but rather bringing those brief titillating activities right into the bedroom. One partner (not always the female) may long to slow the action down, return to those adolescent dating days when all was potential, when the intense arousal level was the biggest kick of all. When the stage is set beautifully, the play itself is so much more enjoyable. How can you slow the place when your partner is in a hurry to get down to business, implying the old line "we're married now, so why play games"?

Take charge. Do a strip tease. Get daring underwear he'll have to notice. Light a candle to soften the mood. Or suggest a timer be set—not an egg timer but an hourglass or oven timer—and make a rule that no one gets too close to genitals until the sand has run out. One man recalls fondling his lover's breasts while they listened to *Scheherazade* in its entirely; it resulted in mind-blowing sex when the music was finally over.

Sex therapist David Schnarch writes that "foreplay is where we negotiate the levels of intimacy, eroticism, meaning, and emotional connection (or lack thereof) in what follows next." When you think of it that way, the possibilities for variance expand, and you get an enlightening perspective on why some individuals tend to rush through foreplay unimaginatively. Try conceiving of foreplay as a way of beginning to remove yourselves from your ordinary workaday selves to join each other in intimacy. Are you both ready and willing to begin that vulnerability-exposing process? You may need to talk more openly than you're used to doing, and it helps if you're willing to share the responsibility. One person can't create intimacy for two.

↝ **DROP THE ELITISM.** I once said to Stephen that I'd like to try listening to music while we made love. One evening he put a blanket on the living room floor and put some French art songs on the stereo. The music was piercingly lovely, but too relaxing and not arousing to me. Later I explained that by music, I meant rhythms closer to Prince's "1999" with an exciting beat. Sex is no time to show off your aesthetic credentials. Of course, this is entirely personal between the two of you.

↝ **RESPECT THE FRAGILITY OF THE MOMENT.** If you're not feeling positive about each other in other areas, sexuality between you might be more unstable. That means if there's some behavior that's an instant turn-off for you, let your partner know it before you approach each other for lovemaking. For example, your partner's obsessive clothes-folding prior to hopping into bed makes you nuts. Or when your husband keeps the computer on in the bedroom right up until you're in bed, naked, with the covers pulled up, your eyelids adroop, before he shuts down the machine and begins amorous overtures. Or he likes to watch the news as he starts touching you. Or he comes to bed without shaving or without brushing his teeth. Or she starts fondling you while reminding you it's garbage night (guilty!).

Address these minor turn-offs (if any turn-off can be called minor) at a non-sexual time. Speak your mind directly, take responsibility for being uptight or distractable or super-sensitive to smells, and ask your partner to help you out so your lovemaking can be as free, easy, and mutual as it can be.

↦ **GET YOUR BLOOD MOVING.** Since an aroused nervous system *feels* similar to other kinds of arousal, it may augment your libido if you take actions that stir you up physically. Take a brisk walk (together is even better) or work out at the gym or on your home treadmill or exercycle. Dance (I use the word loosely) to music but stop before you're exhausted.

↦ **FOCUS ON YOUR EMOTIONS.** Some of the best sex evolves from a session in which you've both opened up emotionally in fresh ways. Try this exercise, suggested by a Jhumpa Lahiri short story: take turns sharing unacknowledged ways you believe you've hurt each other. In the short story, the couple has been drifting apart, but this exercise is so effective at peeling away layers of defensiveness that it gives the husband hope. (I won't spoil the ending, but the wife's perspective is affected by how long it took them to begin paying attention to intimacy.)

↝ **WELCOME FAILURE.** If you always stick to the tried-and-true, no wonder at least one of you gets bored. One woman told me that when she pleaded with her husband to try some not particularly daring sexual position, he resisted, saying they should stick to what they know works for both of them. She prevailed, and he was right: it didn't work (i.e., she couldn't come) until they switched back to the old way. He even said, "I told you so." But if her husband's attitude had been more open-minded, they could have had a positive experience instead of feeling foolish and disconnected.

I'm thinking of a man I know whose wife, he said, turned down his overtures for a more varied sex life with the line "My body is a temple." It's hard to have fun in a temple where the expectation is staid and hushed reverence. Creativity often leads to flow, and a precursor to full creativity is a willingness to experiment, to risk failure. The fact is that there can be no failure between two loving partners who are seeking to broaden their sexual repertoire. One husband attempted to infiltrate a food item into an adventurous lovemaking session, until he discovered his wife believes food of any kind doesn't mesh well with eroticism. All such experiments are part of the learning process, and at least worth a shared laugh over after.

↝ **DEFINE SEX BROADLY.** The myth that one kind of orgasm is more pure and all others somehow lesser is long outdated. That includes believing that coming simultaneously is the best, even though you and your partner have never managed to. Mutual masturbation (whether watching or getting involved), oral sex, sex toys, and all the other types of erotic behavior gathered in all the sex manuals of the world's cultures: each is as worthy of attention as the unfairly maligned missionary position.

↝ **DO IT YOUR WAY.** If your sex life is coughing along a bit phlegmatically, try this idea that our therapist suggested to us: the one who has the lesser libido agrees to do it *whenever* the other one wants, but the higher drive partner agrees to do it *whichever way* the other chooses. Thus, you're tired, and your partner's tired of being put-off, so you agree to have sex as long as you don't have to move a muscle. Role-play "bored prostitute" or "stage-shy porn star" or "blow-up doll." Obviously, this list of ideas won't suit everyone. All that's required is to be available so your partner's sexual needs can be satisfied, and you can choose how much energy you want to expend. You may start out uninvolved and, as Christine explained in the previous chapter, you could enjoy yourself regardless. Of course, any such experiments must be mutually agreed upon. *Real* coercion isn't the least bit erotic.

➥ **BE THERE NOW—WITH YOUR PARTNER.** Sex therapist David Schnarch points out that many of the techniques suggested to couples who are struggling with low desire succeed only in making the situation worse. We're told not to think about our partner but to fantasize about someone—anyone— else, or to maintain a tight focus on our own sensations to the exclusion of an awareness there's a lover in bed with us giving us those sensations. Schnarch's remedy is to make love with your eyes open—for as long as you dare—and to concentrate more intently, rather than less, on our actual partners. "Your feelings have a bigger impact on genital functioning and orgasm than do physical sensations," he writes. Turning "your attention to what's going on between the two of you" should be your priority.

It's more challenging than it sounds to be that intimate and in-the-moment with a real live person, no matter how much you love him or her. But it can give a boost to your lovemaking. And it can lead to what Schnarch calls "wall-socket sex," another phrase for flow: sex in which time stops, external reality fades, your consciousness changes, and boundaries between the two of you cease to exist.

•→ **SEEK THE "AS IS" FACTOR.** You experience profound relief when you're confident of being loved without your partner wishing you were different in any major way. For example, when Howard talks about his sex life with Jane, he says, "I'm attracted to the fact that she is just who she is."

Marylis explains that she and Conrad learned to respect each other and to know that any disagreements they may have about frequency don't reflect on the relationship, but that it's totally about their individual bodies. "I know he adores me, and I know he's comfortable with the way I am. No matter what, that love pulls you through."

Theo Park tells why it barely matters that his desire level isn't perfectly matched with his partner's: "Part of it is, for me, that nothing matters that much. I just mean the number of times you have sex or the list of 101 things you do that bug me—those things are just part of a relationship."

Sometimes you need to compromise and reframe what might seem like a deficit. Harriet says she once asked Myron what you have when passion is spent, and he said, "Love." Says Harriet, "Who could want a more romantic answer than that?"

## THE PORNO PERPLEX

WIFE: "Who was that lady you were with last night?"
HUSBAND: "Oops, did I leave my porn video in the VCR again?"

In my perfect world, husbands would find the idea of their wives enough to arouse them perpetually. Of course, to be fair, wives would then also never need to imagine anyone but their husbands to heat their own erotic kettles to a boil. Here we are, though, in the real world, where a little judiciously applied fantasy may be an aid or a treat. Some people like to use pornography—whether magazines, videos, CDs, or Internet-based—to imaginatively pad the flesh of their fictions. I realize this is a controversial subject. Such material is offensive to some due to the exploitation of those involved in making it, or its perceived demeaningness. Others believe it all depends on the type of porn you're discussing. In the convivial relationships I explored, such differences of viewpoint are managed through loving compromise.

At the risk of oversimplifying (there are many exceptions), a great many men, especially in the first half of their lives, have a much stronger sex drive than most young women realize. I've heard of men masturbating regularly five times a day, and of men who have sex daily with their wives and still have enough energy for pornography. Young people are rarely offered such detail, and certainly not with the idea that this is normal behavior. Of course, girls may be told to watch out for men, that they only want "one thing"—as I was told by my grandfather when I was eleven. What I couldn't have known was that even when they get that one thing, they often want more, and then even more. This can come as a shock, and that shock—based as it is on erroneous expectations—has been known to rock marriages.

Says Asher, one of the more sexually candid men I interviewed, "I grew up using porn. Every guy I knew growing up used porn. If not, they jerked off *imagining*—which isn't as different as you might think." Asher explains that most men, including him, "keep right on doing what they're used to doing, when they date, get engaged, et cetera. It's not as though sex is regular or ideal during those times. Why would they stop? No woman commits to fill every gap in her husband's sex life—and we men sure know it! We just don't tell our dates, fiancées, etc., about masturbating. Why would we?"

When Stephen and I were dating, we had a rollicking sex life each weekend. So I was unprepared when he told me by phone one mid-week, "I've been saving myself for you and not masturbating this week." Wow, I thought. Our weekends were so sexually depleting to me, yet they barely made a dent in my lover's libido. For a while, then, it seemed to me that I wasn't as cherished and special as I'd thought. I later learned I'm not the only woman to come to a similar erroneous conclusion.

The frequent use of porn may or may not signal trouble in the marriage. The way a couple confronts this subject reflects and reveals a lot about how they handle all differences.

The porn industry in the United States accrues an annual revenue of at least $10 billion, which, as a recent *New York Times* article pointed out, is more than people spend on movie tickets and on all the performing arts combined. And as the article's author was told, "We realized that when there are 700 million porn rentals a year, it can't be just a million perverts renting 700 videos each."

So what's going on? One possible reason porn is so appealing is that the viewer is in control, explains Stephen A. Mitchell in *Can Love Last?* When you want a romantic response, in addition to sex, from a real person, there's a chance you won't get it. According to Mitchell, that can make you angry on some level—dependency often moves in that direction—and so to remain in control, you head for the porn. Mitchell calls it "risk-free desire."

Or, more benignly, using porn is a convenient way to have sex more often without going to any trouble (and without troubling your partner when all you want is a quick fix). It's fun, fast, feels good, and whom, after all, does it hurt (putting aside considerations of possible exploitation during its production, and with the obvious exceptions of sadistic or child porn)? Of course, these are not universal attitudes. A distant relative told me that when she discovered her husband was using porn, she never wanted him to touch her again.

Asher tells me his wife Audra thinks he's the first person she knew who used porn. "I'm sure *all* the guys she knew used porn, she just didn't know it!" Audra, however, isn't bothered by it at all. One wife I interviewed told me that when she found out her husband masturbated—he told her during a vacation when they were relaxed and he was explaining why his sex drive was so thwarted by her low interest—she said it was a total revelation to her. She admits to feeling disgust. "Though I do it myself sometimes, I do have some sort of puritan feeling that we're not supposed to do this," she says. "I was grossed out about it. There was the 'aren't I enough?' feeling." The other facet that disturbed her was realizing that for him sex had such a huge physical component, whereas for her it was more an act of cherishing. Finally, after that enlightening conversation, "It was 'Oh, *now* I get it, now I understand.'"

I have to admit I was taken aback when Stephen admitted during dinner with friends of ours, "I use porn because I need variety." The other husband seemed to take pride in the fact that he wasn't like Stephen, saying to his wife, "Why would I need anything else when I have you?" But a few years later, it turned out that he had a large stash of porno magazines of his own. For whatever reason—diplomacy? embarrassment? a false sense of romance?—he had been lying.

Authors Ellyn Bader and Peter T. Pearson note in *Tell Me No Lies: How to Face the Truth and Build a Loving Marriage* that when a woman says she doesn't like porn and won't have it in the house, the message often is "I don't want to know about it." The male will then be sneaky about it or else resentful. "'Don't' is a strong word," write Bader and Pearson. "A marriage needs to have room for each person's complex truths. You want it to be possible to express complicated, even conflicting parts of yourselves and tolerate the uncertainty that results."

It took me some time to come to an accommodation with my own spouse's use of porn. When we'd been married only a year and a half, I began missing the former frequency and intensity of our sex life, including the kisses, and, as I complained to my diary, the "no breathing in my ear, no foot massages, no long, slow, languorousness at all, it seems." But Stephen didn't notice the change and said he was happy and things were perfect. Perhaps that's why I pounced on his cache of naked pictures as a handy scapegoat for our building difficulties, although he insisted it was my problem and he didn't like feeling responsible for it. I knew on some level that that was true, but, I told my diary, "I feel fat and less attractive than when I was making love almost every day. Those magazines he reads (!) upset me mightily. I feel the most intense jealousy, while he insists I am wrong to try and make him feel guilty. They are getting the lustful attention I lack and feel incapable of inspiring anymore."

This was the crux of the matter for me: why wasn't I inspiring as much lust as these paper bimbos? It had to be because I was somehow lacking physically, I figured, since this is one of my insecurities. It never occurred to me at the time that our day-to-day interactions were primarily at fault for our sexual slowdown. What was especially galling to me was that, due to Stephen's innate obliviousness, he'd leave his magazines around after using them—on the bedroom floor or in the bathroom—where I'd bump into them unexpectedly. I couldn't keep from leafing through them at such times, staring at the women he had recently ogled and comparing myself unfavorably to them.

At the same time, I have never had any negativity about fantasizing. I have mine, he has his. Perfectly fine. The key for me was realizing that I hated seeing his fantasies in the flesh, as it were. Our eventual compromise was an easy one: he learned to keep his porn out of my sight. That helped a lot. Fantasy and reality are not the same when it comes to sexuality, and I finally accepted that my mate's use of porn in no way detracted from our more substantial life together. If we weren't doing it as often as one or both of us wished, *that* wasn't the reason.

I was fascinated to learn that although Asher's wife is unflustered by his use of porn, Asher himself is occasionally somewhat bothered by it. His ambivalence mirrors my own reasoning. "I used to feel that I was cheating Audra out of something. As my sex life with her evolved, I kept doing it, but less often. Then I relaxed about it. It's kind of apples and oranges with me now, although when the fertilizer is limited one must still conserve." He says he has to remind himself that men and women have different drives, and that "it's just a power fantasy that they should serve each other's whims and needs 100 percent of the time. I'm firmly convinced that's neither honest nor sexy nor even possible."

Some of the wives I interviewed, evidently more self-confident than I am in certain ways, seem to have an intuitively sane grasp of the subject. They aren't threatened and have managed to relegate their partners' porn preferences to a negligible corner of the relationship.

For instance, one of these women told me that she doesn't mind watching porn with her husband. She doesn't think of it as his getting excited by the other women, but that he's getting excited by watching the sex. "It's not the women," she says, "because most of them, if you look at them, they're kind of skanky. It's a means-to-the-end type thing." They've laughed together at the unbelievably bad acting on some of the videos.

Christine, the wife with the at-least-once-daily sex life, says she and Jed have rented videos and that she never feels at all threatened. "If he wanted those women, he'd be with them. Just give me five minutes and I'll point out every imperfection of every female on those tapes. I think it's just the fact that she's somebody else naked. I know what's wrong with my body, but he doesn't have the best shaped body either," she says, laughing. "Whenever he sees me naked, he compliments me. And I tell him I think he's sexy. I tell him if I was rich, I'd pay him to walk around my house naked all day. I find him attractive, he finds me attractive. That doesn't mean there's not something else that's going to excite him. Sometimes he's been up awake for forty-eight hours straight, and he still wants to have sex, so looking at porn will just excite him that little extra."

Other women have learned over time to accept their partners' interest in porn. Frieda told me that when she and her husband Rodney were dating, he wanted to show her some pornography, but she refused. "My first husband used to drag me to the theaters, and I hated it." With Rodney there was a "little struggle," as she puts it, "and that got to be a problem. So we came to a compromise. When we play the videos, I don't like to hear the sound on them. I like to hear music, nice soft love music, whatever. So we turn the sound down on the video and we turn my music on. Most of the time he doesn't look at the video anyway. I think he likes it maybe just in the beginning, as a visual stimulus. Most of the time, I don't watch them at all."

Rodney uses the videos to masturbate at times, which used to make Frieda uncomfortable, but "only because I didn't like the girl he was particularly hot on at that time," she explains. "I'd kind of tease him about his favorite ones. I'd always tell him that he says he loves me, but if so-and-so shows up, he'd be gone." Though that sounds a bit insecure, she elaborates about why she's not threatened. "Because I know my husband. If she was a banker and walked to the front door, then yes, I'd be jealous, because I think he *would* be gone if she wanted to go. But that type of woman, he just likes to look at them. The men I know that watch them do so because they like to *look* at them, they think they're sexy, but would they want that type of woman for their own? Oh no, definitely not."

Once Frieda found it disturbing when a porn actress looked a lot like her that. Watching Rodney watch the actress do things Frieda would never do made her feel oddly exposed. "I'm not a prude, but I'm very private, and to see someone who looks like you doing that, and knowing other people were seeing it...There have been a couple of positions he's wanted to try that I'm kind of afraid to do. Really kind of wild. No, I don't think so, honey."

I do believe that some pornography may potentially be harmful to the development of healthy, loving sexuality. I'm not convinced that seeing all those artificially enhanced images of always available fantasy figures might not, in some instances, lead some men to believe they could do better than settle for the flawed woman they have. I asked Asher whether he ever feels that the ready availability throughout our lives of pictures of gorgeous and sexy women might have some effect on a man's reactions to his own gorgeous and sexy woman. He responded: "Yes, it has an effect. So does the imagination itself, without porn. Imagination has an effect on real life in all areas. Does real life ever measure up to the imagination in any area? Sex isn't any different."

An honest answer. His own preference anyway, he admits, is not pictures alone, but text porno which suggests enticing situations. He also likes altered memories of past situations which are even more effective since they invoke real emotions. "Needless to say, fantasizing about one's own wife also hits a deeper nerve—some porno mags devote whole issues to it."

Still, I persisted, isn't it true that seeing "perfection" so easily makes ordinary imperfect bodies seem more ordinary and imperfect? "It's not 'perfection,'" insisted Asher, "it's what turns you on, which often isn't perfect at all. A lot of guys, if not all, can be turned on by an element of skank, real down and dirty sex, even whoredom, more easily than by some Victoria's Secret iceberg model who won't even take her top off. Face it, most hookers and strippers aren't Kate Beckinsale. Women with dirty minds can really steal your heart without being cover girls."

Stephen has said, similarly: "the grosser the better." He doesn't mean disgusting, he has told me, but direct, unromanticized, unprettified outright sexuality. I asked him whether it bothered him that I don't wear high heels, and he said, "Whyever would I care?" I said that the porn babes he responds to are displayed in high heels." "They wear shoes?" he asked, without guile.

When it comes to porn, each couple needs to agree on the details for themselves, with honest conversation sans the negativity. For instance, in our home we agreed that lusting in your heart after unresponsive images isn't infidelity, but that carrying on a sexy conversation over a chat line with another woman would be. The difference, we both agreed, has to do with the interaction being consciousness-to-consciousness. Anything short of that is one-sided and falls under fantasy. Of course, if porn use is a bona fide addiction that causes massive friction in the relationship, then outside help would be beneficial as with any addiction.

## COMMUNICATING ABOUT SEX

It's difficult to talk about your sexual desires, even—or especially—

to your lover. I recall admitting to a close friend, at the beginning of my relationship with Stephen, that I was having trouble telling Stephen about some minor habit that was troubling me. She responded brusquely, "You have to let him know what's on your mind! Just put a little yellow sticky note on your body."

One woman who enjoyed full body hugs didn't like it when her husband went straight from the shower to their bed. He'd still be damp and their all-over hugs just didn't "slide." She finally got the courage to tell him his wetness was a turn-off.

Putting off sexual conversations can turn them into momentous and forbidding obligations, and that makes you avoid them longer. Together nearly two decades, Naomi and Janice have moved apart sexually over the past few years, and neither is overjoyed about the change. Naomi explains: "There are different reasons for both of us. Some has to do with body image, discomfort with our own bodies in different ways, and also, for me, I think peri-menopause may be a big part of it. My libido is practically gone, but that's not the case with Janice, even though she's older than I am and already went through menopause. Also, sex is an area of our lives that is so fraught with old and unfinished emotional stuff. It's become a big deal to get into it and talk about it and work on it, and I think we're both just not going there."

Naomi relies on the hope that they will eventually get beyond this long dry spell, their only obstacle to an otherwise deeply satisfying relationship. But meanwhile, neither of them is taking the initiative. Fortunately, they continue to cuddle and snuggle, with no abatement of their mutual affection and warmth.

Communication, of course, doesn't always require words. Words have been known to get in the way when it comes to messages about what feels sexy. The easiest nonverbal technique is to let your partner know when his or her touch is just right by murmuring, and by staying silent when it's off a bit. If a particular touch is uncomfortable, or it hurts, move your body or move the innocently offending hand. Suffering in silence will get you nowhere, and in the long run only brings you more of the same and an increase of resentment. If those gentle purring sounds and slight body shiftings aren't clear to your partner, take his hand and show him. If your partner is nondefensive outside the bedroom, this will go smoothly. If he gets defensive at the slightest hint you're suggesting he change a little, go back to Chapters five and six and focus, for now, on making him feel safer during your non-sexual interactions.

What can you do if your partner seems to hear your request for change, whether verbal or not, adapts his behavior in the moment, then reverts back to his old habits the next time you make love? It's a common complaint. But instead of assuming he isn't paying attention to you or doesn't care, make the effort to repeat your preferences. It's possible that he'd been doing this same movement for a long time before you spoke up, and once he's immersed in sex, his cognitive faculties aren't fully engaged anymore. He could use a gentle reminder of what you prefer, but lovingly. Yes, it would be great if each of us could focus on our own sensations and at the same time be attuned to our partners' responses every moment. It may not be for lack of will or effort that your partner seems forgetful. It takes a while for habits to become entrenched, and by that time, what arouses you may have changed. There's no way around keeping those communication lines open *all the time*.

I found sex expert David Schnarch's discussion of differentiation relevant in this context. He explains that differentiation is how well you can maintain your sense of self when you're near someone very important to you. Schnarch says not to underline passages in his book, for example, and hope your partner will read them (or in other books and articles, as I used to do regularly and ineffectively with Stephen). "If you're not ready to speak for yourself, then you're probably not ready to hold onto yourself through the ensuing discussion," he writes.

Over time, and having been through the clarifying fires of our personal troubles, I learned I had nothing to lose by being frank about my sexuality. I stopped holding back my wants and found a way to state desires that kept the responsibility on me, not my partner. In our non-bedroom conversations too—which the erotic ones mirrored—I learned to say, "This is my own quirky preference, and it says nothing about you. But could you help me meet this need?" There's only so much you can do on your own when it comes to improving your sex life. The rest requires loving support and a nondefensive attitude.

Marylis and Conrad are both extremely monogamous experimenters who like to try novel scenarios once in a while. "There are actually times when I've written him a little note or he's written me a little note, because we're a little shy to talk face to face," Marylis admits. She'll write, for instance, "I've been thinking about this. What do you think about it?"

Does every great couple talk (or write) with equal ease about sex? Not at all. I found that some of the older couples, as one might expect, were not only more reticent to be candid with me about sex, but admitted they weren't always able to speak openly to one another.

"Because of our ages and backgrounds," says Zhita Rea, "talking readily about sex is not comfortable, certainly not for me, and probably not for Jim. I would say we talk about it very little. I think we each feel it's satisfying and certainly a very enjoyable part of our relationship. Even having met in our mid-forties, it's very, very important." Her husband tells me the following: "There's a little compromising there, as well. I feel a little inhibited about discussing it with her. Earlier, when it was fine, I didn't feel any need to discuss it. It's still fine, but less frequent and I'm not sure to what extent that is because of declining testosterone. She recently mentioned a book that we got some years ago and I never got around to reading, about love, sex, and aging. I took her mentioning that book as a sign that it might be helpful to take another try at reading it. And maybe we'll find that there *are* things to discuss."

As we have seen, sex, whether there's more or less of it, is an integral part of a flourishing relationship. It can also—when allowed to deteriorate—be one of the precipitators of the most common and disastrous crisis couples face: infidelity.

# 12
# HITTING BOTTOM

Maybe it was impossible to be a strong country or couple or family unless you'd fought a little war, either against a common enemy or amongst yourselves.

—Jane Hamilton, *Disobedience*

Ten years ago, Stephen and I passed through what we now tongue-in-cheekly refer to as The Troubles. We—and numerous others—are proof that it *is* possible to survive and transcend such a maelstrom of misery. If your own relationship has already hit bottom, I'll share solid reasons for long-range optimism, and if it hasn't, you may glean some insight here that will keep you from ever having to fall that far.

In this chapter I'll begin with the earliest hints of trouble in my own relationship to show how easy it is for a well-matched couple to join the dispiriting statistics on infidelity. Then in the following chapter, I'll share several other couples' stories, in order to reveal more of the underlying factors in such crises. Along the way, we'll learn the assorted ways that resilient couples rebound after toppling over the brink.

## HOW MUCH LOVE IS ENOUGH?

I would stand before the windows of the numerous borax furniture stores that dotted the neighborhood and stare at the "parlor suits" and "kitchen onsombles" there, immersed in the most abysmal depressions as I evoked, from the patterns of tritely set tables and chairs, whole married lifetimes of banality....These glimpses were like visions of hell, of an intellectual and spiritual perdition into whose attendant quagmires of E-Z credit terms and twenty-years-to-pay I must at all costs avoid putting my foot.

—Peter DeVries, *The Blood of the Lamb*

It's sometimes thought that "not enough love" in their committed relationship is what causes people to stray from their vows. That's misleading. It is a common question: do you love each other *enough*? It expectedly occurs first before you make a commitment, but often comes back to haunt later when one of you is considering whether to stay or stray.

Stephen admits he was partially in the throes of a romantic delusion early on, brought about by his fervent adolescent reading of the Edgar Rice Burroughs novels. He believed then that when you're in love the whole world is supposed to burst with glorious pinwheels and continue to do so forever. I suppose these would be equivalent to the teenage girls' and women's magazines I was raised on, as well as all the romantic English novels that used to form my view of what true love should be. (My own fantasies had already been moderated by my first marriage's thirteen frustrating years of reality.)

Stephen wasn't quite sure what *was* possible. He'd left a previous girlfriend with whom he got along beautifully, because the "magic" was absent. As I wrote in my journal four months into the relationship, "I'm sure he loves me, but I don't think he loves me *enough*. I'm worried about his possible boredom." The minor neuroses dovetailed here: he wanted from love what it could not deliver, something all-encompassing and mind-obliterating and, well, *perfect*, whereas I wanted to be a man's failure-proof love-of-all-times, and yet I'd chosen a perfectionist, a skeptic who hedged every bet, qualified every statement.

Everyone has heard of midlife crises, but there isn't only one such possible crisis. Around age thirty or so, most of us go through a normal developmental transition. Stephen, who was around that age when we met, was struggling with how much reality he could settle for, and how intently he ought to hold out for achieving his ideal of a total soulmate. Like the character in the Peter DeVries novel quoted at the beginning of this section, Stephen was apprehensive of ending up ordinary, no different from his parents, living a restricted suburban life behind my white picket fence (with my two children). But then when we grew to know and appreciate each other, our love deepened and he made his decision (I'd already made mine), and we committed to one another.

At this point, when we were both more romantically fuzzy-minded than we would ever be again, we wrote letters to each other in which we listed each other's best qualities:

Dear Susan, What else do I like about you. Well: you're cute. You're intelligent. You can motivate yourself and others to positive action. You're honest and open (not just your legs). You're sexy. You're willing to change. You're open-minded. You're a good conversationalist. You have a good sense of humor, even in trying circumstances. You're generous with your time and savings. You help me to be a more consummate soul. And you're loving and lovable.

I responded with the following list of my own:

Dear Stephen, I LOVE YOU FOR: your instant understanding of my feelings, for thinking me pretty, your total honesty, being uninhibited in bed, your willingness to show your vulnerability, playing miniature golf with me and the kids, asking me what I like in bed, your artistic sensitivities, your smiles, your values: loyalty, integrity, fidelity, respect for good people; kissing me in public, the nasty jokes followed by abject apologies, reading books on childrearing, the poetry in your touch, the hugs and the kisses, your extraordinary sexual technique, your creatively practical approach to problem-solving, your strength, your softness, sharing your doubts (yes, even that), encouraging me to be me.

Three months after we were married, sex was fabulous and occurred almost daily, and I told my diary, "I wouldn't change a thing." How did we get from here—this euphoric enumeration, this total satisfaction—to a time, not long after, when we focused almost entirely on our less loving selves, became much less charitable toward each other, were downright stubborn, withholding, carping, even vindictive?

## THE LONG SLIDE DOWN

By the time we'd known each other for three and a half years altogether (married two and a half) disillusionment had definitely set in. As with any awakening-from-the-dream-of-courtship couple, it isn't necessarily that any of those particular personal qualities we'd counted—and counted on—had vanished. But they hadn't told the whole story of who we were. Like many couples, of course, we blamed each other and were miserable. Looking back, it is easy to recognize the roles played by Stephen's earlier hesitation as to whether I matched his romantic longings, his bouts of depression and my own, his habit of withdrawing from conflict, and my own pesky personality (previously, in Chapter six, I described how hard it was for me to figure out what Stephen meant by my "negativity").

In the following journal entry, notice how my own demands and expectations contributed to our downward spiral. Clearly, our mutual neediness and inability to assume goodwill on the part of the other left us both frustrated and, eventually, desperate.

I've re-started therapy and am in the midst of a suffocating depression/anxiety. Stephen left for work mad at me again. He said I was critical several times this morning. Yes, I was. Probably because of my own repressed anger toward him. I'm mad at him because I don't feel anything coming from him toward me. All he wants is for me to love him, touch him, scratch him here or there, reassure him, bolster his flagging ego. But I get nothing at all. The briefest of touches, distracted conversation, no help at all with the multitude of tasks facing me except the suggestion that the problem is in me, for being aware of those tasks. I've complained repeatedly about my inability to get started, to get organized on my articles—but he never offers to help, even when I scream HELP.

Unsurprisingly, our sex life, amidst all this anger, was not going well. When we were first together, if I wasn't aroused as often as he was, I went along anyway because we felt so close. Now I had begun to rethink my constant availability. He's still masturbating anyway, I figured, and if I can't possibly be his whole sexual source, then why put myself out at all? Whereas he used to be utterly attuned to me sexually and in every other way—psychological projection, as I noted in Chapter one, is an amazingly deceptive practice—now I felt as though I was merely an afterthought. Mimi Schwartz describes in her own memoir how she felt when she wasn't getting enough attention: "Stu was working night and day at a new job as department chair, and I was ready for sex, murder, whatever it took not to feel like his worn-out slippers night after night." That's exactly how I felt, too.

When I mentioned the absence of our former passion, Stephen said it wasn't that he didn't like me, but that he was feeling defensive, and if I wouldn't complain so much, he wouldn't feel so attacked. But by the time he would agree to talk, I would already be on the point of hysteria and tears, and most of what would come out would be negative, angry, and frustrated.

## FROM BAD TO WORSE

They exchanged glances of iron and fire over the dinner table and across the seemingly still spaces of the living room. It had been one of those marriages where the worst is to be tolerated and endured, and hatred burns steadily like a pilot light.

—Charles Baxter, *Shadow Play*

At this point we wondered if perhaps the impasse would melt if we exchanged lists of behaviors we each wanted. We hoped, as our therapist suggested and numerous others have written, that by acting more pleasingly toward one another, we'd feel more loving. My own list of "desired caring behaviors" included items such as these: read and *comment on* an article I leave on the kitchen table; hug me; tell me something good about me; take the initiative in dealing with any chore; ask me what I'm working on and take an interest in the answer. To help me feel more loved in bed, in particular, I asked him to "approach me with a sexy gleam in your eye as early as possible in the day or evening, indicating a possible interest for later when it will be feasible to carry out; when you are feeling loving, use words to let me know—you do not lie with words, whereas you seem to be able to commence lovemaking when not feeling truly loving." And this big one: "Stop being afraid of me. I love you and I value our relationship above all else. Remember this."

Stephen's lists for *me* went on for several pages, divided into "general" and "sex." The gist of the former was to "minimize critical comments," including the nonverbal, for which he gave an example: "The look or laugh that says it's obvious that all decent people flush toilets immediately after urinating." Here he meant contemptuous behavior, one of psychologist John Gottman's "four horsemen of the apocalypse," which we only learned about in depth much later.

Stephen had the wisdom, even back then, to add this to his list: "Understand that I have a different reality than you in some respects, and respect it." This book is built around that, but at that time, even with professional help, I wasn't ready to put such non-judgmentalness into action yet.

Stephen's sex list felt intimidating to me. He wanted me to initiate half the time, give clear signals when I was in the mood or ready to be in the mood, be more casual and spontaneous, focus on the positive and what works, communicate calmly exactly what I want, and show lots of enthusiasm. There were a few specific erotic suggestions included on his list that seemed unlikely to me, considering how wary we had been feeling around each other, and for some reason, I focused unduly on those. I told him he wanted too much from me, though now I can see how reasonable he was being overall.

For our troubling sexual drift, I thought we ought to try some advice I'd read that suggested a couple refrain from sex for a couple of weeks and check with each other frequently as to their current interest in making love. This would supposedly show that their sex drives, separated from any performance anxieties, would be more equal than they thought (which, by the way, isn't necessarily true).

"Okay," Stephen agreed. He is, after all, an agreeable person. But only three days passed before he let me know it was time for him to have sex, one way or another. He was willing to masturbate, but to me that seemed to go against the plan.

"But that's not long enough for me to feel unpressured," I told him. "It feels like I've always got the balls of Damocles hanging over me!"

It felt to me as though his short-term concession—admittedly based on simplistic self-help advice—was a compromise in name only. "That's how long you're willing to wait? Three days is the sum total of the sacrifice you'll endure to help us make our sex life better?" I asked huffily.

"There you go again, making light of my efforts to make things better," he responded. "It's just more of your negativity. Let's just forget the whole thing!"

And, complicating matters, Stephen began wanting to include porno films in our sexual repertoire, *every* time. But that reduced my feelings of desirability, contributed to my feeling old, ugly, undesirable, like a feeble substitute for his two-dimensional but colorful young fantasies (I wasn't forty yet).

"I don't want to make love ever again," I fumed at my diary, "as of right now. It's gone wrong for me too many times. I don't feel free to speak up, to say what I want or don't want. Sometimes it's such a tiny thing that's ruining it for me, and I can't even say it for fear of bringing up his defensiveness. So I end up sad and frustrated instead. I don't feel hopeful about the long-term happiness of this relationship anymore. This is the first time I have said this, and it scares me."

Is it any wonder one of us had an affair? Looking back, I realize it might have been either of us, whoever had the opportunity first.

As the years went by, the fights became more frequent, with Stephen withdrawing for an evening or a day or two. What were all these fights about? Anyone in a long-term relationship knows that far-reaching imbroglios can result from the most minor beginnings. One I recall in detail began innocently: I was lying down, feeling exhausted, but as we'd earlier agreed to take a walk, Stephen started putting my socks on for me. He often asked me to do this for him, but he'd never done it for me. The first sock didn't feel right, and I said, "Be sure you get the heel on the right place." He pulled the sock off and did it again, this time catching my toenail on the inside of the sock.

"Ouch!" I yelped. "Don't rip my toenail off. If you rip my toenail off, I'll...something." He didn't respond well to this unappreciative onslaught, and he walked away. Then we tried talking about what happened, but ended up frustrated with each other, as usual. He said I was being directive and that this was a pattern with me. I said I was just telling him how I liked my socks put on, and if he was doing it for *me*, why couldn't he do it the way I liked it? Stephen insisted it was a power thing. Neither of us would back down.

A few more years ensued of these tense stand-offs over mis-understandings or hurt feelings, and then, one summer, Stephen spent what he called "the best week of his life" at a poetry con-ference in Northern California. He admitted that libido ran high throughout the week. In fact, he insisted one drunken evening after his return, "All men want to fuck all women." It's got to do with biology, he explained, in one of his uncharacteristically simplistic moments. Later he rephrased this *slightly* more realistically as, "All men *consider* fucking all women." That didn't do much for my sense of security.

Then, when my younger son was about to leave home for college, and Stephen was preparing to attend another poetry conference, I figured it was time for some excitement for *me*. I began doctoral studies and was away for a week in North Carolina for a school-related session. Upon my return, we had what turned out to be a critical confrontation over, of all things, a garden bower. As soon as I got out of the car, Stephen showed me what he'd designed and partially completed while I was gone: a lovely winding brick walkway, and a less-pleasing-to-me bower over the front entrance to the yard. We stood there arguing quietly about it for quite a while. I felt estranged: I came back and the first things I encountered were changes I didn't like and had no part in.

Stephen decided to go ahead with his bower-building in spite of my strong opposition, which seemed to me evidence of a lack of true partnership. He explained later that due to his own strong need for autonomy, he had taken my interests to heart in planning the walkway but felt compelled to execute his own design for the bower. He viewed my extreme displeasure as further proof of my greed to control him. I suppose he felt like a failed bower bird: a species that gathers leafy and other detritus to construct elaborate displays to win the favor of a picky would-be mate. But, as he already had me and wasn't so sure I was worth the trouble, he wasn't going to rebuild his bower according to my blueprint. I needed to take *this* one or leave it. Or, as it turned out, he would leave *me*.

## GREENER PASTURES?

That is how disconnected we were, nine years into our marriage, when, a month following the bower incident, Stephen flew to a conference in New England. He called me a few days into the two-week session and said he wanted to come home, that Bread Loaf was an intimidating, unfriendly place. I reassured him that whatever he decided would be fine with me, that the money he'd spent was irrelevant, but that as long as he was there and the surroundings were so lovely, why not take some long walks in nature and give it a few more days?

And then I didn't hear from him for the rest of the two weeks. When I picked him up at the airport, he was just a shade more quiet than usual. Our hello kiss was awkward—as I learned much later, reality itself felt unreal to him—but then our whole relationship had been strained before he left, so I wasn't more worried than usual. But all that week he seemed distant. Then, after seeing his therapist for his usual bi-weekly appointment, he said he'd made an appointment for the following week.

"Is something going on?" I asked. Since money was tight, I knew an extra appointment was serious.

"I'm reevaluating our marriage," he said.

I was flabbergasted. Over the next few days, he told me more about what had gone on while he was in Vermont. It turned out that this is a conference well-known for its eroticized atmosphere, where liquor flows freely each evening, where there are numerous dances, and where everyone walks about intertwined, limb to limb, with someone not their spouse. "I felt jealous," Stephen admitted to me.

The next three months were intensely strained. We sat hour after hour on the sofa, hashing over the pluses and minuses of staying together. He would come down on one side of the fence one day, then be back on the top, checking out the green grass on the other side the next day. He broached the idea of separation, but I insisted we had to work this out together.

I couldn't figure out what was going on in his mind, but since he'd been utterly honest with me about even the smallest things, and he is so sloppy about details, it seemed impossible that he could be keeping a dark secret. I confided the little I knew to numerous friends, and they invariably asked, "Is he having an affair?" And I invariably responded, "Oh no, that's impossible. I would know, and he would never do that anyway." Years before, when I'd expressed insecurity, he told me, "Don't worry, if I ever plan to have an affair, I'll call you from a phone booth first." Somehow, I continued to cling to that, as ridiculous as it seems in retrospect.

During those three post-conference months, Stephen spent a lot of extra time at the college where he teaches and received a number of phone calls at home from a female friend he'd met while away. In fact, I trustingly handed the phone to him. One time, while dusting, I broke a tiny glass hummingbird he'd hung in our bedroom, a gift he said he'd bought himself at the conference. I apologized profusely. He put the pieces in a desk drawer, wordlessly.

Throughout this period, he surprised me by haunting the self-help shelves in bookstores. This wasn't like him. Even when he bought Frank Pittman's *Private Lies*, with its subtitle that should have screamed the truth directly into my brain—*Infidelity and the Betrayal of Intimacy*—I still wasn't suspicious. His choice made a stretchy kind of sense, since we were spending a lot of time talking about sexuality and monogamy and his questions of why couldn't we have more than one lover? what were the limits of intimacy with a "friend"?

## REVELATION AND RAW EMOTION

> But, as soon as the power of any one of Odette's remarks to make Swann suffer seemed to be nearly exhausted, lo and behold another, one of those to which he had hitherto paid little attention, almost a new observation, came to reinforce the others and to strike at him with undiminished force.
>
> —Marcel Proust, *Swann's Way*

As soon as Stephen got partway through *Private Lies*, it was as though he'd been slapped helpfully hard in the face. He told me he had been having "an emotional connection" with a woman that he'd met in Vermont. Now the pieces began to fit together: I had talked to this woman on the phone, I had seen him reading her unpublished novel in our bed, it was her hummingbird that he'd hung in our bedroom. And then he did one very good thing: he called her up and broke off their relationship.

I was numb with shock. When Stephen went to work the next day, I wandered the house in a daze, desperate to understand the implications of his "emotional affair," as he had referred to it. I called several friends, and no matter what they suggested, I *still* didn't get it that he had been having a *real* affair. That night, I asked him point blank. "Yes, we had sex," he told me. I went wild.

I screamed myself hoarse, wept my eyes nearly swollen shut, hyperventilated until my hands and feet went numb. I climbed on a chair in the kitchen and tossed wine glass after wine glass to the floor. I stormed through the house with each new revelation—it had begun with drunken dancing and led quickly to sex in meadows, they exchanged daily love letters, they talked of a future together—I ripped items from the walls and threw them as hard as I could. Even *in extremis*, though, one retains one's personality, and I didn't destroy mindlessly: I picked and chose, figuring in some cranny of my resilient spirit that I might go on to live beyond this awful time. I chose one memento deliberately: a love gift I'd given in the first month we were together, in which I'd written how much I cherished him and that I'd never hurt him. I tore it to shreds and left the pile of detritus for him. It caused the desired effect on him: intense sorrow and remorse—but all of this was useless to me this soon.

For a week following Stephen's disclosure, I couldn't get out of bed. I laid there and wept incessantly. He tried to comfort me, but it was impossible. He said he had no idea I cared so much. Which only made it worse—had we ever been in the same relationship at all? I lost seven pounds in four days.

When I finally crept to my journal, I wrote this:

I have been seriously considering suicide. I have no work of importance left to do, can't imagine ever working again. I don't want to live in a world where I cannot trust. It's too empty, too lonely. If I could not trust *him*, how could I ever expect to find a man I could trust? There is very little holding me here but not wanting to hurt the very few people I love, my family. I thought he was my family too.

We were the most open couple I knew, and the loss of that is incalculable and inconsolable. Three-and-a-half months of lie upon lie. And I, a suspicious person by nature, a clue-gatherer, still trusted, never for a moment could have believed anything this horrible could happen. Even when puzzle pieces appeared, I never connected them. I didn't know this was a test and it was. The biggest test of my life and I failed to notice, to believe, that one plus one are fucking.

This is the one breach that could never be allowed, the one we talked about more than many couples do, all out in the open, the one, single thing that could never, *must* never ever happen because it could not be borne, it would be eviscerating. And yet he did it. And did it. And did it again and again and then talked to her about it and wanted more and yet lied to me that he loved me and wanted to work on our marriage and still he talked with her and remembered her body and what they shared. Then how can *I* forget? I see her sitting on his lap, moving over him, giving him head (I know how much he used to like all that with me), of course giving her oral sex, his specialty, comparing our orgasmic responses whether he intended to or not, whether he will lie about it now or not, I know some things, and so far I have always been correct except when I trusted him and thought such a thing could never happen, that no matter how upset he was with me or how hopeless he might temporarily feel about us, that he would never, never, never choose to hurt me in this deepest and most unforgivable way. But he did.

I think I love him very much. And yet of course I hate him with a painful fury for hurting me and for not loving me enough, which is the only reason he could have betrayed me like this. One minute I think I can get over this and the next, the images come flooding back and I want to vomit, I want to die.

None of my friends is much help. One suggests I have a fling of my own to balance things out. Another keeps pressing for the juicy details. A third says I shouldn't let him attend any more conferences, while another insists I should go with him from now on. A couple have commented, "Bullshit!" and "Cop-out!" when I tell them what he has told me, putting me in the unwanted position of having to defend Stephen's sincerity in his inner struggle, when all I want to do is gnash my teeth and rip out his pubic hair—or chop his headstrong dick into a hundred slices and sprinkle them in the garden. They'd make good mulch.

Someone suggested I devise a ritual "killing" to alleviate my fury, perhaps with candles and music and a knife, and of course with Stephen's cooperation. Although he was willing to go along with any playacting intended to offer me relief, and although I allowed myself to imagine plunging that knife into him repeatedly, I knew there would be no release for me in such a fantasy. Recovery would be long and hard for both of us.

# THE CLICHÉ CRISIS

Billboard spotted while driving south on the Golden State Freeway in Orange County, California: "Cathy, I love you more than you'll ever know. Please forgive me. Tom"

How did we traverse that long distance from when I ripped up our early love mementos as a paltry substitute for tearing *him* (or myself) to shreds to my feeling such love for him that being in the same room with him is all the heaven I desire?

After a crisis of the magnitude of infidelity, it seems as though every story you read, every video on the shelves, the trailer for every film, is about betrayal. There's no place to turn that feels safe from hurtful reminders. As you struggle to overcome your own emotional injury, going through all the stages of grief more than once, experiencing post-traumatic stress, these supposedly titillating images only salt your wounds.

It took me at least a year before I could relax my guard a little. It's not that my life got back to what I used to consider normal. Nor, from the vantage point of hindsight—as much as I'd prefer we didn't have to go through what we did—would I want our lives to be the same as before the crisis.

## HOW WE REBOUNDED

A few days after all was revealed, we left for a previously scheduled weekend trip—a location I was assigned to write up as a travel article. The hours passed in a surreal haze for me, with the two of us going through the motions of being a couple, but feeling like mere phantoms now. At one point, Stephen said he couldn't get in touch with any feelings of love for me, and that seemed to mean only one thing. "It's over then," I said quietly, factually. And, paradoxically, that was the moment we began moving back up from the bottom. When I let go and stopped pushing him to reconnect with me, he said later, that was when he was able to loosen up enough to feel positively toward me again.

It's not easy to explain the process I went through, and I don't want to give the impression that there is one best way to recover from this or any trauma. In fact, most of the couples I interviewed didn't do precisely what we did, and what worked for them would not have been sufficient for us. But that's not surprising, as your own personalities will dictate how much "processing" you'll need before feeling safe and reconnected. I can only share what worked for me, my fairly complex mental and emotional exertions, and how Stephen played a vital supporting role. Without that role, I'm sure our marriage would have ended.

First of all, I had to figure out why I was suffering so much. I recognized that I was operating, in that immediate post-revelation period, on at least two levels of thinking and feeling. On the overt emotional level, the most concrete level, I felt intense jealousy, mistrust, anger, and hurt. I told Stephen that it was as though gravity had suddenly stopped. I could not get my bearings. Was he the same person I thought he was? If so, how could he have acted this way? Did it mean he cared nothing for me? Was he an untrustworthy person? Could anyone ever be trusted? My sense of security was obliterated, and no matter how he reassured me that his tryst was over and that he had made an appalling mistake and that he truly loved me, I believed that all of my previous perceptions of him and of our relationship had been flawed, and I could no longer trust my own perception of what was real.

As one is wont to do, I bargained pointlessly with the past: if only he could have simply slept with her; if only he could have simply fallen for her but *not* slept with her....(I remember once reading about a woman whose arms had been chewed off just below the shoulders by a bear. Lucky to be alive, she wished she had been left with at least one elbow. I imagined that I now knew how she felt.)

The anger, of course, came from my conviction that I hadn't deserved this, that my husband's affair was unexpected and unfair. I realized, though, that much of this anger I was freely expressing was merely the overt expression of an even more intense hurt. I couldn't bear that he could not now recall *our* initial passion.

Understand: it's not a matter of accusation. I did not, after the first days, spit out invectives or call him names. Much later, Frank Pittman told me in an interview that if the betrayed partner keeps up the anger, he or she makes it much more difficult to reestablish an atmosphere of honesty.

"If you can get past the anger to the hurt," he explained, "then you can deal with the hurt. Everything starts to make sense. The anger just enhances the shame felt by the adulterer even more, which causes him or her to see the marriage as uncomfortable, as unpleasant, as unwelcoming. The hurt offers the opportunity of closeness as a resolution, whereas the anger only offers distance as a resolution. And somebody who's angry at the same time they're trying to get somebody to come close is sending crazy-making messages."

Although I had to do most of the hard work of healing myself, and fell into a deep depression for a few months as I struggled, I couldn't have come out the other end without Stephen's active participation. What helped most was his willingness—unlike many of his colleagues-in-crime—to let me go on and on, and on some more, about how much I was hurting, how betrayed I felt, and what I needed from him. This was all the more difficult for him because his main defense had been withdrawal. We sat for hours in the living room on what at this point became known as the talking couch. I talked much more than he did, but he listened, and he responded each time I asked a question.

If you are ever on either side of such an affair, I recommend just such a nondefensive and profoundly vulnerable stance. If the most wounded of the partners feels free to say what is on his or her mind, then such painful events can be both integrated and risen above. They can also be used in unexpected ways to help the subsequent relationship flourish.

## MAKING SENSE OF THE UNTHINKABLE

I spent a lot of time teasing apart what led up to our personal night of broken glass. Although, like everyone else in such circumstances, I berated my partner with endless Whys and How could yous, I now realize how futile it is to try tracing the precise determinants of a relationship rupture. Nonetheless, it can be illuminating—and ultimately healing—to trace as best we can the origins of major troubles: mine, other couples', or your own past ones.

I was forced to understand that my husband's experience of our marriage was dramatically unlike mine, and that is what made this event possible, likely, or perhaps even inevitable. He had come to think of it as a bad marriage. Me and my reality were not a part of this for him, since he was not in touch with them. I had to get to where I could accept that because of his lack of insight into other alternatives we might have tried, he was less capable of making the best and most moral choice when confronted by temptation.

The two levels of thought and feeling I was experiencing are analogous to a spitting cat facing a phenomenologist. Bringing the two together would require, I believed, a spiritual element or a letting go that would only be possible when my healing became complete. It would take *time*.

Like many people, when I experience any crisis, I would prefer to go back to "the way it was before," regardless of how flawed life was previously. Even a year after The Troubles, I complained to my diary that even though things were far better already than they had been, I wished I could go back to how we used to be.

Crisis, though, can be an opportunity to discover unknown facets of yourself. I had a dream while this was going on that my treadmill was not functioning properly. The stable handlebar I normally hold onto was swaying, and I was having to bend over uncomfortably to keep up with it. Then, just off to the side but in plain sight, I discovered an adjustment lever I had never noticed before, with which I was able to stabilize the bar. I found this to be an encouraging set of images. For further insight while writing this book, I consulted Joan Mazza, a psychotherapist and the author of *Dreaming Your Real Self: A Personal Approach to Dream Interpretation*. She pointed out that it's never a good idea to make a big decision based on an interpretation of a single dream. "It's better to look at a pattern of dreams and their emotional content that carry over from emotions in waking life. What is the arc of the individual dreams—does a problem go from mild to nightmarish? Or are you faced with an obstacle that you can overcome in each dream?"

That reminded me that my "treadmill with the hidden-in-plain-sight control lever" dream was one of several around that time. They all had one major theme: frightening situations in which I seemed trapped—such as several where I, a non-swimmer, was trapped by a huge body of water—turned out to have exits that became apparent when I took a second look. In each case, my anxiety was alleviated and I awoke feeling—dare I say it?— empowered by my own ability to save myself by my persistence.

Mazza also suggests we look for clues to specific solutions in the symbols of the dream, "which will often offer some insight that you haven't quite grasped in waking consciousness." I realized I could regain the security and safety I craved if I kept laboring at it. I needed to continue pursuing understanding, since that's how I've always felt all right.

Meanwhile, I both blamed myself and refused to blame myself for what had happened. I questioned whether perhaps I seemed too competent. He *had* accused me of being controlling... Maybe he needed to feel he could take care of me more (he pleaded at the beginning of our relationship: "Let me give, too"), but then I remembered how competent he was at asking for and receiving, too.

I learned that an affair can be the ultimate passive-aggressive expression of anger. When I held back sexually (when I was angry, which was regularly), I was asking him to control himself too—which couldn't have been pleasant. Did that contribute to him wanting out of our marriage? Then there is the role of alcoholism in affairs, which neither of us downplayed. It's no excuse, but his heavy drinking contributed to reducing inhibitions. In its most basic form: he got drunk, danced with a stranger, got aroused, agreed to her urgings that they go for a late-night walk in the woods, and, once he'd given in to the inevitable, figured there was no turning back. Hadn't I always said this was the one unforgivable act? That if he was ever unfaithful, that was the end of us? Why not go back for more, then, since he'd already botched up the marriage?

Depression offered another clue. Psychiatrist Peter D. Kramer writes that it's often depression, anhedonia, that causes individuals to lose differentiation of self and feel taken over by their wives, and then they seek intensity outside to save themselves and to feel more alive. "The perspective of altered mood is utterly convincing to the person who inhabits it. You know that you once thought you loved your wife, but you cannot for the life of you remember why, not in any way that matters." This helps explains why Stephen, who often suffers from depression, told me, soon after the revelations, that he couldn't get in touch with what he used to feel. Of course, his emotional life was still entangled then with the other woman, and it's difficult, if not impossible, for most of us to feel that intensely about two people simultaneously. He didn't yet want to reconnect to our past, which makes sense since he was still striving to get over the idea he'd had of starting a future, however fantasized, with a new love. He said it was like a drug—all love is at first.

Eventually I concluded that, in spite of my own contributions to our unraveling pleasure in each other's company, his hurtful actions were *his* responsibility, not mine. If it began accidentally, it was not simply an accident, not liquor's fault. He made a definite decision, albeit a wrong one. I did not push love away. If anything, I wanted it too much: asked for it, demanded it, pleaded to work at it.

The truth is that nothing short of *years* of trustworthy behavior brings you back to where you were, more or less. One woman, quoted anonymously in a *New York Times* article, says of her previously errant husband, "He doesn't leave the office without calling me. There will never be a time when my husband is an hour late and the affair won't be the first thing I think about."

But by the time all the factors are fully struggled through, the person who's waiting at home can feel confident that because the circumstances are not the same, and neither are you quite the same people you used to be, the hurtful behavior will not be repeated.

## THE MATH AND CHEMISTRY OF CHEATING

One-fifth of the couples I interviewed mentioned an affair— whether fully consummated or not—as the low point in their relationships. Additional infidelities may have taken place as well, of course. These are all couples I chose on the basis of how satisfied they are currently; in only one case was I already aware of the affair when the interview began.

A friend of mine, Lavonne, once said to me in a whiny tone: "But why *can't* I have an affair with Will?"

Lavonne, however, had been married for more than twenty years, and was so devoted to Stan that she joked she planned to have him stuffed after his death. That's why I tried so hard to counter her temporary obsession with Will, a mutual friend. I pointed out how devastated her husband would feel. I insisted she'd feel lousy about herself afterward. I told her she risked ruining the special friendship she shared with Will. To clinch my arguments, I reminded her that her husband had threatened to sue for custody of their child if she ever betrayed him.

None of these warnings stopped Lavonne, but she came to her senses after a single kissing session at a party. To save her marriage, she had to end her friendship with Will. Watching this from the outside made it clearer to me than ever how hormones and chemistry have the power to alchemize us into regrettable decisions.

In spite of the higher figures bandied about, recent reputable surveys of infidelity have found that about ten to twenty percent of all individuals have sex with someone other than their spouse. This coincides with what I found in my own sample of couples. Riffle through your mental contact list of couples: every fifth one may be hiding a similar skeleton in the marital closet.

Even the briefest of flings can seriously challenge your relationship. One source suggests that at least half of the couples in therapy may be there due to infidelity, and affairs are one of the most difficult problems to treat in therapy, according to a survey of couples therapists.

Affairs, and especially their beginnings, take different forms. Pittman divides them into philandering, accidental, and romantic affairs, but I found it wasn't possible to categorize precisely the affairs that took place among the couples with whom I spoke. Too much overlap. That is, an affair that begins semi-accidentally, where someone takes advantage of an opportune sexual thrill, can turn ardently romantic.

## THE SERIAL BETRAYER

Among the group I interviewed, only one of the husbands was a repetitive adulterer. Rita is an energetic and independent-minded artist who easily looks at least a decade younger than her actual age of seventy. When I ask her about the thirty-four-year relationship she had with her husband Elmore, who recently died, she offers a Mona Lisa smile, then tells me in her no-

nonsense way, "We had a wonderful last twenty years." And before that? Her husband, a doctor who thought rather highly of himself, according to Rita, played around a lot.

When they'd been together for eleven years, Elmore unexpectedly asked for a separation "to find himself." Until that point, Rita hadn't known he'd been philandering. Not long afterward, even when Elmore realized he'd made a "terrible mistake" and decided his heart (and other parts) belonged at home after all, Rita was in no hurry to take him back.

"He wasn't in control of himself," she explains, and in the meantime, she'd met someone else. "I had to make a decision, and I decided in favor of history. There were our kids [her stepkids], and we'd worked hard to make ourselves into a family." With the help of a therapist, Rita agreed to live with Elmore again.

She made sure Elmore knew the extent of her considerable hurt and anger. She was getting heart flutters, but a treadmill test found her physical health to be fine. Rebuilding trust took a couple of years, Rita explains, but then she got to where her trust level was again 100 percent.

After reconciling, they took trips and spent time together, no matter how busy their schedules were. "The main thing is that when problems came up, we didn't let them build. If a concern seemed serious, we talked it through until both of us were comfortable or we'd go see a good therapist. The thing that made the real difference is I don't think Elmore had ever had anybody in his life that was as important to him as I had become. He was absolutely determined he was going to make this work, whatever it took."

## ONLY AN ACCIDENT?

So-called "accidental" infidelity occurs when two people, friends, co-workers, or strangers far from home, begin talking intimately, perhaps because of some turning point or major stress in one or both of their lives. And then things heat up.

Arousing situations—any time you are in an unfamiliar place among strangers, any context that makes you anxious—cause physiological effects that you might interpret as sexual. Think vacations, conventions, parties, or life transitions. It's easier under such conditions, say social psychologists, to find a stranger attractive, and to convince yourself something "real" is happening that you owe yourself to pursue.

After the so-called accident, the infidel has two choices, according to Pittman. If it was a single event and he admits it and takes full responsibility, recognizing he was out of his head, there's hope for the marriage. If, on the other hand, he decides his marriage was irrevocably flawed, the whole mess was his wife's fault, and he must be in love with the affair partner anyway, the situation gets much more complicated.

Several of the affairs that were described to me might fall in the category of the-devil-made-me-do-it accidental-start, and each went on to become emotionally muddled. I believe that's because they weren't accidents at all, though those participating might like to think of them that way. Rather, the choice of *partner* was arbitrary. Arbitrary because the preliminaries for these affairs had been building for some time, and when the circumstances were conducive and a likely partner turned up—*any* likely partner—the result was an instant affair.

Matthew and Georgia, the long-married Ivy League psychologists I mentioned earlier, rate their marriage, now and for the past ten years, at 95 and 100, respectively. To her, that means their "bond is strong enough that it's not going to have anything external shake it."

Matthew had an affair twelve years into the relationship, when the youngest of their three children was still a toddler. "It was like a nuclear bomb was dropped in my house," says Georgia. "I was thirty-two years old, slim, a size five, and I used to think, if I'm attractive and I keep my figure, he'll never stray." Georgia admits that she was preoccupied with caring for one of their children, who was quite troubled. Whereas, says Georgia ruefully, Matthew's affair partner, his secretary, was "a southern belle who laughed a lot and nurtured men's egos."

Although Matthew had been acting strangely for three months, and Georgia wondered why he seemed so angry at her, he never mentioned being unhappy. "That day, I had just spent five hours driving back and forth to the psychiatrist with our son. I came home, made dinner, and we were walking in the park, looking at the squirrels. Everything was good, and then he told me, 'I just want you to know I want a divorce.'"

She told him: "It's like everything that *was* is gone, and my whole past life has been a lie. And you are dead and now I have to mourn you." She started crying, but she was already figuring out how she'd manage without him, how she'd take care of the children, work harder, *not* move in with her parents.

Like many women, Georgia used to tell her husband that if he ever had an affair, she'd divorce him. She believes that contributed to his giving up prematurely on his marriage—"he'd already weakened and done it and was now dead meat"—and starting to picture his future with the other woman. Much later Georgia said to Matthew, "How could you not have realized that those words were said early in marriage and were changed now?"

They talked that whole post-revelation weekend and "a lot of true, but painful, words were spoken," says Georgia. "I gave him the ultimatum of either you call her up and break it off right now, no in-between, no easing it out, and promise me that this is over, or you're making that decision final. It's up to you." He told Georgia, "I will give it a chance." She pronounces this phrase with a nervous laugh.

When it's Matthew's turn to describe events, he admits he had an inflated sense of himself. Combine that with the fact that Georgia had pulled away sexually, so that they were then having sex only once or twice a month, on Saturday night. He says he figured he deserved better. He admits he had no insight as to Georgia's depression—she was going through a hard time with the children—and how that might have been related to the sexual dropoff. He interpreted it as rejection.

"It was probably the height of my disillusionment with the marriage," says Matthew. He now had the job that had been his first choice, and their third child was no longer ill. "The feeling was all systems are go now. Why are we still so unhappy?" He knew he wasn't strong enough to leave his family, but Georgia had made it clear that if he were ever unfaithful she would never take him back.

Matthew insists he and his secretary never slept together, that there was waist-up touching only. "I couldn't do it, I was just incapable," he says with a laugh. It was the fact that he was in love with another woman that mattered to Georgia. He expected her to say, "Get the hell out, you're the worst person I ever knew," and that would have been it. But then, Georgia didn't walk away. Nor did she simply take him back. He says she told him, "I want you back, but not if you want her. You have to love me."

"All along," says Matthew, "I'd interpreted her sexual rejection of me as not loving me. But her reaction made me reevaluate the quality of the relationship I had. I remember very clearly one conversation where I said to this other woman, 'I know right now that if somebody had a gun pointed at me, Georgia would step in front.' And the other woman said, 'Well, how do you know I wouldn't?' I didn't answer her, but I knew she wouldn't. The other thing I remember is when she spoke of marriage, I was thinking, 'Oh my God, that's not what I really want to do, I just want to *get out*.' Georgia's response made me realize there was much more depth to the relationship than I was giving it credit for."

Getting through the next couple of years was extraordinarily challenging. The children were time-consuming, and babysitters were too expensive. Still, Georgia was willing to make the extra effort because, she says, "I'm good at delaying gratification. I had hopes that the time would come when things would be better." She decided to complete her dissertation and get her long-delayed degree. "Matthew facilitated that for me, did the housework and childcare once for a six-week period while I wrote. And one

Valentine's Day he gave me a thousand dollar credit for photo-copying in the library."

Starting at that time they vowed to eat breakfast together daily and talk. "We eat breakfast out 365 days a year. It used a be a problem on Christmas Day, but we found a place open."

"The first year," continues Georgia, "we talked about the affair openly. Occasionally, we'd be going to sleep at night, and he would start crying, saying how terrible he felt over what he did. But when we'd continue talking, it turned into 'But you made me do it, because you didn't do this and that.' He never took full responsibility. On the positive side, what it did for me was it made me think every single day, this might be the last day I'm married. The undertone of all this was 'Don't be too depend-ent on the marriage because it may be gone.'"

A couple of years after the affair, they moved, with Matthew leaving his job so Georgia could begin a better one herself. "He put his career second, a big change, quite a statement," she explains. "It meant it was my turn. Though that took care of some of the fury I felt, it still wasn't enough. It's twenty-four years now. I don't feel stirred up at all about it now, thank God. It took a long time. There used to be a kind of anniversary of it, in both of our minds. He used to get scared: am I going to be snapping at him, am I going to be critical, will I mention something?"

Matthew admits that he still feels that it *was* partly her fault, "but still, I take the blame for it. But I can't live the rest of my life apologizing for it." Psychology backs him up: if you contin-ually throw a wrong in your partner's face, it might backfire, according to equity theory, since it may begin to feel that no matter what the errant partner does, it can't be made right, and he or she gives up.

Besides the career shifts and the daily talking breakfasts, Matthew and Georgia made much more of an effort to deal with their differences in another way. Georgia doesn't like sports, and they used to fight about how excluded she felt from Matthew's obsession with baseball.

"I was more suffocating," she admits. "It was quite a significant moment when I bought him season tickets to the baseball game. Then he bought season tickets to the symphony for himself and me, where before he'd never had any interest in classical music."

As often happens after affairs, sexuality between the couple was affected. Explains Georgia: "I had been extremely shy, and regardless of what I might have looked like—those were the years when I had a good figure—I was very repressed sexually. My mother used to tell me, 'You have to do this so you can have kids, it's destiny.' After the affair, I thought, 'He went ahead and did this anyhow, what could I possibly do now that would matter? Would he think less of me if I tried this or that? And it allowed me to be less inhibited. Because it didn't matter, I had nothing to lose. And now I'm overweight, and he tells me I'm the most sexy thing in the world. It's so weird when I can easily think back to my size five days. Looks meant nothing."

## STARRY-EYED LUST

Romantic affairs may as well be called temporary insanity. As I've said, while many affairs begin without conscious intent and thus could also be termed accidental, it's the quality of the attachment that qualifies them as romantic. It's like that heady in-love feeling that begins most fine relationships. The problem occurs when you're already married and your hormones somehow convince you that you're *now* in love with the intriguing person you just met, someone who may be wildly inappropriate for a lasting relationship. You're convinced *this* one is perfect, unlike your mate. And this time the feeling will last.

Alas, it won't. "In my practice," notes Pittman, "while over half the people who get into romantic affairs end up divorced, only a fourth marry the affairee. Even then, three-fourths of those marriages end up in divorce."

Most of the affairs in the group I investigated fit the romantic template, with idiosyncratic variations. For example, a decade into the marriage of Derek and Teresa, when "everyone" the couple knew in their small Midwestern town was having an affair, says Teresa, Derek began having one too. Teresa says that this woman, a friend of a friend, "just literally put herself right in his face. We were having some financial problems, he was about to quit his job and we were going to move, and his mom was dying around this time. I wound up going back with our two kids to Florida to stay with my mother, for financial reasons, and it was while I was gone that all this happened. This woman built up his ego left and right."

When Teresa returned from being away for six weeks, he confessed the affair and told her to move back with her mom and he would keep the children, since she had no job. "I adored this man, he was my whole life, and I was in such a state of shock that I don't think I would have been a very good mom," she says, explaining why she agreed to leave her kids behind. "I pitched a big fit that night and told him I was not going to give him up, but he told me he'd already made up his mind. They were already living together in my house," she adds. But a month later, he wanted to get back together with Teresa. "He began to realize she was not the kind of woman he wanted to be around his children. They really hated her." Obviously, disillusionment had set in as a grubby life with kids overshadowed the fantasy elements.

"Our faith had a lot to do with getting us through this," Teresa says, adding that Derek partially blamed her, and they hardly mentioned it. "Over the years, he's mellowed out to the point where we were talking about it the other day, and I said, 'If anything ever happened to you, I'd never marry again,' and he said, 'No, I would never marry either, because I wouldn't want to have to break another wife in. I don't want to have to go through any pain like we went through.' It has bothered him; he just won't say it."

Teresa sighs. "I don't ever think about it, but it's there. If I hear her name—she has a very common name—I remember."

Another version of the romance scenario is told by Lila, a fifty-year-old teacher, who has spent thirty years with Harry, who works in construction, in the same small Southern town. "Our whole life has always been real huggy touchy, filled with 'I love yous,'" Lila claims. But then she returned to junior college a few years into her marriage. When she had to get up at 4:30 in the morning to take their baby son to day care, Lila says, then drive an hour to school, "Harry never said, 'Oh, I feel so sorry for you that you've got all these lessons.' He couldn't have cared less. Well, not that bad, but he meant that I was doing it on my own, nobody asked me to do it. And I guess I resented him."

That may have contributed to what occurred next: Lila and one of her teachers, about her age, discovered they had "so much in common." The problems at home receded, and when this instructor hired her to work in the computer lab, "there was an attraction." Still, she says she loved her husband and their baby. The other fellow had children also. "Things went a little bit too far. He even asked me to leave and go away with him. I almost went. It did get quite physical. I was probably only out alone with him one time, but we were in his office a lot. We slept together once. I have very strong religious views, so I was torn to pieces."

All during the time she wasn't having sex with the other guy—though she desperately wanted to—sex at home with Harry was better than ever, "because I felt like by having sex with Harry, I was making up for this time I was with the other guy. Of course, he loved it. But he didn't have a clue."

The affair ended after ten months when the teacher became overly possessive. "That opened my eyes. I kept thinking, 'Am I willing to give up everything?' I thank God today that I did not."

Harry suspected something was going on, but Lila never came right out and told him. Yet, quite recently, when they were talking about something else, he said, "Well, don't forget what you did."

These events have subtle ways of lingering for a long, long time. For instance, one day Lila said, "I wish you'd quit this smoking and drinking. You know it's killing you and I worry about you all the time." His response was, "Oh, well, if something happens to me, you can just find yourself a better man."

Harry's comment may have been evidence of low-lying resentment, as well as a quiet way of asking for reassurance.

Recovery for the infidel is harder than those betrayed usually realize. Lila grieved for her impossible lover all summer, though she didn't doubt the rightness of ending the affair. "I can't remember exactly 'coming back,'" she says. "About a year or two later, that guy came by to see me, and I did get a tiny odd feeling in the pit of my stomach. He said he felt it too. Kind of 'Oh, I still have that feeling.'"

## MIDLIFE EXAM

> He would lie in my bed on the last nights of his visits ... and tell me
> he wished we already had years of shared life behind us. He longed
> for a common past. So someone else has a copy of it, he said.
>     An emotional archive with me as curator.
>     And me as yours.
>
> —Michael Redhill, *Martin Sloane*

A midlife crisis is the standard rationalization for affairs, particularly those of men, though experts disagree on the prevalence of such a crisis. Some say only a tenth or so of middle-aged men come close to experiencing a midlife crisis, and those crises aren't necessarily any different from those that occur at other times.

Daniel J. Levinson, on the other hand, found that eighty percent of his subjects aged forty to forty-five underwent a midlife transitional crisis: "Every aspect of their lives comes into question, and they are horrified by much that is revealed. They are full of recriminations against themselves and others. They cannot go on as before, but need time to choose a new path or modify the old one."

This describes my husband's experience at forty-one. For instance, Stephen said in therapy after the affair began, but before he had told me about it, that if he knew he was only going to live for six more months, he would *have* to leave me. He complained that he was afraid I was not growing as fast as he was, and that we watched too much television and did not spend enough time reading great books. He couldn't handle the fact that I wasn't the enemy to our mutual growth—after all, I was the one in school. He couldn't see me clearly because of his infatuation with someone else. She held out hope of an easy answer to his midlife questioning of his own accomplishments and goals, just as my own premature and ill-advised attachment to my first husband seemed an easy way out of my adolescent tumult.

One of the hallmarks of how a midlife crisis can affect a marriage is that when you're undergoing internal upheaval, you may decide to turn your back on those very people, including your longtime partner, who knew you "back when." It's a way of running away from home when you see yourself as having grown beyond whatever home represents to you. Some people seek out new partners, are relieved when only their revamped self is known by these unfamiliar others.

The biggest loss in an affair is the possibility of a truly intimate partnership, one in which you are known and cherished in all your messy complexity. Sweating it through with your partner is far more gratifying than abandoning your joint past for a few sessions of temporary passion.

Theo, the Episcopal priest I mentioned earlier, and his partner of more than two decades provide a perfect example of how couples drift at midlife. Theo says he's entirely satisfied now with their relationship. But a decade ago, when Theo decided to pursue his calling, he and Dennis had to be apart for a year while Theo was in New York for the final stretch of his seminary training. Theo had a great time. "For the first time in a very long while I was not part of Theo and Dennis. And I was spending my own money without having to ask. It was the whole piece I had missed in my life."

Not so surprisingly, then, Theo had an affair. "It was the headiness of independence and then running into somebody— the classic stuff—who seems to appreciate me, and there's no history connected to it. New and clean. And really, it was only about looking for the things I wanted from my relationship with Dennis but looking for them outside."

It wasn't that there hadn't been areas of discontent before this. "We kept butting our heads against the same issues. I wanted a particular kind of more spontaneous emotionality, bigger, more surface. That's just who I am. We didn't recognize it at that point, but we were running into some of his depression. There was a bunch of underground disgruntlement. Not enough that we'd say 'Oh, I have to leave this person.' But something easy came along, and it was exciting."

Theo and Dennis had discussed fidelity prior to this incident, and had agreed that sexuality outside would be all right, but not making an ongoing emotional commitment to anybody else. But Theo's affair was an emotional one as much as a sexual one. "The two got very messy, and I *wasn't* able to keep those lines clear," he explains.

Theo ended the affair around six months after he returned from New York, after couples therapy. "I finally wrote a list saying *this* is what I want. It went everywhere from 'I want you to be more affectionate,' to 'We're going to separate our finances,' to moving in order to downscale. I had come back from this year away of just being 'me' with an even more solidified awareness that I didn't want to continue a lot of the old patterns. And that was very threatening, obviously, and Dennis found it really hard to accept."

Then, as sometimes happens, Dennis had his own period of doubt about staying in the relationship. "Just when I thought we were back on keel, suddenly boom," says Theo. "Dennis was having what you might call the classic male midlife: 'I've never had the opportunity to...'fill in whatever blank you want to." More counseling helped them get through this, too, and both of them decided to stay in the relationship. On the occasion of their twentieth anniversary, they renewed their commitment by exchanging rings.

"The last five years have all been sort of gravy," Theo concludes. "It was a matter of going through all that bumpiness for a while there."

## SOUL MATE (?) TIMES TWO

People stray out of a desire for *more*: intense sexual excitement, emotional connection. Sometimes the sexual thrills follow, and at times they precede, the extramarital emotional involvement. Of course, it's often *because* of the affair that an individual no longer feels connected at home.

I was able to interview one woman soon after an emotional affair ended and then again five years later when her twenty-seven-year-long marriage had become re-invigorated. Kaitlin, 47, is an artist, and her fifty-two-year-old husband Mark is a businessman. Their children are grown.

Kaitlin knew Mark less than two weeks when they got married: "We had a powerful soul connection, as corny as that sounds." But nearly twenty years into their marriage, Mark apparently lost sexual interest in Kaitlin. He would dismiss her with "You're too fat," accusing her of being "no better than a dog in heat." That played into Kaitlin's pre-existing insecurity about her body, shattering her self-esteem. By then, they were only having sex a few times a year.

The emotional abuse wasn't new: Mark had a history of using contempt to get his way in the relationship. Later, when Kaitlin entered therapy, she learned how her own role of super-nurturer had led her to behave like a doormat around his inappropriate furies. As with all emotional abusers, Mark had what Kaitlin calls "his sweet precious side," and she used to think the outbursts must have been her fault.

It wasn't until much later that Kaitlin found out why Mark had withdrawn from her. He was alarmed by how his body was changing in his mid-forties: he was no longer able to readily get and maintain an erection. He was fearful of sharing this delicate information with Kaitlin, so he pushed her away and turned to easier arousers such as phone sex, as long as that remained effective.

Even when Mark did make the effort to have sex with Kaitlin as often as once a month, after she mentioned she was close to having an affair, neither of them liked what was transpiring. "I noticed it was so different," Kaitlin says. "It was not like he got a hard-on. It took all kinds of different manual and oral stimulation to produce that, and then, oral stimulation would be too intense, so that he'd want to come immediately in my mouth, and I'd get nothing. Or he would have to handle himself because he knew just the degree of pressure. So there I was, hungry and lonely and insecure, figuring I just didn't turn my own husband on anymore."

In actuality, Mark's physical change was not unusual. But since he wouldn't talk about it, neither of them was able to explore how they might have either remedied the situation or adapted themselves to it. Instead, Kaitlin started losing weight and began getting attention from other men.

When she met a man at a dance during an evening out with some female friends, "he turned out to be my soulmate," Kaitlin told me when we spoke five years ago. "We talked two hours, sharing so many amazing things we had in common. When we kissed, it was the most incredible electricity I can ever remember feeling. He was married with kids too. And for the next two weeks, he called me each day and we would have an hour-long talk. He said that he never felt about his wife like he felt about me.

"Then, after three weeks of my not hearing from him, he called, sounding like death warmed over. He said, 'I'm messing up my marriage. My wife knows something is different, and we ended up in this huge fight. I have to make it work with her.'"

Kaitlin decided the message in all this was that she had to bring out the best in her marriage or else she needed to end it. She gave her husband an ultimatum: Show me you cherish me, give me specific signs, or I'll leave.

"And lo and behold, he really heard me." Kaitlin believes that, in addition to her ultimatum, it was Mark's mother's death that was the catalyst for him to finally open up about his sexuality. That brought them much closer emotionally. Kaitlin would have liked to discuss her outside involvement, but Mark never wanted to know details. As her sense of self grew, Mark's respect for her grew at the same time. As she coped with his outbursts differently and dealt valiantly with their children's health problems, the marital connection grew.

"At last he saw how incredibly strong I was, yet sweet and nurturing, and it was as though he thought, 'Hmm, maybe I have the best of every world here. And she understands my problem now that I've opened up to her.'"

The Viagra that a doctor prescribed rejuvenated their sex life, says Kaitlin. "Mark felt like the king of the world. I was so reassuring about it and how wonderful it was, and it's our little secret."

When I recently asked Kaitlin if she thinks her affair partner had truly been her soulmate, she admits, "He called me a year ago, and it became obvious to me that I'd been fooled. He was such a good talker, and at the time, I felt such an urgency to be understood and desired."

She's now fully recommitted to her husband. "I love him. After all, we have such a bond. We've been through almost every imaginable scenario together."

Do they talk much about their relationship? "Every day," she says. "He came home yesterday and told me his buddies were asking about Valentine's Day, and he said, 'With my wife and me, every day is Valentine's Day.' Because every day we say how much we mean to each other and love each other, and how grateful we are that we found our way back to our relationship." She laughed and added, "Our kids get nauseated by it: 'Oh please, get a room!'"

## FORGIVENESS: ALL IN GOOD TIME

Often after the very worst moments in their marriage, she had experienced a blithe instant in which she was all lightness, all reckless tenderness toward Charlie, as if nothing he did was beyond her power to understand and endure, yet as if those

things were immensely easy to forgive, far easier than it could
ever have looked from outside—but there was nobody outside, of
course. It was a marriage.

—Elizabeth Tallent, "The Forgiveness Trick,"
from *Great Short Stories about Parenting*

In our efforts to get past the crisis of infidelity, my husband and
I didn't do everything right—far from it. I needed Stephen to let
go of the other woman completely, but this wasn't possible for
him in the way I'd have preferred him to, not all at once. As Frank
Pittman told me in an interview, "A lot of guys can't bring themselves to break it off altogether and want to continue being
friends and worry about the other woman and try to be protective of her. It's impossible." Although Stephen called her to break
off their relationship the same day he revealed it to me, he also
told her he'd write to her one more time to explain. I wasn't
shown this letter, and when he told me about it, it seemed to me
that by writing more than a line or two, he was still romanticizing their relationship. She wrote back, of course, once or twice,
and I never got to see those letters either, which was hard for me
to handle. Stephen went so far as to wonder briefly why she and
he couldn't remain friends, which is a common pitfall seen by
Pittman in his practice.

The last remnant of the affair, in my mind, was Stephen's cache
of love letters from her. After some urging, and while I preferred
that we burn them together, Stephen dumped them in the trash at
his college. These are tiny matters, and Stephen did more to "come
clean" than many other straying mates, but such niggling foot-
dragging behaviors prolonged my battle to regain equanimity.

The whole process was a gradual one, not a once-and-for-all
matter of his asking for and my bestowing a word called "forgiveness." Like some of the others I interviewed, I never got
around to using that word. I knew Stephen had made his decision to connect with this other woman based on the best analysis
he was able to make at the time, figuring our marriage was

beyond repair, yet I couldn't readily stop blaming him for not recognizing how much I cared, how hard I had been trying all along, and especially for giving up before I would have. As Cohen and Sterling write in *You Owe Me,* "Once forgiveness has been granted, the *forgiven* is liberated from any burden of repayment— he is free to resume life as though nothing ever happened. However, for the *forgiver* there may still be an ongoing battle against vengeful emotions toward the offense and the offender." And that's my point: that's not forgiveness at all, not if you've let someone off the hook to make peace but you're still distressed.

I asked Rita, whose husband had been a philanderer before deciding to recommit to his marriage, if she'd ever said, "I forgive you."

"No, it wasn't a question of that. It was a question of trust. We never used those words. Those were empty words. It's not like he broke a teapot. A wise friend of mine said, 'Once you've been hurt, you can never be hurt in the same way again.' I think that is probably true."

Forgiving is a process, not a word. It comes when you're again able to feel empathy for the transgressor, which motivates you to behave constructively toward the relationship. A set of forgiveness researchers found that by forgiving, you demonstrate that your caring for the offending partner now takes precedence over the hurtful actions you've experienced. For me, full forgiveness could only come *after* understanding—preferably both mine and his—and thus recovery. When I read somewhere, in fact, that I didn't have to force myself to forgive prematurely in order to make things better between us, it was liberating. Later on, using the word seemed superfluous.

But if your own distress has diminished enough that you're ready to help lessen your partner's guilt, doing so is a generous act. An elderly man, when I asked if his wife had forgiven him for a long ago affair, said, "No, but forgiveness would be golden."

One vestigial reminder of all this in our lives today is that when I'm heating two meals in the microwave, or making omelets, I heat

Stephen's meal first, so it cools off a bit while I heat mine. Before, I always let mine be the one to cool. A tiny statement.

## CAN YOU AFFAIR-PROOF?

Only a fool would claim illicit thrills aren't enticing. It's not always easy to summon up the discipline to turn down excitement and short-term gratification in any form. Undeniably, a choice must be made and the trade-off acknowledged to yourself and to your partner. Loving in flow couples have all learned, some through painful experience, that feeling good about themselves as individuals and living in an honest and trusting intimacy with their partners far outweighs a forbidden, and temporary, thrill.

Here, then, are a few thoughts about how both you and your partner might make your relationship less vulnerable to being ripped apart by the cliché crisis:

- ↦ **NEVER KEEP SECRETS.** The intensity of affairs is more based on their secrecy than it is on sex. A strong bond quickly develops when one of you shares a secret outside the committed relationship. This relative stranger becomes the only other person in the world who knows this secret, whereas at home you must keep up your guard.

   A fascinating study found that if you can get two strangers to surreptitiously play footsie under the table, they will later rate their secret partner as more attractive. Why are furtive relationships so alluring? They affect your brain: you have to keep the secret in mind at all times, lest you give it away inadvertently, but you mustn't think about it, or it might leak out. And this doubly complicated cognitive task causes you to become obsessively preoccupied with the affair partner, which makes it much less likely that you'll focus on your spouse or be able to relax in his or her presence.

   George Seeds Sr. told me that once when he was away for a three-day meeting on some dry subject like psychopharmacology, a woman flirted with him. "She was real pretty, and she kept making remarks like, 'I've got this bad hip. I have a hard time spreading my legs apart.' Things like that. She had a room in the hotel where I was staying. I thought, 'What if I have sex with her? How would that affect my relationship with Norma? How could I *ever ever* tell Norma this?' And I would *have* to tell her. I couldn't live with a secret. It would be like a poison, like a wall dropped down between us over the years. I *knew* it would be. All those things just flashed through my mind in a split second."

Use the power of secrets to enhance your marriage: come up with jokes and couple innuendo that you share with no one but your partner, or try an occasional clandestine (but legal!) sexual hijink that would raise eyebrows "if only our friends knew." (There's more about honesty in chapter 16.)

↔ **RATIONALIZE IN THE RIGHT DIRECTION.** I asked Howard, who takes frequent long business trips, how he manages when temptations arise. He admits to having had more than one opportunity to pursue a fling. But his respect for his wife is such, he explains, that "the temptations I have felt have always been quickly smothered by remorse at the prospect of hurting her. Fundamentally, the question becomes: what's more important, sex with this woman, or maintaining my wife's respect and faith in me? The answer has always been very clear to me."

Howard adds that self-discipline plays a part. "I love cookies," he explains. "I don't eat as many as I'd like because being healthy is more important to me. One can rationalize infidelity—or eating too many cookies, or any other over-indulgence—in many different ways. It all comes down to identifying your priorities. Where the mind goes, the body follows. I won't proceed down the intellectual path of a prospective affair because the relationship damage is too great."

➥ **AGREE ON WHAT FIDELITY IS.** To make monogamy feasible, couples need to decide exactly what each of them considers an infidelity. One spouse may feel that an erotic online chat harms no one. If the other partner disagrees, however, then such behavior has no place in an honest relationship.

Each couple has to draw their own lines, and some draw them in places that may seem surprising to others. For instance, Sol Gordon, 78, a sex educator and author of many books, including *How Can You Tell When You're Really in Love?*, explains the policy he followed with his wife Judith throughout forty years of marriage: "We both agreed to be monogamous, but my sense of intimacy doesn't mean just sexual intercourse. For me intimacy includes massage with people I liked and cared about. Judith knew and didn't object to it. I might masturbate by myself later, after such a massage. I have always made it clear that Judith was my priority and that I didn't want another sexual relationship or even an ongoing relationship."

Also, by talking about adultery, you bring the subject into the light and acknowledge the temptations. It's unrealistic to assume neither of you will ever feel the slightest inclination toward an extramarital liaison. But that does not mean that all open sharing with someone other than your partner need be dangerous to the primary relationship. Agree on boundaries that feel safe without being so confining that you're no longer allowed to be a genuine human being with anyone else. If your relationship is healthy, it's not negative to reveal your inner self to another, as long as you're not doing it in a flirtatious way, or with someone who might construe your openness as more meaningful than it is, or you reveal details your partner wants kept private. Many men and women make certain they mention their spouse at least once when they're conversing with others about what might seem personal matters. If you avoid the fact that you're married, ask yourself if you have a hidden agenda.

An addendum: even the smallest everyday deception may affect trust levels in certain couples. Some of us don't even want to be told we look great in an outfit we are sure we *don't* look great in, while others are delighted with this sort of ego-boosting exaggeration. It's best to agree on what constitutes a lie that matters.

↪ **MAKE TIME FOR RISK AND ADVENTURE.** Adultery is not a healthful drug: it stimulates in the short run but can have devastating effects on several lives. Better to seek ways for both you and your partner to get some of those glorious effects, passion and novelty, within a context sustainable over time. Loving in flow provides a chance to continually renew yourselves.

When I attended a reception for new Peace Corps volunteers (my older son was one), I was surprised to see several midlife and older couples committing themselves to spend two years in an underdeveloped country for beneath-modest pay. That is one way to reinvent yourselves and share an incomparable adventure.

If you're at all creative, you can locate ethical ways to bring excitement home to share, rather than taking the clichéd route of infidelity. Try embarking on a joint project, planning a vacation, taking a course, or learning a skill together. See chapter 18, which explores play and complexification, for more ideas.

↪ **BUILD YOUR INTIMACY.** Intimacy is a worthy and achievable replacement for the passion that accompanies unfamiliarity with a particular body. In my first marriage, one of the most intimate moments that comes to mind more than thirty years later is one afternoon when my then-new-husband shared some moments from his youth with me, including vulnerabilities exposed, weaknesses admitted, and various poignant anecdotes I hadn't heard before. But that was the only time, and over the years we came to have what I've heard called a "Greyhound bus" relationship, the kind you have when you are forced to spend idle time in a public place and all you exchange are pleasantries.

I once met a man, also married, at a grad school function who, as we talked late into the night on the patio, told me about incidents he said he'd never told anyone else. It was quite chilly, but I didn't want to leave since this level of exchange is so rare, and, yes, exciting. He was nobody to me and I couldn't even picture him a month later. But I remember the thrill of being told secrets. In that case, it was an ephemeral intimacy that led nowhere.

The same level of sharing, of course, leads to many affairs, but also to the deepening of committed relationships. Discovering what's being covered up by a public face can be an exhilarating experience, and it's still possible after many years together.

**BE NICE TO ONE ANOTHER.** Sheer niceness and comfort are often the main things that keep couples pleasurably connected. Numerous times I've met women who are filled with fury at their husbands, and I wonder if they will overcome their conflicts before their husbands stop coming home. Of course, angry and critical husbands are just as likely to send their partners in search of someone who appreciates them.

**TAKE LOGISTICS INTO ACCOUNT.** Some studies have found that *opportunity* is at least as related to infidelity as marital quality. Opportunity, which can range from number of days traveling in a year, to job requirements, to financial means, is far from a quantifiable concept. How, then, might you reduce the chances for a partner to be unfaithful? One suggestion by experts is that if only one partner is employed outside the home, pay special attention to righting any potential imbalance of power so that you both interact with other individuals and couples together. Also, if one partner travels a lot, it would be smart to talk about temptations and how they might be dealt with. A daily phone call—not a perfunctory one—can keep you connected emotionally. Consider discussing how much alcohol, if any, will be consumed by one partner out of the presence of the other, if this has proven an issue in the past.

Infidelity isn't the only threat to loving in flow, of course, and in the next two chapters, we'll explore some of the other challenges couples have overcome.

# 14

# CHILDREN: FLOW INTERRUPTED?

A relationship crisis occurs when an event takes place that requires more change than a couple can readily accommodate. It might be a shift in the family's composition, a job loss, or a major illness. It has been found that relationships typically go through at least one hard period, and how couples cope impacts the rest of their lives together. Many of these low points might evolve into full-blown crises if both partners aren't able to adapt and bounce back to a more tenable status quo. Now we'll see how resilient couples avoid letting trying events degrade their relationship.

## ADJUSTING TO THE STRAIN OF PARENTHOOD

> Life, at least our life, was too fragile to survive the onslaught of Michael's needs—his cries, his rashes, his sleeplessness, his abhorrence of having his diapers changed, his little stuffed nose, the narrow nostrils plugged with green, his eyes glittering with panic as he tried to howl and breathe through his mouth at the same time.
>
> —Scott Spencer, *Men in Black*

Relationships are often strained by children: normal babies, sick children, stepkids, teenagers, returning-to-the-nest kids. Children are especially likely to strain what is already stretched thin. According to a ten-year study of more than 100 couples who took part in the Becoming a Family Project at the Psychological Clinic of the University of California at Berkeley, a majority of parents experience a period of higher conflict, less emotional closeness, and less satisfaction with their marriages in the year or two after a birth.

In the weeks after my first baby was born, my then-husband went to work and I stayed home. Our lives began to diverge sharply. Before the birth we'd felt closer than we ever had—talking quietly on the sofa each evening about our plans for our family-to-be—but he now came to seem like a stranger. He was so *big* next to the tiny infant with whom I was spending all twenty of my waking hours.

This post-baby adjustment period hits many couples hard. New mothers—fathers too—lose a lot of sleep and are exhausted by the seeming boundlessness of baby-related chores. For a while, it's hard to see ahead to when you'll feel normal again.

"Afraid to put into words what they are really thinking, new parents let their emotions fester inside," writes Rhonda Kruse Nordin in *After the Baby: Making Sense of Marriage After Childbirth*. The groundwork for many divorces is laid at this time. Of course, if both of you have unreasonable expectations of yourselves and each other, the outcome of self-expression may not be positive. Once when I was beyond exhausted and couldn't bear my six-week-old's screams any longer, I blurted out, "I hate this kid!" Proud-but-clueless Papa looked shocked and hissed, "You mustn't say that!" Piling guilt on top of guilt didn't help me cope any better.

Luckily for the longevity and ultimate happiness of their relationships, some of the couples I spoke with reacted to their own parenting stresses with more innate wisdom. For instance, Elizabeth never blamed her husband Dan for what she experienced as the low point of her marriage. "I allowed myself to be overwhelmed by a man who, as intellectual and bright as he is, wanted a little house in the suburbs and some kids and a dog," she relates. "He wooed me and pursued me and I fell madly in love. Then I woke up right after we had our first child and realized that the path that I had planned, the career I very much wanted, was gone. And I thought 'What the hell have I done?'"

Elizabeth says she threw up for about a month *after* the first baby was born. "I was upset because he was a four-pound baby with an infection on his head and in his belly button and under his arm. I had never been interested in running a house. I longed for the career that having children made less likely." When Elizabeth spoke of returning to work, Dan told her he would prefer her to stay home and raise their family. That's what Elizabeth did: she had three children in her twenties, and she made the best of it.

Nearly twenty years later, when she was at last ready to venture forth, Dan told her, "You've given twenty years to running the house and raising the children. Now it's time for me to support you in starting your career." He was willing to grab a peanut butter and jelly sandwich so she didn't have to cook for him when she attended evening meetings. His letting her off the hook of taking care of him eased her way into the life she had wanted all along, and she seems genuinely appreciative today.

## GETTING BACK ON TRACK

Even while you're immersed in baby care and figuring out who you are as a parent and what it means to be a family, you can strengthen your connection as a couple. Marital researchers at the University of Washington found that you can do so by building affection for your partner, being aware of what's going on in your spouse's life (and caring), and approaching problems together with a sense of control. These factors are all exhibited by the couples I interviewed, to the obvious benefit of their loving feelings.

When women marry, they become, in many ways, the nurturers of their spouses. Then when children arrive, wives turn into mothers, transferring most, if not all, that caregiving to their needy infants. Neither energy nor desire remains to coddle the other half of the partnership, that adult male who they feel should be halving their burden, not doubling it.

As we've seen in earlier chapters, at the beginning of a relationship, you often blind yourself to the faults of the other person.

Later, normal disillusionment sets in and you notice your partner isn't so perfect after all, and that's when babies typically join the family. Such a shifting of couple dynamics forces the process of compromise to take place more rapidly. And that's stressful. But it is possible to rebalance your lives if both of you make a determined effort to keep the marriage foremost in your minds.

Letitia and Lenny admit that with a preschooler, the only issue causing what might be called suffering is finding time to do what they used to enjoy together. They can no longer attend movies frequently, eat out, travel most weekends, go to the beach and rollerblade—all joint activities they loved before becoming parents.

"Those things aren't as easy to do by any means, or much fun, with a three-year old," explains Letitia. "It's a little easier to be home. I don't think we're bored with each other at all, it's just more that occasionally we go, 'Oh my gosh, we feel a little boring.' We're still adjusting to that." Even with their current constraints, this energetic couple goes out once or twice a week to see a movie or eat and visit a bookstore.

Lenny, when asked about his perception of their quandary, responds, "A while back Letitia and I had a couple of counseling sessions to deal with the balancing issue, since it seemed we were both getting too swept up in work. We try to do too much all the time." He mentions they're considering having another child, and they talk a lot about managing the time crunch. What ordinarily takes place with a newborn is that either the three of you are together, or your partner gives you a break and takes the baby for a while. "But that meant I wouldn't ever be alone with my husband," Christina Baker Kline, editor of *Child of Mine: Writers Talk about the First Year of Motherhood*, told me in an interview. "And also my husband would get home from work, not early, and he wanted to spend time with the baby too."

Some couples hire a babysitter so they can go out for a brief respite beginning when their child is very young. Others take a half hour each day, beginning within weeks after childbirth, to sit together in the dining room and talk about anything but the baby. If you can arrange it, try allotting an hour or two a week where both of you are free from concern over your child. No movies, no visiting relatives, no TV, no bike rides, since you can't talk then. Taking a walk without the baby is perfect. Sharing dinner preparation tasks, even with baby nearby, can become an oasis of together time.

It's not a matter of avoiding your feelings about the baby and your changed roles, but of making a conscious effort to not limit yourself to such topics. You need to awaken to each other—and yourselves—as individuals again, and as friends, now that you're parents. Your time together will be more enjoyable if you don't focus on problems, but instead talk about a video you'd both like to see, where you'd love to go when you can take a short vacation, an amusing early date, an outrageous event from the news. If reading the newspaper seems overwhelming now, listen to the radio or, if you're online, keep your browser at a site such as the *New York Times* which is updated frequently. It's a way of feeling part of a larger universe when your own world seems to have shrunk.

One easy behavior that many couples don't bother to try is to get the father involved in all aspects of the baby's life. We tend to ease into traditional roles and drift apart with little in common to converse about. Dads do feel left out, though they may not say so. Invite him clothes-shopping for the baby, or have him drop off and pick up the baby.

If you have a smidgen of energy left over to help your partner feel special, knowing that when he feels cherished he can be a more loving helpmate, consider trying one of these: put up a banner that says, "Welcome home, lover"; compose a brief handmade card of appreciation to remind him of what you love about him; make a coupon book containing promises for three or four things, such as a massage or a living room picnic.

And then there's sex. Finding time, energy, and the right mood for pleasurable lovemaking becomes more complicated when you're parents. Some men, when they experience their wives turning into mothers, may sense a subtle overlay of their own mothers, and they may lose sexual interest for a while. So long as both partners can talk about such feelings, attraction does return. This is all complicated, of course, by a woman's own anxieties about losing her attractiveness. When this is communicated to a partner, he can offer reassurance. He might buy you a new negligee (so long as it doesn't have a hidden agenda of rushing you into sexual behavior when you're nowhere near ready), or say nice things to bolster your esteem.

How, in reality, can you manage in the bedroom? People have said they do it faster than they did before they had kids. You can learn to focus on the moment more quickly, perhaps by using relaxation techniques together.

Keep in mind that both estrogen and progesterone levels drop dramatically after birth, often leading to a lowered libido. Talking and cuddling may provide a sense of intimacy for you—and perhaps for your husband—but, as we've seen, some individuals normally crave a sexual connection in order to feel most intimate. Now is the time to expand your sexual repertoire and, perhaps, consider making love for your husband's sake even when it wouldn't be your first-choice activity.

If you find yourself avoiding sex for more than, say, a few months, reflect on whether you might be angry with your partner and tell him about it. Dealing with the underlying issues may help dissolve the resentment, and you'll soon be willing to get in the mood.

It may take less effort, when you're pooped but wish to please your husband, to satisfy him without intercourse (although some women find lazy intercourse the most energy-conserving of all). Or you can be good-natured about the ways he takes care of himself, and you might even agree to be involved in his masturbation.

Let your husband know that these physical changes are only temporary and that you appreciate any patience he is able to manage. While some women are primed to go in weeks, it can take others a year or more to get back to enjoying sex. Talk about the fact that you both need to make some sacrifices for a while, but be appreciative of each other, not demanding or self-righteous.

"What helped us," explains Christina Baker Kline, "is that we both had a sort of long-distance-runner mentality about this grueling period. We both felt and knew that we would get through it. Keep it in perspective. People have had babies for thousands of years. You didn't invent this. You're not going to redefine it. It's an experience that sweeps you along, like white water rafting. You just have to get past the rapids."

Once past those postnatal rapids, however, you still have to raise the kids. The fact that some couples have a hard time agreeing how to do so can lead to more serious trouble in the relationship.

The only dark note in Mei-Ling's twelve-year marriage involves the arguments she and her husband have about raising a child. He's more traditional, while she's more concerned about what she calls the final product: a person with confidence and inner strength. Their little girl has "a few of what might be called bad habits, like sucking her thumb, pulling hair from my head and tying it around her finger, and she still sleeps in our bed," Mei-Ling explains. She fears causing anxieties in the child if they're too hard on her about such trivial matters—after all, Mei-Ling grew up with a family bed, so it seems natural to her—and she draws the line when she hears her husband criticizing the girl.

Indeed, psychologists delving into parenting attitudes and marital intimacy found that couples in which the husband held more traditional attitudes, as well as partners who disagreed about child rearing, experienced steeper declines in closeness over time than couples who thought more alike. This held true not only for first-timers but for the rearing of subsequent children as well.

For some couples, of course, intimacy increases after children are born. One woman told me that bringing up their child was the biggest project she and her husband had ever undertaken together, and they were having great fun at it. Hewing to the same parenting philosophy helps; otherwise, keep communicating until you find areas of agreement, such as your basic values, to keep your relationship from becoming contentious.

## PARENTING WITH EXTRA PROBLEMS

If so-called normal children push against a marriage's weakest pressure points, how much more so does a child with a disability or who presents some other extra challenge? Unfortunately, when a couple is undergoing major stress, rather than feeling more supportive of one another, they often reduce those supportive reachings-out just when they're most needed. But if the two of you continue sharing your reactions and impressions throughout any stressful situation, you can get through anything together.

Consider the example of Lou and Norman Owensby, the North Carolina couple mentioned earlier as having solved the chore wars after forty-three years of marriage. Right after they got married, they moved to another city for Norman's medical residency, and the hospital had no place for them to stay. "It's a wonder we stayed married at all after the first month," says Lou in a soft Southern accent.

"So for two months we stayed in one room in a rooming house, Norman gone two days and one night at a time, and me in that one room, four walls, and the owners did not appreciate company, and we had one car. I was trapped *and* pregnant. After we were married for five months, our little apartment burned down with everything we owned, every wedding present, so we started from scratch. And he was making fifty dollars a month.

"We had four kids real fast, one a year. The first seven years, without a question, were the hardest. Also, our third child had Down's Syndrome, and that was very difficult. Not difficult between us, except—it was an interesting thing—we were both devastated, of course, and he stayed home for a week, and we were very close to each other during that time, you know, miserable. And then he went back to work and I was devastated that he could *possibly* go back to work. How could he do that? It was weird because, in retrospect, what would we have done if he *hadn't* gone back?"

Lou laughs at this point, as she does often while relating the intimate details of her early married life. I ask her if they had to learn how to talk about such difficult matters productively, and she laughs again and says, "Absolutely! To be real truthful, for the first seven years, I honest-to-God, deep down thought that I was right and he was wrong. Because I *knew* how to make this the perfect relationship and all that kind of crapola.

"After about seven years of being miserable—I don't know how much had to do with our Down's child and how much had to do with being exhausted from having four kids—I decided that I couldn't live like this anymore. Something's got to give. The core issue was that Norman wasn't paying attention, no matter how many times I told him I needed something different, more attention, more time. He is a one-track person. I felt martyred, overwhelmed, and I never could articulate it very well.

"But what could I do with four young children if I left him? I decided that's not an option. Then I thought, 'What would make a difference to Norman?' I decided I would tell him every day that I loved him. I was so angry and hurt when I started that I couldn't even say 'I love you,' I had to say I loved something *about* him. 'I love the way your shoes look.' But I was hoping he would pay attention.

"I also decided I would look at him differently: if he's 100 percent, how much of that 100 percent do I love about him? It floored me to come up with about 80 percent. So I realized that I'd been focusing on the 20 percent and not the 80 percent. I made a decision to focus on the 80 percent and that changed everything around.

"So it wasn't him at all," she admits, laughing. "It was me! He changed too, absolutely. He became more loving, though he'll never be as communicative as I am."

Concrete changes also helped. Lou returned to graduate school and finished her master's, and then seven years later Norman did his psychiatry residency. "That's one of the things I love about him, that we're both very flexible and we also feel that if something doesn't work, you figure out a way to get beyond it."

As for childrearing, Lou admits she thought of herself as a perfect mother until their Down's child was born. "We put John in a nursing home when he was born because I couldn't handle it—he's severely and profoundly retarded—at about age two, and now he's 39 years old. He's sweet and adorable, but we have to be home by three o'clock, and we don't go out at night. But all that's okay. He's in a workshop during the day, and Norman helps a lot. He may actually be more nurturing than I am."

They haven't always agreed on child discipline either. "I would have been a lot stricter than he would have been," says Lou. "I always thought you should have a solid front with your kids and all that theory stuff, and then I saw that wasn't so good after all, that it's better for them to learn that people treat you differently. We had the same values on the important things and totally agreed on them."

I asked Norman how he perceived the same low point. While he'd been aware Lou was miserable, he believed it was depression caused by her inability to do what she wanted, due to overwork, boredom, and his inability to spend enough time with her.

"She had completed one year of graduate school, and she always likes to finish things, so I talked her into going back to school," explains Norman. "And I think that turned her around almost immediately. She never even would have thought about that." I noticed how Lou herself gave so little weight to this, but her husband almost attributes the whole marital recovery to it. Of course, finding an engaging pastime outside the home has saved many a marriage (and broken up as many).

"I've always felt that we were a team," adds Norman. "And that whoever had the greatest need at the time needs to be focused on." That's a suitable rule for couples to live by, and

ng with just going back to business as usual,
 were coming home? Here's an example of our
 few months prior:

in was home over spring break, remodeling our
yroom. After replacing the seventeen-year-old
h shiny linoleum tiles, he began on the wallpa-
r afternoon, he papered his way into the corner
ing machine, grumbling because there was no
e the machine out of his way. He crouched
he could, and scraped off the layers of orange-
 paper while the same music played over and
blayer.

ived close to his local university, coincidentally
hort visit after school that day carrying his laun-
im he couldn't do it because of the wallpapering.
Stephen was racing from room to room, anx-
 with multiple phone calls and computer-
ed business, playing the role of poet-playing-
nessman, to make up for having lost his main job
He was feeling the stress of playing against type.
ater, Simon entered the bathroom, and soon I
heated exchange. "GET OUT! GET THE FUCK
OU SEE I'M WORKING!?!"

tered into the kitchen and I looked at him
hat happened?" He blustered, "What's the mat-
? No one has the right to yell at me like that."
u doing?" "His tape was over and I said, 'Whew,
.' He told me to get out, then he yelled at me."
ou leave when he asked you to?" "I was just
" I said, purposefully calm, "He wasn't grumpy
rprised he yelled like that. But maybe you need to
t other people's requests the first time they ask."
get a job this summer so I can get my own apart-
take that from him." He returned to his dorm
t.

when they neglect to—or they can't agree on who's neediest—
tough times follow.

Difficulties with parenting played a role in the rough start of
the marriage of Georgia and Matthew, the mid-fifties couple discussed earlier (they rebounded from his emotional affair some
years into the marriage). They married young. Georgia claims she
gave up her own plans to support him in his career choice, which
included being away from her family. They were quite poor, she
became pregnant, and she devoted herself to being a mother.

Matthew's view of that period differs from Georgia's. He says
she never wanted a career and all she wanted was to have babies.
"My mother was powerful and I wasn't yet independent of my
parents. That was what my family felt Georgia should be doing,
and therefore she felt she had to do it."

When they had their second child a couple of years later,
while still living on loans, it turned out he was "a not-normal, a
very mentally ill child," says Georgia. "And this colored the entire
rest of our lives. I was young and not equipped to understand
that it wasn't just a clash between the baby's temperament and
personality and myself. It was very frustrating. He's been in a
mental hospital. I knew there was something wrong with him
when he was a baby. When he was a year old, taking his shoes off
would give us two hours of screaming. Oppositional defiant,
anxiety, rages, temper tantrums, and later on bizarre behavior,
lying, stealing."

But no one else saw what Georgia saw, including Matthew. "I
got blamed because the child knew how to get sympathy for himself. So this was a crisis between me and Matthew. I became the
bad guy and he became the good guy."

Ironically, when their third child was born with physical problems that required hospitalizations throughout the first year, that
unified them. "Physical illness, people can see it. It was such a contrast having an ill child, with operations, internal bleeding, a year
old and couldn't sit up. However stressful it was, on the other hand,
it was at least something I could deal with," explains Georgia.

After several years and some sessions with a counselor, Georgia and Matthew began to deal with their childrearing problems as a united couple, no longer allowing guilt and anger to get in the way of their connection. "The counselor didn't take sides," says Georgia, "but allowed us to hear more of the feelings behind each other's words."

When Christine (she of the rollicking daily sex life) had a colicky baby nine months after marrying, she found it a strain, to say the least. Her husband Jed had wanted to have children much more than she had. "Oh, gosh, it was so hard," says Christine. "Neither one of us slept. She would cry fourteen hours a day every day. We couldn't figure it out. I hated him, I hated her, I hated everybody. And Jed was very supportive. He would try his best to relax her, take her outside, sit in the car with her. I was still resentful because I felt like it was his fault. I was more angry, trying to engage in bickering. I was getting really depressed." At the time they lived in the country. Then, a couple of farms away, a family moved in with an infant four days younger than Christine's. "That gave me someplace else to take the kid to scream, which really helped. My new friend had a husband who didn't help her at all. So I got to see that I had it pretty good."

Obviously, not all potential childrearing crises come in the first years of a child's life. For example, when Barbara and Thomas S. Greenspon of Minneapolis took custody of a teenage girl about twenty years ago, they admit they ended up "taking a hard look at" their relationship.

Tom, a psychologist and author of *Freeing Our Families from Perfectionism,* and Barbara, a sex counselor and educator, work in side-by-side offices. They were advisors for a church group when the courts gave a troubled near-suicidal fifteen-year-old girl to them. At the time, they had two school-aged children of their own. The girl, whom they soon considered their daughter, shoplifted, took drugs, and frequently ran away. She also played one parent against the other, so that they had to figure out how to set limits.

"It was a huge s[...] worried about her, [...] that point, with you[...] argued over how to [...] ship, but it did push[...]

Tom agrees, addi[...] solve problems. And [...] ing things through, [...] realized this was affec[...] answers." Eventually t[...] the same goals for the [...] did the relationship pr[...]

## FAMILIES IN FL[...]

A dozen years ago, just [...] when our marriage wa[...] enced one out-of-the-o[...] from college and livin[...] arrangements that hadn[...] live with his father wher[...] had grieved over the emp[...] before, even though that [...] were back home.

Busy with school and [...] couldn't go back to the o[...] for my attention and w[...] (Stephen is very conflict-p[...] mothering role for myself[...] scious by means of a journ[...]

Family systems don't [...] adapt to outside events (a [...] in or out), change does oc[...] boys with each other, me[...] changing the sometimes gr[...] tomed to interacting.

What was wro[...] now that the boys[...] interaction from [...]

Handyboy Kev[...] bathroom/laundr[...] carpet squares wi[...] per. One particula[...] behind the wash[...] easy way to mov[...] behind it as best[...] and-silver stripe[...] over in the tape [...]

Simon, who [...] came over for a s[...] dry. I had to tell [...]

Meanwhile, [...] iously coping [...] consulting-relat[...] the-role-of-busi[...] months earlier. [...]

Sometime l[...] heard half of a[...] OUT! CAN'T Y[...]

Simon sau[...] quizzically. "W[...] ter with Kevin[...]

"What were y[...] it's about tim[...]

"Why didn't [...] watching him[...] before. I'm su[...] learn to respe[...]

"Maybe I can [...] ment. I can't [...] right after th[...]

As usual, I'd meant to be gentle and "helpful," but I was getting in between my two sons' interaction, serving as an interpreter of Kevin for Simon. I was also judging Simon without having been present.

That evening, while Kevin and Stephen and I were eating dinner in front of the TV, I asked Kevin what had made him so grumpy at Simon. He snapped at me, "I knew you would blame me." "Wait!" I said, "I'm not blaming you. I'm asking you. I know you haven't been in a bad mood all week and then suddenly I heard this big yell." (Even the hint of being "blamed" would set Kevin off on his typical "but I'm totally innocent" routine.)

His explanation: Simon had come in and criticized his music. Kevin was in the middle of struggling with a piece of wallpaper and asked Simon to get out. He didn't leave. Kevin said Simon wanted him to say "please." Finally, when he looked back five minutes later and Simon was still watching him, he yelled at him. "I know I probably reacted too strongly, but do you want someone watching *you* when wallpaper is falling on *your* head?"

My internal reactions: 1) Uh-oh. Is this how the summer is going to be? 2) I hope Stephen doesn't get too anxious about the summer from hearing this. 3) Did I do the right thing? Should I have stayed *completely* out? Not even ask what happened? 4) This is such a familiar helpless feeling. After all these years, I still don't know how to handle their battles.

One day not long after that, I had a chance to speak with Simon, who expressed his annoyance at me. I apologized, explaining that I was concerned about what had gone on between him and Kevin and was hoping it wasn't a sign that the summer would be conflicted. He said, "You didn't talk to Kevin this much about it." I said I *had* talked with him, and that he had admitted he had overreacted, which was when Simon finally seemed to relax—taking it as an apology in absentia.

That's the background of that singular summer. My staying conscious of the process did help—with the boys, at least. I changed my own reactions (and they cooperated amazingly well) so that between May, when they arrived, and August, the household ran more smoothly and peacefully than Stephen or I had dared hope. (And now as adults they get along so well that they take trips together.)

Behind the scenes, though, more was going on. In fact, I later found out that Stephen's disequilibrium had been extreme while the system was changing. Having my older son move back home for that short period of time was an event I welcomed and enjoyed, while Stephen withdrew into the security of our bedroom for much of it. I was certain our marriage would offer me that margin of safety to indulge in the pleasure of spending time with my boys (perhaps to make up, in part, for the guilt I felt for Simon's having gone to live with his father all those years before). Since Stephen, however, is an intense introvert and lives only in the present, he was anxious that the enlarged, less private, configuration might become the new status quo.

The most excruciating episode of our marriage, which I've already detailed, began at the end of that same summer. So, although we eventually turned our marriage around, this period was one long crisis that had multiple aspects we didn't recognize at the time. The blending and reblending of our family was only a meagre part of that larger turmoil. We felt as though we were struggling against the forces of chaos, so that flexibility was needed now more than ever. As conscious as we tried to be of what was going on within ourselves and each other, nothing short of an intense commitment to stick with it pulled us through—even when we weren't sure of how that "it" would look.

## MISCARRIAGE AND INFERTILITY

When a couple is unable to have a baby, the emotions unleashed can be devastating. Those who have suffered through a miscarriage report that relatives and friends don't realize what they're going through. Would-be parents bond to their expected child and grieve when they lose it, even when they chose to terminate the pregnancy because there was something drastically wrong with the fetus. Subsequent pregnancies are much more fearful and anxious. It is common to build walls of protection against potential disappointment, Pam Rillstone and Sally A. Hutchinson found when they interviewed fifteen women and nine partners who were in the process of a pregnancy after ending an abnormal previous one. A side effect of protecting yourselves this way may be a general shutting down in your relationship. The most loving couples manage to avoid such negative effects.

Howard and Jane, the couple mentioned earlier as having overcome so many personal differences in their twelve years together, have two young children. But they had a miscarriage when Jane was four-and-a-half months pregnant, right after the couple moved to a rural town, far from her family.

"Jane never blamed me or the move," says Howard. "At the time, when you're going through all the emotions, you go through the typical stages of grief, and a lot of things go through your mind. But even then, I don't think that either of us blamed the other, and I think that we've both come to a point where we just look at it as these things just sometimes happen and that's the way the machinery works. Four months later we were pregnant again.

"The experience brought us much closer," he added, and then emotion stops him a moment. When he resumes, he explains, "It's kind of a happy emotion. I'm emotional because I'm remembering. It's hard to explain. It wasn't intellectual—something from within bubbled up inside of me and I needed to take care of my wife. Seeing to her was my whole reality at that point. It was a very visceral thing, to take care of her. When we talked about it later, she told me she felt that she was completely taken care of and her perception was that I was very unselfish. You know the old saying that people show their true colors when the chips are down? What I was feeling right then was not important, especially that first week. I just made the decision that I needed to be there for her."

For some individuals, having children is one of life's major urges, and when that urge is frustrated, relationships may be threatened. Frieda, 49, and Rodney, 45, together fourteen years, say the lowest point in their relationship was when they found out she would be unable to conceive.

"We both love children very much and had always expected we would be a family," explains Frieda. "It was a hard period for us. I would have adopted, but he was adamant about not doing that. I went through a deep depression for about a year when we found out. Rodney was depressed too, but less than I was."

They considered artificial insemination, but they knew there'd be no guarantee, and Frieda had gynecological problems that would have required a very expensive operation.

"Rodney was very supportive going through all those meetings with the doctors, but he just didn't know how to deal with my depression. We had arguments, I cried, there was blame. It got to the point where, after a year and a half, I was tired of crying over it, and I told him if he wanted to divorce me, though I loved him very much, I wouldn't try to stand in his way."

Frieda and Rodney continued to discuss their options for a few more months after they reached this crisis point. Finally, Rodney agreed to at least consider adoption. Three years passed with the idea still on hold. "I got to the point where if we have children, fine, but if we don't, that's okay, because our relationship is very strong. And then two years ago, our nephew had a son, and that brought the subject of children back up. A girlfriend of mine had a little boy for whom she wanted us to be godparents. So *that* brought it up again. We decided to see if we could adopt a child, perhaps a little older one. We'll probably start the process shortly."

It becomes clear through all these couples' stories that the strength of the couple connection can be sorely tried by additional members in the family, and also by the failure to have children when that is your heart's desire. Yet we also see that those who talk openly, share their full range of feelings, and keep the larger picture in mind do triumph over challenges that might be fatal to the love of less resilient couples.

It's intriguing, too, to realize how primary the couple link can be, even though it's not a blood tie. Adult to adult, we give one another strength and comfort as we deal with life's vicissitudes. Some of the challenges couples face, as we'll see next, can be daunting indeed.

# 15

# MONEY, ILLNESS, AND OTHER POTENTIAL CRISES

I thought, I suppose, that we would be poor but happy to begin with—
meaning that we would be living in a small, cute flat, and spending a
lot of time watching TV or drinking halves of beer in pubs, and making do with our parents' hand-me-down furniture. In other words, the
difficulties I was prepared to tolerate in the early years of my marriage
were essentially romantic in their nature.

—Nick Hornby, *How to Be Good*

Some couples find flow in spite of horrible low points. In a vast
study of more than 600 long-lasting marriages in eight nations,
researchers learned that both partners were highly resilient and
exhibited learned resourcefulness, both flow-enhancing traits.

If you and your mate can be resourceful as early as the newlywed
years, other research indicates, it will make a difference in whether
you stay satisfied with one another or begin to lose that loving
feeling. Such findings merely confirm the old adage that what
doesn't kill you makes you stronger. By accumulating a rich
repertoire of successes—"we got through that!"—you feel better
about yourself and each other, and about your prospective
longevity as a couple. Then you'll problem-solve even more
effectively in the future, as opposed to having to first overcome a
feeling of helplessness due to past failures. You've done it, and you
know you can do it again, so you're able to face each new gauntlet
optimistically and energetically.

Merely being together with your mate when unexpectedly bad
things happen is a known stress-reducer for both animals and
humans. When the worst of the challenge is over, that togetherness

brings an even bigger payoff. One couple described a typical crisis aftermath: "All of a sudden we were staying up late in the night and talking. As we held onto each other through that time, we both saw that no matter what happened, we would face it together."

To learn more, I asked my selection of successful couples—united like veterans who have fought together against a common enemy—to describe how they overcame their most difficult challenges.

## FOR RICHER OR POORER

Despite marriage vows to stay united for richer or poorer, most couples expect their financial situation to improve over time. Money has so many deep personal resonances that financial hardship is one of the better tests of a relationship's durability.

When Jim and Zhita Rea got married—he for the third time, she for the second—they each already had two daughters. Long before this, Jim had reluctantly left a career teaching philosophy when he became blocked while completing his doctoral dissertation. He then became an electrician and wanted to start his own wholesale electrical supplies business. In spite of Jim's supreme optimism, Zhita was skeptical—realistic, she calls it—about the endeavor's prospects.

"The business had been kind of a, I wouldn't say life dream, but certainly something that was very powerful for him," explains Zhita. "And I felt 'OK, you know how I feel, and I see what this might mean to you.' I had supported my family for years and years, sent my daughters to school. I'm not a person who needs a great deal of material things. I said, literally, 'Let's just hold hands and go forward.' The rest of our relationship was strong, and that was an important test. It was very difficult and stressful, but not a low point in our marriage. Part of what partnership means is that you support the other person in things that are important."

When the business didn't do well after six years, Jim sold it to a larger company and continued to work for them as a branch manager. The couple lost a lot of money. "I was prepared to lose our house," says Zhita, "and I wouldn't have been resentful if we had. And we did sell the house when we retired seven years later."

Jim, for his part, declares that the way Zhita supported him when he started the business, "with no reservations and no complaining," endeared him to her forever.

A younger couple, Isabel and Anthony, together for a dozen years, has an ongoing potential crisis around financial matters that impacts Isabel's satisfaction level. She knocks ten points off the score she gives the marriage because, she says, "I'm looking for us to be a little bit more financially stable. He says to me sometimes that money is very important to me, and it is, though to him, number one is that we're healthy."

Anthony's grandparents came from Mexico. Isabel was born in El Salvador, but has lived in the United States her whole life. She hates having to struggle at all, she says, but "my frustration is not at *him*, it's at the situation. That's the only thing we argue about, especially since the kids were born."

If disappointing income is often a challenge, job loss by one of the partners can be a major relationship stressor. When one of you is unemployed, it's been found, the strain takes a toll as both partners feel depressed, and the depression of the non-unemployed partner reduces her ability to express concern and offer help to the job-seeker. He then feels more depressed than before and is less content with the relationship, thus negative interactions increase, creating the usual vicious circle.

The best couples, though, never turn against one another for long. Marylis told me how, for instance, when Conrad was laid off for six months, they both had to get used to roles they didn't want. As a writer, she hated the idea of a nine-to-five job, and he, the first full day home, polished all the shoes in the house. "He was going crazy. And I would come home stressed out and weeping from this ghastly job I had, that I'd taken because I felt like I had to. Still, through it all, I think we both felt like we were on the same team."

When Raleigh, an elderly Missourian, is asked what was the low point of his own long marriage, he says it was when he lost his first job. "My firm went down the tubes after the war. I thought at the time that Hope was more critical than supportive." Such memories can be intense enough to last a lifetime.

Other couples learn to deal with financial issues in a healthier way as they become more bonded. Jorge tells me that he and Rosalisa no longer argue about money, but that it was a big issue for the first five or so years of their sixteen-year marriage.

"We both thought money was much more important than it is," admits Jorge. "In the early days, we took it out on each other. But I think we now see that the arguments over money are only temporary. Are the bills paid? Are we going to have enough? That type of thing."

## IN SICKNESS AND IN HEALTH

> It seems to me now that the plain state of being human is dramatic enough for anyone; you don't need to be a heroin addict or a performance poet to experience extremity. You just have to love someone.
>
> —Nick Hornby, *How to Be Good*

When one of you suffers distress due to illness, the other is of course affected, too. And even though the best relationship is liable to feel some strain, either partner is usually able to offer the support needed by the other. The problem is exacerbated when the difficult situation persists. Support may start slipping. Researchers who studied breast cancer families from four to ten months after diagnosis learned that the partners tended to be most supportive related to the physical impairment, but less so for the patient's emotional distress, especially as time went on. Most people have no idea how to nurture someone suffering emotional pain. It may also takes a huge toll on one's psychic energy to continually be relied upon to give more and more when the need is so one-sided. If both partners are aware of how long support might actually be called for, it is less likely that the patient's neediness will drive away the supportive partner.

The nearly-four-decades-long marriage of Barbara and Tom Greenspon is an example of how couples adapt to continued health strains. Barbara Greenspon says that a real low point in her marriage to Tom was when she had an IUD that gave her an infection doctors couldn't diagnose. Even after the device was removed, she continued to have pains and symptoms that were misdiagnosed for nine long years. A doctor finally discovered that the problem was a grossly inflamed fallopian tube and removed it. Admits Barbara, "Three or four of those years were really tough. I hurt and was in misery, yet I thought I was nuts because no one was finding anything."

She was irritable throughout that time, and Tom was frequently accommodating to a fault. "That's not to say that I didn't consider leaving emotionally or physically, or fighting, or keeping my mouth shut and fuming," says Tom. "But I continued to be committed to our relationship, and to be looking for ways to work out whatever this was."

Tom's essential optimism led Barbara to feel the most nurtured she's ever felt in her life. "It was incredibly emotionally fulfilling to have somebody who loved me enough to be there. Which then—none of this was conscious of course, for either of us—stood us really well at other times because we had this history."

Tom adds, "Barbara was looking for a place of safety where she could be heard, and I was looking for affirmation, to be competent and accepted. I got that from her if I listened, and she got what she needed if she affirmed me, so that kept us connected and created a resilience in the relationship."

A health problem was a catalyst for another couple's nightmare years. Several years ago, when Moira, now forty-two, was put on and then abruptly taken off a steroid medication for a serious auto-immune system disorder, it catapulted her into an uncontrolled manic state. She disappeared from home to stay in five-star hotels, thus draining their funds and driving her husband Jason mad with worry. At around the same time, Jason lost his job. And then, as though things weren't bad enough, they lost their home in a tornado.

"Those two or three years were a tremendous dark hole," says Moira. "At the end of it, we had to declare bankruptcy. We faced that together and were supportive of each other through that. Jason was very frightened by my mania, and I didn't realize how it was affecting him. It took a lot of time to heal from that period."

According to both of them, they have an outstanding relationship now. "We both held each other up during the difficult times," says Moira. "We didn't turn outside of our marriage but *to* our marriage for support. And we became extremely close-knit friends, in the type of friendship that no matter what, I'll always love you. Unconditional love."

Serious illness that comes years after a couple has learned to love in flow may not threaten the relationship's essential stability even as it threatens its longevity. Lila and Harry have been married three decades, and they haven't had sex in more than a year, since Harry's prostate cancer has to be treated with Lupron shots.

"And that's fine. Every once in a while he'll say, 'I'm so sorry,'" Lila says, "and I just keep reassuring him that I love him so much, that there's so much more to marriage than that." During such crises, concern for more *time* together vastly overtakes regret over lost sexual possibilities.

Depression is common in strained marriages. When one member of a couple is depressed, it can become an overwhelming challenge for the couple to engage in honest, healthful, and helpful exchanges, especially if the undepressed partner is fearful of further stressing the other. No matter what, the depressed person usually feels no one understands or supports him enough. It may devolve into a self-perpetuating negative situation, with relationship stress worsening the depression.

Getting help from professionals made a difference for several of the couples I interviewed. Significant improvement resulted from obtaining the right medication for the depressed partner, and counseling provided help on how to interact when depression is distorting perceptions.

The lowest point in Frank and Margie's twenty-four-year relationship was towards its midpoint when Frank's parents passed away. Frank, a high school teacher in Los Angeles, experienced a deep depression, and he admits he "wasn't dealing well with things. It sort of amplified anything else we would have dealt with more easily, and made it very unpleasant." At such stressful times, Margie and Frank have visited counselors for a short period to improve their communication habits. "Part of it was learning how to listen to each other," says Margie.

One stable couple I interviewed has managed to remain loving through more than a decade of marriage in spite of the wife's persistent major depression, mental breakdowns, and frequent hospitalizations. Neither of them has any real hope that she will ever be permanently cured, yet the husband is consistently supportive. "We laugh a lot even on my worst days," she tells me.

A colleague told me his own marriage's first year was "hell on wheels." Depression—they both suffered from it—played a big role in their misery. When she's between medications, or waiting for a new one to take effect, he says, "I'm back to walking on eggshells and reminding myself constantly that she'll be back to 'normal' in a few weeks." Lately, though, after they both began effective antidepressants, they experienced a major turnaround. "I no longer wake up each morning wondering if this is the day I'm going to leave," he says. "And we've been 'in love' for the last three months in a way even better than when we met twelve years ago."

## OVERCOMING ASSORTED CRISES

She seemed to have no inkling that life wasn't as orderly as her pencil case and that everything is chance and at any moment any number of remarkable things can happen that are totally beyond our control, events that rip up our maps and re-polarize

our compasses—the madwoman walking towards us, the train
falling off the bridge, the boy on the bicycle.

—Kate Atkinson, *Emotionally Weird*

Indeed, "any number of remarkable things can happen" during
a lifetime, more of them distressing than anyone would wish.
Here are some of them and how the happiest couples overcome
such shocks:

↠ **DISILLUSIONMENT.** Normal periods of disenchantment
can be exacerbated by an anxious personality or piled-on environmental stresses. Consider how Harriet describes her first
marital crisis:

"We were married just two weeks and I thought, 'I've definitely married the wrong man! What did I do?!' We were in
Italy, buying dishes at a place called Upham's. I couldn't
speak Italian, and Myron could, beautifully. I turned around
to ask him how to say saucers in Italian, but he was gone. I
went outside and asked him, 'Why did you go outside?' And
he said, 'Well, you have to learn to speak the language.' 'What
do you mean—you're deserting me?' He got very angry and
said, 'You have to learn to do this yourself. Don't count on
me.' And then we went back to our apartment, it was five stories up, eighty-eight steps, and every step he was marching
ahead of me. He slammed the front door. I opened it. He
slammed the door to the living room. I opened it. He
slammed the door to the balcony, and I opened that one too,
and I remember saying, 'Guess you can't go any further, and
we have to talk.'" And they did.

Harriet concedes, though, that the genuinely lowest point
came three years later, when they moved to Ohio and had a
daughter.

"My husband was a medical student, and we were given an
apartment with a subterranean balcony, across the street
from where the winos hung out—they threw their bottles into

our balcony. I was terrified of being left alone with my daughter, and I was alone a lot. I didn't have work, I didn't have creative outlets, I didn't have a dollar for a babysitter, and I thought of suicide. I never thought I could bother anybody, there was no one who would ever care enough about my feelings. I was a smiley sunshine little person.

"It finally came pouring out of me one night, and my husband, who is not flowery, jumped out of bed and threw up. He said he would give up anything in his life for me." Her voice gets very soft here. "So that was both the lowest point in my marriage and the curve to come around up again."

"She had a tremendous anxiety attack, which was very frightening for me," explains Myron, "because I didn't know what was going to happen. If she couldn't handle the situation or if she had to be hospitalized, I would just have to leave what I was doing and support her. This was all a new experience and I didn't know what to make of it."

"It was then that I realized what love really is," concludes Harriet. "Having that response was enough."

**↔ THE EMPTY NEST.** None of the couples I interviewed mentioned a crisis precipitated by kids leaving home. Most loving in flow marriages have worked out how to get along before childrearing ends, so that even while empty nest sadness may affect one or both partners, the couple doesn't let it get in the way of their connection.

An empty nest brings increased zest to some couples, for a year or so anyway, as they no longer have to consider other people when they make plans to go out or away, or to make love. But such freedom can be risky. It matters a great deal what you do with that space, how willing you are to face your changed dynamics and adjust accordingly—and lovingly. Don't fill up all your time immediately, however, suggest the authors of *Empty Nesting: Reinventing Your Marriage When the Kids Leave Home.* You may be saving up all sorts of activities to leap into the moment you're free, but if you don't take the time to reconnect as two adults, strengthening your marriage might end up a lower priority than ever. Loving in flow might not even make it onto the list.

↔ **RETIREMENT.** How you feel when you reach the end of your career could be related to the quality of your marriage—but no one is yet sure as to the direction of influence. You'll have more opportunities for spending time together and thus your intimacy might increase, but other changes aren't so positive: less income, loss of home and friends if you move, declining health, and the potential stress of shifting household roles. The transition itself might be the hardest. When the wife still works and the husband doesn't, that can reduce the wife's satisfaction. Not everyone can handle the extreme role change with panache. But if you realize what's going on, you can share those feelings and empathize with one another. The opportunities for revived romantic spontaneity, as with the empty nest, can frighten as well as excite. More reasonable expectations, and taking it slowly, are a better way to go than anticipating retirement will be a glorious and unending second honeymoon.

↔ **IN-LAWS.** In age-old fashion, extended family members occasionally complicate a couple's life. Sherry Suib Cohen, for instance, admitted that a hurtful note all the way through her marriage was her husband's mother. "Larry is a gentle and loving man and, even when his mother was at her most terrible, he simply would not yell at her or stick up for me. He'd say, 'She's an old woman and she doesn't mean it. You don't ever have to go there if you don't want to. But I can't yell at her.' That was an awful and very difficult period to go through. She was a hard woman. As we both got older and my writing started to sell, and her friends began to read my byline all over, then she started to feel proud of me and was much nicer."

After Ida married Sam, she worked seven days a week for six years in the office of a development they owned, taking over sales and marketing. She worked directly with Sam's son Ronald. "It was great for the first two years, and then there was a lot of conflict between Ronald and me," she says. "I'm very goal-oriented and I want to get it done yesterday, and he's not a good communicator. He's wonderful and I love him, but when you're in a business, you've got to communicate. There was a serious rift for a while. It was so bad that we were barely speaking, and then it carried throughout the whole family, and I was getting hate letters. I'd come home in a very bad mood, tired and angry, and Sam had to listen to it every night. But he never took his son's side. That's harder than illness, because it pulls at all your loyalties. We got through that together. Sam understood what was happening, non-judgmentally."

➼ **SCHEDULE CONFLICT.** You might not think of including lack of time on a list of potential crises, but consider: Jeanette says a time crunch was "the only difficulty we had in the past thirty years." It was before she and Bob had children, when they'd been together for nine years. Jeanette is now involved with a couple of volunteer programs, but back then, she danced the nights away while Bob worked frantic hours in a medical setting.

"I was doing eight shows of *Evita* a week, gone nights and weekends, while Bob worked days. So for a year and a half we didn't see each other. He would make me dinner Saturdays and Sundays between shows, and I'd see him for about 45 minutes, and he would try to stay awake when I came home at 11:30 or midnight, for about five minutes. He was starting to feel abandoned and neglected and not part of *my* exuberant theatrical world.

"He also started to feel a little threatened. I was getting a lot of attention, a lot of people coming on to me. I never acted on it, but I was tempted because I was never seeing him. He said something to me once that really bothered me, like, 'I'm going to have to find a way to live my life without you.' But we both remained committed to the marriage. After a year and a half, I was exhausted in every way, I was injured from head to toe, and what I wanted was to stay at home, cook dinner, see Bob, and have children.

"You know you're in it for the long haul. I do think that even when other people were coming on to me and all that stuff, that wasn't real. Bob is real. The bottom line is I kept track of the big picture, that my life was with him. Maybe we both got perhaps to an edge of a precipice, and we pulled back and said this is a temporary state we're in."

When I asked Bob how he remembers that period, he admits it was stressful, but not in any sense that might have separated them. He can't recall saying what Jeanette claims upset her so much. "But there were times when we, literally, just bumped into each other late at night. We have this close interactive relationship, and so it was like your buddy's not around. I think we were losing the kind of intimacy that comes from just doing things together."

Bob says he never resented Jeanette's dancing career, rather that he was proud of her and appreciated her great talent. "In our relationship it's always been important to give each other the opportunity to do what you want to do and even encourage that, to help each other think through what it makes sense to be doing."

↦ **PET LOSS.** Losing a beloved pet can be deeply painful. Marylis describes how, in the early years of her childless marriage to Conrad, they endured what she calls "a whole pet disaster. Our first several cats contracted feline leukemia and we had a series of just wasting and death. Those were really hard times. Conrad had never had a pet as a kid, so this was dreadful: I was trying to bring something new and wonderful into his life, and I introduced a lot of horror instead. If anything, I think that forged a bond. When you see that somebody's emotionally there for you, that's real loyalty."

➜ **MULTIPLE STRESSES.** When stresses occur simultaneously, they stretch a couple's inner resources to the limit. And if one member turns against the other, the marriage may drift into dire straits. Mei-Ling describes one such set of problems that tested her still-new marriage: "There was a lot of stress when we bought our house, which was a fixer-upper. At the same time, Ramsey's mother was diagnosed with Alzheimer's and was very sick, but was still denying there was a problem. Dealing with his mother, his last living parent, caused an identity crisis for him, and he was very angry. His frustrations were misdirected toward me, which made me feel picked on, and it was becoming hard to live happily. We were in therapy, and I was trying to decide what to do. Then I made the decision that I was going to work on it. For me, not to be on the fence anymore freed me from focusing just on my own personal pain and me me me. It made me focus on 'what are we going to do together?' instead of being adversarial and taking matters so subjectively.

"Ramsey is a very loyal person, and he wasn't ever interested in talking about breaking up. Another part was that he was willing to deal with it in therapy. Eventually, the house got fixed up, we consolidated a lot of our debts, and we made a lot more money. And as lame as it sounds, one of the things that we did was get someone to clean our house for us. Paying for help took a lot of pressure off both of us."

When his rent was raised, Tina Tessina's husband lost his dance studio and had to go to work for someone else. He hated it. This tossed him straight into one of those life-reevaluation crises. At the same time, Tina was grieving the death of a deeply loved dog. "He began neglecting me and the house," says Tina, "and I started feeling like I was part of the problem in his life." Instead of splitting, though, they went to a therapist, who reminded them of the importance of listening to one another, "instead of Richard focusing on his agenda and me on mine," says Tina. "Going through that was what really cemented our 'this is how we deal with bad stuff' thing."

## RECAP: FROM LOW POINT TO FLOW

A firm commitment to remain together and work things through—come hell or high water, so to speak—has helped most of the couples I interviewed overcome difficulties and reexperience flow. And although researchers have divided commitment into three components—personal dedication and love toward one's partner, a sense of obligation, and fear of the consequences of splitting up—the couples I spoke with all discussed commitment in terms of devotion to the partner and the relationship.

What the most flexible couples seemingly write between the lines of their marital contract is that they'll keep revising the agreement as they go along, and that they'll continue to support one another as they evolve. A woman with a long-lasting and essentially gratifying marriage told me, "I might go live in another country, but divorce? Never."

"A marital promise must be made to withstand and weather all human emotions, and inhuman ones as well," insists Frank Pittman in his pithily titled *Grow Up!* "It must withstand change, aging, loss of youth, loss of beauty, loss of youthful hopes, and a lifetime of disappointment. But if that promise is made to hold, one is never alone, never in despair, never lost in the universe. One always has a home."

Resilient couples believe in their ability to modify their environment rather than feeling helpless, and they know that change happens and, in fact, it must if they are to grow. They take responsibility for creating the lives they want. This vital hardiness isn't a trait that is either inborn or necessarily developed in childhood: it can be adopted as an attitude at any stage of life.

In summary, then, here's what the happiest couples do when confronted by a potential crisis:

- **They don't use denial often or for long.** Denial can be a temporary coping mechanism, a way to reduce stress briefly: What? Me worry? While such short-term denial may be useful in giving individuals time to recognize the problem, it only leads to greater distress later on. By facing up to problems early, effective couples avoid some crises altogether.

- **They don't universalize.** That is, when bad things happen, they don't assume the worst case scenario, i.e., this whole mess is just too huge to deal with, we'll never get through it, we're doomed as a couple. Rather, they summon the skills of optimism, explore what they can do to effect change, and take action. Sometimes they are able to reframe negatives as a chance for development.

- **They don't blame one another** for events outside the control of either partner, and they don't let each other blame themselves. They share their feelings, including anger and disappointment, and don't allow such negatives to dominate their lives.

- **They are self-aware and flexible,** understanding that bad days don't last forever. Surprises don't throw them off irremediably. They realize, on some level, that relationships are subject to chaos theory: they are systems continually going through change and turbulence, stabilizing and destabilizing cyclically. Satisfaction levels go up and down as the equilibrium shifts, as daily, weekly, or seasonal moods swing, as external events exert more or less pressure on the unit, as the childrearing years take their toll, and as normal developmental change occurs. They know intuitively what recent research has confirmed, that before long they'll be fine again. After all, more than four-fifths of those in a national survey who said they were unhappily married indicated they were happier when re-interviewed five years later.

#  HOLDING ON, LETTING GO

It is not true that people in long marriages dissolve into each other, becoming one being. I touch Tom's elbow, the sleeve of his tan jacket; he places his long arms around me and his hands cup my breasts in the friendliest possible way. We are two people in a snapshot, but with a little cropping we could each exist on our own. But that's not what we want. Hold the frame still, contain us, the two of us together, that's what we ask for. This is all it takes to keep the world from exploding.

—Carol Shields, *Unless*

The couple in flow exists within a constant equilibrium. It's like a friendly game of tug-of-war, except you are not on opposite sides. Either you both win or no one wins. When should you hold tightly, metaphorically speaking, and when would it be better to loosen up, perhaps let go? How do you balance the stimulation of novelty, growth, and change with the deep comforts of routine and ritual? The next three chapters explore these questions.

Have you ever noticed another couple who appear to be amazingly close, relaxed, and connected, as though they must have the independence vs. autonomy quandary fully worked out? Perhaps you've wondered if it's possible to remain always in such a smooth state. You can't avoid the ebb and keep only the flow, point out Richard Schwartz, M.D., and Jacqueline Olds, M.D., in *Marriage in Motion: The Natural Ebb and Flow of Lasting Relationships*. Although, according to the authors, such closeness may only be possible intermittently—on a vacation or during a shared project—I believe you can learn how to make such flowing moments and hours occur much more often in your daily life together.

Author Sam Keen writes that he was told by his mother that love is "the willed intent of the heart." He elaborates, "Sometimes it seems love is pure grace, easy as falling, effortless as flowing. Sometimes it is hard work, hammer and tongs, the gradual forging of something of fragile beauty from steel and bronze. Love is given, *and* it must be made."

Loving in flow is all about coordinating and integrating a range of seeming opposites. On an everyday level, this isn't mystical, but practical.

## INTIMACY: RISKS & REWARDS

Passion scores high, but intimacy rates highest. That's what Robert J. Sternberg found in a survey of marital satisfaction among 101 adults who'd been together for one to forty-two years.

Intimacy is being fully known by another person and being loved because of who you are—as well as in spite of it. This requires taking a leap into rare honesty and allowing yourself to be vulnerable. The deeper the intimacy, the more you'll have that pleasurable experience of total absorption with your lover, in and out of bed, existing in what feels like a timeless state, which is one of the hallmarks of flow experiences.

Relationships move from one level to another as a result of intimacy. The more we disclose, the closer we feel. "Intimacy is a process of discovery with another," writes Joel B. Bennett in *Time and Intimacy: A New Science of Personal Relationships*. Over time, though, without continued attentiveness, it is easy to lose that urge to keep discovering all there is to know about one another. People who psychologists have dubbed "openers" have intimate conversations with others because something about them encourages disclosure. These researchers found that in long-term relationships, high-openers were preferred to low-openers. Those who don't open up or make it easy for others to do so, known as high self-monitors, have a more difficult time with close relationships.

People vary in the strength of their intimacy needs: how much intimacy they require to avoid loneliness, and how much they can tolerate before feeling saturated. Those of us with stronger needs will expend more effort to ensure intimate contact with our partners by listening more closely and encouraging our partners to be more expressive. If our needs are weaker, then there will be a weaker correlation between intimacy and relationship satisfaction. In other words, if you don't crave total closeness, then you probably won't mind if your partner isn't that keen on sharing his or her own inner life. Mismatched couples are the ones who suffer most.

I asked all the people I interviewed to describe when they feel most intimate with their partner. Some of their answers might seem surprisingly ordinary—but only if you've never had a gratifying long-term relationship of your own.

"I believe we're soulmates," Bea tells me. "I'm not sure what that means, except that I look at Herb and think, 'You're really my best friend, I love you forever.' Sometimes I look at him and, for a moment, I wonder who he is, but then we're almost like one again."

For some, it's that sense of being "home" in the presence of your mate that captures the essence of intimacy. Similarly, it may be an increased sense of relaxed pleasure—a rapturous sigh from deep within—when you see your loved one's face after an absence: "If I'm out and coming back home and Jim is here," says Zhita Rea, "this is my haven. When I see him in a crowd or walking through the front door, I want to go up and hug him. One of the best parts of the day is getting in bed at night and hugging. Just being in each other's arms is reassuring, lovely, comforting."

The majority of couples told me that they don't have to be doing anything special to feel closest to one another. Typically it's "sitting around doing nothing," as Tina Tessina puts it. "It's nice just sitting there surrounded by the two dogs and the cat and watching television," she says. "Sometimes there's a real warmth that comes over me about how wonderful it all is, and I feel very close to Richard."

Naomi shared with me several instances where she and Janice feel closest, from cuddling and snuggling to when they have a productive talk about a matter on which they disagree. "Also when we produce something together. 'Raising' of the cats, doing something nice for friends or family. Like when we're in sync about 'let's do such-and-such for so-and-so.' Or when we want to do something anonymous for a charity, one or the other will come up with it, we'll talk it over and realize we like that idea and want to do it together."

When I ask Lou Owensby what intimacy means to her, her response is immediate: "The way Omar Sharif looks at women. It's the eyes, it's that intense 'You are everything to me' look. Norman doesn't do that anymore." She's laughing, though, and it's obvious she knows she's fantasizing. When I press her for what intimacy means in the context of her relationship with Norman, she tells me that they're each other's best friend, and "we also know without question that if one or the other of us needs or wants something, then the other will knock themselves out doing it."

Letting go into total intimacy takes trust, and sometimes that takes time, or in some instances, a particular defining moment. George Seeds Sr. told me that he'd been single for about a decade after his first unsatisfying marriage. Though he dated a lot, he'd given up on meeting anyone who might inspire that "this is it" feeling—until he saw Norma at a friend's house. "Within a week or so we were living together," he says. But, as Seeds explains, genuine closeness was much more difficult for him. Very early in the relationship, they spent one fateful evening in his apartment.

"We talked very seriously about our relationship, and I started getting very frightened. We were sitting on the floor, and without realizing it, I kept moving away from her until I was fifteen to twenty feet away. She said, "Now why don't we try to get closer?" So I spent the next three hours moving toward her, and then back, then toward, and I'd get frightened, and then back. And she kept saying, "Don't be scared."

"I had this fear that I was going to be hurt the way I'd been hurt by my mother. Norma helped by saying, "Come as far forward as you're comfortable with," and I'd move forward less than a foot. We were physically intimate at that time, but this was a deeper intimacy we were aiming for, a complete acceptance of the other person.

"Later I made the connection to why I was so fearful. When I was about four years old, I had such a longing to love my mother and have her love me, but she was always busy. One time I ran up to her while she was doing dishes, and I threw my arms around her knees and hung on them. I said, 'Oh, Mommy, I love you, I love you, I love you so much,' and she turned around on me, and with this anger in her eyes she said, 'Quit bothering me. Go away. Can't you find something else to do than bother me?' I was just stunned. I felt dizzy and lightheaded, and I got to the hallway and I sat down and thought my heart would break. So I told myself at that time that nobody would ever do that to me again.

"That night with Norma was a major breakthrough. We finally came together in the middle of the room and held each other for a while, and I told her I wanted to live with her forever. That sustained us through the next twenty-six years."

Relaxed leisure time, deep conversations, and trust are only part of the intimacy story. According to Robert J. Sternberg, who has studied how love changes over time, our interactions in close relationships tend to go along in well-worn grooves, called scripts. Most emotion is the result of some interruption in that common pattern. Keep doing the same old thing, and no emotion is experienced, but stop what you've always done, and suddenly someone *feels*. When we're unknown to one another, everything we learn is unexpected, resulting in intense emotion. Then gradually over time we become predictable to one another.

The plus side of this predictability, as Sternberg discusses, is that it leads to intimacy, and "the partners are so connected with each other that the one doesn't recognize the other is there, just as the air we breathe can be taken for granted, despite its necessity to life."

Sternberg says you can find out if the relationship is "live" by generating an unexpected bit of emotion, such as by one of you going away, however briefly, or by vacationing together. But sometimes it takes extreme action to realize how much intimacy there is, or was. Sternberg makes the sound suggestion that you plan for occasional minor interruptions so you don't need a major one to wake you up. Consider making some change in your routine that allows you undistracted time to freshly notice one another and those qualities that initially drew you together. Intimacy that doesn't renew itself regularly tends to deteriorate.

Susan Tyler Hitchcock describes how they fortuitously hit on an unusual solution to a near-crisis borne of their growing disconnection. Since her husband David had been a teenager, he'd dreamed of sailing the Caribbean. A few years into their somewhat stale marriage, he suggested such a trip as a family project. Susan responded with an immediate "Yes!" They borrowed a boat, removed their children from school, and sailed the Caribbean for an entire school year.

As soon as they made the commitment and began planning the extensive journey, they felt "pulled together," says Susan. A joint project, one that is complex, novel, exciting, and fun, can be a superb way to reconnect a couple who have drifted into living separate lives. An earlier relationship of David's had involved working in a lab and writing papers together with his partner. He had frequently mentioned to Susan how gratifying that had been to him at the time. It was about "having something bigger than just…" she tries to explain. Though they had built a house together, that wasn't what he meant. This sailing trip was perfect.

The most lasting advantage of the trip, and some shorter ones that came later in the marriage, was to improve communication, and thus intimacy. "One of our patterns," explains Susan, "was that if I expressed anger or disappointment, David had a tendency to withdraw first emotionally, then physically. He would become absent even though he was there." And her habit had been to become fearful of the confrontation, figure she'd been pushing too hard, and drop the conversation altogether.

Now imagine the confines of a sailboat. Susan found that the space limitations "made it easier for me to keep at him, since he couldn't just walk away." Although she acknowledges that it sounds awful put that way, somehow it worked and they were able to communicate at a deeper and more honest level. They learned details about each other's inner lives on that trip that have changed their attitudes toward one another and halted what was becoming a long, slow estrangement.

Whether at sea or on land, some individuals are not comfortable with a communicate-what-you-feel style of intimacy. What if you are part of such a mismatched couple, where you crave a deeper level of communicative openness than your partner ever will? Comfort levels with verbal sharing typically do increase with practice in an emotionally safe context, so learn to become a non-judgmental listener. In addition, it may only be fair for the free-and-easy-talker to recognize and give credit to the other's preferred modes of expression. Women tend to equate communication with intimacy; more than two-thirds of the divorced couples in one study say they didn't get the level of conversation that they'd expected in their marriages. The women complained they wanted to talk about negatives as well as positives, and they especially wanted to talk about work. They said the "give and take," the emotional exchange, was missing for them.

Only one-third of the men in that sample said they didn't get the emotional intimacy they wanted. What some of the men missed, though, was for their wives "to be there for them in much fuller ways." They wanted concrete demonstrations of intimacy such as being kissed and asked how they are at the end of the day, and being greeted with open arms at the door. Such desires are as valid as the urge to talk and be heard. As long as the less articulate demonstrate their love in their own ways, they deserve credit for their thoughtful behavior, as well as extra patience and understanding on the part of the talk-deprived.

## HOW HONEST?

> I had been the man I had become over the years with Astrid, but
> I had only been that man because I believed she knew all there
> was to know about him....I had always been afraid of the
> thought that there might be something I hadn't managed to tell
> or show her, something she had not seen or seen through. I only
> dared to believe in her love if I could count on her loving me
> despite all she knew about me, despite all my faults and failings.
> —Jens Christian Grondahl, *Silence in October*

How honest do you have to be in order to reach the more transcendent stage of intimacy and loving in flow? Very. As Ida puts
it, "I tell Sam absolutely everything and he does the same with
me. This is the first relationship I've ever had where that's true. I
have never felt so safe in my life."

Those couples who don't dare open up about what *isn't* working for them are sending out warnings about the vulnerability of
their relationship. One woman told me, "Talking about what
you don't like is opening up a hornet's nest." Another said,
"When you talk about your relationship, that's when it starts to
go bad." But those couples who don't share the negatives, keeping their annoyances to themselves, sustain a fragile status quo.

Are there significant topics you hesitate to approach with
your partner? Think about what you say to yourself when you're
having those inner conversations we all have. Are there secrets
you would unburden to a friend but not your mate? It struck one
wife, about two years into her marriage, that she could get naked
in front of her husband, but that she was unable to tell him her
feelings. She decided those barriers had to come down.

Tom Greenspon tells how it used to be hard for him to
express anger until he realized that it's more honest to share your
concerns than to keep your partner guessing about what you're
experiencing. How can your mate change behavior that's distressing you if you're silent about it? Over a long period, explains

Tom, his wife has learned to ask him what he is thinking. "I couldn't have asked in an easy way and he wouldn't have heard me in the same non-threatening way ten years ago," Barbara admits. "I let him know that when he tells me some of his thoughts, it helps me feel less alone."

Barbara enjoys sharing a particular turning point the couple experienced: "Tom was always the one who didn't express anger, and I was the one whose role it was to show anger, so then we could argue and fix things. One day after we were married fifteen years, he got mad at me first and overtly picked a fight. I was standing at the sink scrubbing potatoes, and he came in and yelled something, and I put the potato scraper down and put my wet hands on my hips and said, 'How dare you yell at me?' I picked up the car keys, left the house, and drove around the block, thinking, 'Who the hell does he think he is?!' As I came around the block, I thought, 'Oh. My. God.' I came back in the house and said, 'I'm really sorry. I've been asking for this for years.'" Because it's not hard for Barbara to admit she's wrong and sorry, this incident, ironically, made it safer for Tom rather than less safe. "I did 'lose it,' but we were able to understand immediately what happened and take steps to improve things," Barbara explains.

Of course, not all happy couples swear by 100 percent honesty at all times. One startling piece of research revealed that in relationships with spouses, a lie was involved in one out of ten social interactions. Since that study was based on diary entries kept by volunteers, it's possible that the actual rates of fib-telling might be even higher—or perhaps it might have been lower if the researchers had focused only on the happiest of long-marrieds. Realize, too, that many of the lies reported were the so-called altruistic kind, where, for example, agreement with a partner's opinion would be faked in order to show caring and concern. One implication, according to the psychologists, is that acts that are seen to benefit one's partner, such as a minor other-oriented lie, also profit the relationship, and thus yourself. In other words, when your partner feels good, you both feel good. But—and this is important—it is also possible to show genuine caring by *not* pretending you feel what you don't feel.

You might make a case for leaving out a few details, though, considering that intimacy derives more from honesty about emotion than from burbling every scrap of fact. While some individuals want to know all the details about a mate's former life, for instance, Sol Gordon told me that he and his wife didn't feel it was necessary to tell each other about their marital histories: "We stayed very much in the present."

Tina Tessina partakes of a pedestrian sort of convenient omitting: "My secrets would only be dumb stuff like maybe I spend more at the cosmetics counter than I think he will feel comfortable with, so I don't talk to him about that. He knows I don't always tell the truth about purchases. He'll sometimes say, 'You paid *what* for this?' So I avoid the hassle. He trusts me to tell him the truth on anything important. It's just when I don't want to have to deal with his comments. I usually don't outright lie—I just avoid it."

Of course, not every passing thought must be told—no more than you are required by the ethics of honesty to tell every dream that flits through your subconscious. Stephen and I once had a lengthy conversation with a gorgeous, tall, young, and Irish male neighbor. He has a delightful accent and shiny long black hair. I later mentioned to Stephen, "He has those chiseled looks you see on the covers of romance novels." He agreed. And then I stopped blathering about this fellow's looks.

Stephen is rarely jealous of passing attractions, but I know how *I'd* feel, and I wouldn't want to push to the point where he *would* feel a twinge of jealousy. Sometimes when I'm with Stephen, I'll notice an unusually shapely woman in the street. I assume he'll notice, too, so I look at him and smile and he looks at me and nothing needs to be said. I feel I'm acknowledging the woman's attractiveness and his normal response to her. Leaving certain things unsaid is occasionally the most loving—and intimate—way to behave.

Couples struggle over the divulging of details related to affairs. We have already discussed this subject, but I'll add here that no firm rules can be set that apply to everyone in all circumstances. Kaitlin, who came very close to having a serious affair before patching up her marriage with Mark, is troubled that his refusal to allow her to "tell all" may reduce their intimacy by a few degrees. "Overall," she concedes, "I don't necessarily think it's a bad thing to not know everything. I think we all have secret places inside of us. I just still feel a little guilt because I am such an open and honest person." Mark may believe more went on than did, but his fears have kept that final onion-layer-thin barrier up between him and Kaitlin. She accepts this as a price she must pay for her husband's comfort.

## LOVE ME, LOVE MY CREATURE RELEASE MECHANISMS

> He bent over the sink, lathering his face, blathering and spluttering, sticking his index fingers into his ears and waggling them. Then, after rinsing the soap off, he placed one forefinger over each nostril in turn and slung great gobs of green snot into the sink.
>
> Prior, his elbow touching his mother's side, felt her quiver fastidiously....
>
> It takes a great deal of aggression to quiver fastidiously for twenty-eight years.
>
> —Pat Barker, *The Eye in the Door*

Some couples believe that full intimacy includes benign tolerance of each other's scents, sounds, and random movements. Others feel it's disrespectful and anti-erotic to exhibit so-called creature release mechanisms in the presence of one's beloved.

Some advice I read in a sex guide back when I had barely entered puberty has stuck with me: if you love someone and his breath bothers you, give him breath mints. If you're bothered by a minor aspect of your partner's body, consider whether there's an emotional component. When you're enraptured with someone, smoky breath or a mutant nose hair probably will go unnoticed. Still, we do need to respect each other's sensitivities—some people are highly attuned to scent, others to sound, yet others to body hair. If you must have a sparkly clean and sweet-scented partner before you can relax into feeling sensual, speak up gently and take responsibility for your likes and dislikes. Such preferences aren't universal: they're influenced by our childhoods and the culture we live in.

One set of researchers went so far as to posit—and prove to their own satisfaction—that individuals who are more neurotic have more problems with the physicality of sex because it evokes their deep fear of death. Quite a leap? Not necessarily, as they explain: "Sex is problematic...because it is a creaturely physical act that reminds us of our animal nature and thus of our ultimate mortality." That may be why, suggest these psychologists, we romanticize sex and give it symbolic meanings beyond being a mere animal act aimed at reproducing the species. The more secure an individual is about his or her sexuality, the less the physical aspects are off-putting.

Of course, this needn't imply that you or your relationship are lacking if you're physically reserved. In fact, I found a continuum of attitudes toward creature release mechanisms among my sample of mates.

Sherry Suib Cohen is one of those who strongly believes in what she calls privacy. She says she'd rather die than use the bathroom together with her mate, as some of her friends do with their husbands. "It seems to me that the dearest familiarity can be shattered by a certain kind of coarseness, a lack of modesty. True intimacy requires a dollop of mystery," she writes in her memoir.

For myself, I've relaxed in areas that I have limited control over, so that when I drink diet soda, for example, air travels backwards up from my esophagus and escapes. Stephen likes to identify these eruptions as he hears them. The other evening we were reading together in the living room when I released a long, slow belch. He looked up from his book, turned his head to the left as if thinking hard, then said, "A nice woodland brook." And then, a moment later, "with decomposing frog."

## HEY MOM, HIS BOUNDARY IS TOUCHING MINE

> "Well," said Mr. Parsons, "perhaps you could tell us how one person hands his soul, I think you called it, over to someone else. It is a farfetched idea, is it not?" "Not to a superintendent of an asylum," said the doctor. "The person simply mistakes someone else for himself. He believes the other person is part of him. We see *that* every day at the asylum. We see it in lovers as well. They often say that 'I belong to you,' or 'you belong to me' and nothing is wrong with it. It is the size and nature of the mistake which determines its pathological nature. Lovers still know they are two people."
>
> —Susan Fromberg Schaeffer, *The Madness of a Seduced Woman*

When you think about boundaries in your most intimate relationship, what image comes to mind? Is it a fence with barbed wire that separates you and your partner, or is it more amorphous, like a scrap of fraying cheesecloth, that keeps you from total overlap? Either can work equally well, as long as it suits the world you've jointly created with your lover. Philosopher Robert C. Solomon calls this "the loveworld, in which we play the roles of lovers and, quite literally, create our selves as well."

This loveworld is always changing in order to maintain itself. When one of you does something, the other reacts to keep the equilibrium constant, providing a sustainable and reasonably comfortable homeostasis between personal freedom and what Solomon calls the "ideal of an eternal merger of souls." Just as children are sometimes asked by adults to draw their families so we can get a clearer idea about how the child perceives her place vis-à-vis the other members, you and your partner may be enlightened if you draw your marriage. If you use circles to represent each of you as individuals, do the circles overlap to the same degree in each of your drawings? Don't be surprised if your perceptions don't match up precisely.

Can you separate your thoughts from your partner's, or do you always believe he feels (or should feel) as you do? Don't take it to heart if you occasionally confuse which one of you made a particular comment. At least not unless you take it to extremes, as in the *New Yorker* cartoon in which a husband says to his wife, "I can't remember which one of us is me."

Even so, those areas where you *do* overlap often bring the most pleasure to a relationship. A theme emerged among some of the happiest couples I interviewed: sheer delight in the joint marital "self." Christine expresses it this way: "We're very close, very compatible. Everything we do, literally, we do it together, even going to the cleaners, to the grocery, or to buy gas for the car. We're just like one person."

Other couples attribute their marital longevity to the right amount of separateness. When I ask Zhita Rea if she and Jim find the prospect of losing one another terrifying (Jim recently had a cancer scare), she responds, "We've had these wonderful years together and marvelous memories. Neither of us is eager to be alone, but it's not a scary place, I think, for either of us. I guess that's partly because each of us has a life as an individual as well as as a partner. That's part of the strength of the partnership. But that also allows you to know that you can continue on."

Whether you're an advocate of plenty of togetherness or you insist on huge dollops of autonomy, sometimes boundary issues turn up where you least expect them to—such as on the desk in the study. When Rose would move her husband Morty's pen from his desk, he would get furious. It's not that he minded her using it, he insisted, but that he felt Rose was being disrespectful to move it. "If he moved *my* things," says Rose, "it wouldn't even occur to me to see it as disrespect. For him, it brought up the memory of how his mother would go into his room and 'fix' it her own way." When she understood, Rose exerted extra effort to remember to leave the pen on her husband's desk. "Sometimes I truly forgot, because I was so busy with twenty things, and he'd say, 'My pen.' I'd say, 'I'm sorry. I'm trying, I'm trying.' He never got mad again once he realized that it had nothing to do with respecting his things. We would laugh about it."

As Ida and Sam are so different from one another, they had to develop dramatic ways to respect each other's space: separate studies, separate TV rooms, separate computers. "The first six months we had to figure out how to live together," admits Ida. "I thought, 'This is impossible. We're so different, my God, we'll *never* pull this thing off.' But we had room, space, and money, which are nice assets."

According to Ida, they're both strong-willed. "We feel opposite on almost everything, except the basic values. Now that's the key. We never have a cross word about anything that's the slightest bit important. I'm more liberal than Sam about people and things, and he's more Southern in some of his judgments, but here's the beauty: I can feel the way I feel, that's okay with him. I don't feel any necessity to change or apologize for the way I feel. He'll tell me, 'You're pissing me off,' and I'll think about it, and I'll say, 'You're absolutely right, I'm being a pain." And I'm more high-strung in my reactions, and he just laughs and thinks I'm funny. And then I start to laugh, because it *is* stupid. His eyes twinkle, he'll hold out his arms and he'll say, 'You know, you're really silly,' and I'll start to laugh, because he's right."

Now that Sam is struggling with serious health problems, Ida's challenge is to not turn into his mother. "I was never a nagging mom, at least my kids tell me I wasn't, but I'll say, 'Sam, did you take your insulin?' There's a line there and I'm sloppy about it and I'm aware of it. I can see it in his face. Or he'll say, 'I'm a big boy now.'"

Sam says his reaction, when Ida over-caretakes, is to "shoot her a finger or something. I just let her know." Here he laughs good-naturedly. "I don't like to be babied. I never have when I was sick. I like to be left alone. Check on me once in a while."

It helps to be aware that when one partner is the overdoer and "parents" the other who takes on a child role, the caretaker is also getting dependency needs met. Notice what roles you're slipping into. It could be that when one of you caretakes a great deal, it sets off alarms in a partner whose parent smothered when she nurtured.

Jeanette points out that one of the reasons her long marriage to Bob has functioned is that they started out as two independent people with independent lives, "and we never had a big batch of demands of togetherness. We give each other enough space." One half-century-married couple (not among my interviewees) takes this "space" rule literally: they sit in separate aisles of the plane when they travel. "A stranger won't cramp my armrest space, but my husband does," explains the wife.

Familiar boundaries may shift as one of you might need to regress a bit under stress, notes Marion F. Solomon, author of *Narcissism and Intimacy*. One woman used to tell her affection-starved husband, "Don't be a baby." Solomon adds that in a functional relationship, individuals can heal each other by allowing childlike needs to be expressed and at least partially filled (with no hard feelings if they can't be altogether met). That way, your marriage is a genuine comfort zone. Solomon writes that partners, when first together, establish homeostasis, keeping things from becoming too hot or enmeshed, or too cold and distant. A great deal of couple conflict is over one partner's efforts to pull away and the other's efforts to keep him from doing so for fear of loneliness and abandonment. Intimacy is positive when you want it but feels intrusive when it crosses your boundary of the moment. That boundary must remain a shifting one that feels acceptable to both partners most of the time.

In order for that boundary to shift in ways that don't crush either of you, it helps for each partner to have a sturdy sense of self. To determine your ego strength or level of differentiation, Peter D. Kramer suggests this test: how long can you spend in your parents' home without reverting to your childhood self, stuck in the old scenarios, and also without emotionally shutting out the other family members? Parents of grown children might pose themselves an analogous question: do you revert to parenting behavior when your child is there? Or can you maintain your current self? It's common knowledge in the psychotherapeutic community that people tend to seek a partner at the same level of differentiation. It's not that we choose wrongly, but rather that we're choosing precisely, even when it might seem we've made a weird and dysfunctional match.

The healthiest boundaries are achieved when neither of you is overly controlling or judgmental of your mate. One of the best facets of her husband's behavior toward her, says Sherry Suib Cohen, is that he never attacks or judges her. "This is the secret of my marriage. He is not a judgmental person. I'm *very* critical, *very* controlling, but due to his marvelous example, I never say to him anymore, 'Why don't you do this, why don't you do that?' Whatever he wants is fine with me."

Cohen offers an example: "I used to want him to change his style of dress a little. He's been dressing Brooks Brothers since he was 18 years old: very conservative, just beautiful, but always the same. 'Could I buy you a black turtleneck? Please, I'll give you a thousand dollars,' I tell him. Nooo. He's very strong."

Cohen's husband is matched by Jeanette in that when *her* husband attempts to exert control, she resists. "I don't know if controlling is the right word," she clarifies. "He has strong opinions. Controlling implies that one allows themself to be controlled. It's not a problem, probably because I have a strong enough sense of myself. I think if I wasn't as strong in some ways as I am, his being so opinionated may have been a bad thing."

Couples like these may struggle with control issues for many years before they find a set of boundaries that suits both parties. But once they have settled on an agreeable balance, each one knows quickly—or is notified—when he or she has overstepped a line and brings the offending toe back a few inches.

## WHAT'S RESPECT GOT TO DO WITH IT?

> On our wedding day, the vicar asked us...to respect one another's thoughts, ideas, and suggestions. At the time, this seemed an unexceptionable request, easily granted. David, for example, suggests going to a restaurant, and I say, "OK, then." Or he has an idea for my birthday present. That sort of thing. Now I realize that there are all sorts of suggestions a husband might make to a wife, and not all of them are worthy of respect. He might suggest that we eat something awful, like sheep's brains, or form a neo-Nazi party.
>
> —Nick Hornby, *How to Be Good*

You may have noticed that in the previous two sections, both men and women often used the word "respect" in regards to all types of personal boundaries. Indeed, respect appears on many of the top ten lists compiled by lasting couples. But it isn't a word Stephen and I have ever paid attention to in our own marriage, and I began to ponder what its actual meanings might be. Whenever one of my interviewees spontaneously claimed that respect was one of the cornerstones of their success as a couple, I asked for more detail. I'd thought of respect as more akin to good manners than to genuine loving—that is, you'd notice its absence, but not necessarily its presence.

I was pleased to see that Robert C. Solomon agrees, stating that "love requires equals. Respect, common wisdom aside, seems to have very little to do with love, although to be sure one would hardly want to be in love without it." Respect, after all, seems to refer more to social and public status than to the personal.

For our purposes here, I'll allow more leeway when defining respect since I discovered it is used by loving couples to represent a range of considerate behaviors. The Owensbys, for example, explained that they both respect each other's vulnerable spots. "For Norman," says Lou, "because of his first wife having an affair, I know that's a big issue for him. And for me, he knows that being second-best and being discounted—I had a brother who was the favorite of the family—is my big one. What would not work would be if he would ever say, 'Oh, you don't know what you're talking about.'"

The Greenspons make it clear that respect, to them, involves each of them acknowledging that "anything we say is worth taking a look at. If I ever found fault with Tom, and believe me I have," says Barbara, "it was because I didn't feel he was paying attention to me, respecting me as a person. Coming from the childhood I came from, the deal was that being heard was respectful."

Howard rates respect as among the top five feelings he has for his wife. "Respect, to me," he explains, "is about acknowledging and backing the other person's stand or beliefs or behavior."

Respect takes on different nuances in private and in public. A partner's respect in public is especially noticeable when it's absent: when this person you've shared everything with turns on you and takes another's side against you, or laughs at you rather than with you. Many a heated discussion on the way home from parties could be avoided by working out in advance the ground rules for suitable jests about one's partner's personal habits. (I speak from experience.)

Jeanette attributes the few fights she and Bob have to her "getting pissed off if I don't feel adequately respected by him," such as when she's just spent two hours cooking a special meal and he makes a comment about how long it took. In fact, being taken for granted in *any* way annoys Jeanette.

"I feel it's a lack of respect when Bob leaves the milk out. If he leaves in the morning with his breakfast dishes strewn around the kitchen instead of putting them in the dishwasher, that might bother me. I'll usually put them away, but to me that's being taken for granted. But if he says something that I feel is a put-down about some opinion I've expressed, I will say, 'I didn't like what you just said,' or 'I don't appreciate that.' And he will almost always apologize immediately, saying, 'You're right,' or 'I didn't mean that.'"

Jeanette tempers her anger by acknowledging to herself how hard Bob's work days can be, with numerous people demanding his attention, and his having to watch people die and having to deal with grieving families. "It's hard to imagine what he goes through. Sometimes Bob will come home and I can tell that he's on edge, and I know that he's been emotionally assaulted all day long. I give him a *lot* of room and don't expect anything. But sometimes he'll get a little snippy. I won't get pissed about it, but I'll say, 'Listen, I know you had a really shitty day and I'm really sorry about that, but I'm not involved in that, so don't take it out on me. That's not what I'm here for.' And that's pretty much the end of it."

What is so marvelous about stable longterm relationships is that you repeatedly have the opportunity to revive your warmest feelings for one another, even if the equilibrium temporarily tips a bit too far one way or the other. Relationship flow is within reach if you're willing to accept the risks of intimacy and are able to be flexible about boundaries in ways that suit you as a couple. This balancing act sometimes requires conscious effort and attention, as we'll explore next.

# YOU LOVE WHAT YOU PAY ATTENTION TO

He was stroking my arm with one hand and peeling the label off his beer bottle with the other. The kind of absentmindedness I was used to....I was his wifely assumption.

—Charles Baxter, *The Feast of Love*

Obliviousness doesn't bode well for intimacy. When you begin responding to each other by rote—my wife is like this, my husband always does thus-and-so—you are no longer reacting to each other in the moment. But each day's experiences subtly change us. When an intimate thinks he or she knows what you're feeling based on how you reacted previously, you may feel misunderstood and unknown. To sustain love, you need to invest profound attention to the shifting complexity of your partner.

Can it ever be negative to pay attention to your relationship? One woman chose not to discuss what she called a "very good marriage in spite of problems" with me for this book because "once you talk to people about your marriage, then you break up." She may have been thinking of this phenomenon: the most unstable times are those when most couples pay the most attention to their relationship, looking at it from the outside instead of living inside it. But looking closely isn't what caused the instability. The happiest couples, in fact, tend to give more thorough answers when asked about their marriages; they're more aware of what pleases them.

# WATCHING ME WATCHING YOU

A couple is sitting on a sofa, looking into one another's eyes. One says, "I'll be right back—I'm going to blink."

—cartoon in *The New Yorker*

Do the best couples have any secret strategies for staying mindful and not taking one another for granted?

Naomi and Janice take pride in being unusually self-aware. They've each had therapy, though not couples counseling together. "We've also become aware of when we're *not* being self-aware," says Naomi. "We get into trouble in the relationship when we don't slow down and look at each other and find out 'How are you *really*?'"

The two women regularly go over their calendars to see what's coming up for the next couple of months. "Also, a few nights a week, once we get into bed, we'll say, 'Tell me what's been good,' or 'What's going on that's not good?'"

Such self- and other-awareness is incredibly effective, even in relationships that are already in excellent condition. When I checked with Naomi six months after our initial conversation, she told me she and Janice felt as though they've fallen in love again. "What makes me feel so good about us is that we communicate about personal and difficult topics more easily, more frequently, and more honestly than we ever did before," she explains. "This has been a journey (not to sound corny, but it's true) of self-exploration, making time, taking our relationship seriously. We're so aware of how enormously busy and stressful our lives and those of our dearest friends are, and of what could happen if we didn't take deliberate steps to nurture our relationships."

One psychologist wrote that we should try to be as sensitive to small changes in ourselves as we're taught to be with our cars, and as sensitive to tiny cues from others as a mother is to her baby. And Gottman's research with hundreds of couples in his lab has proven that partners who, when a bid is made for attention, turn toward each other—rather than ignoring the bid or turning against their mate—are far more likely to stay together. A bid for attention can be as minimal as a touch on the arm or a comment while reading the newspaper. Paying attention each time your partner reaches out in some tiny way, even if you must say, "Now's not a good time," shows courtesy and caring, and keeps you both current with each other's lives.

You might think this sort of attentiveness would get easier and more natural with the passing years. Not so. In fact, an unexpected correlation was discovered between how long couples had been married and empathic accuracy—how correctly they are able to assess the mental and emotional states of their partners on a day-to-day basis. Couples married a shorter time (the average in the group studied was about fifteen years of marriage) tended to be *more* accurate in their assessments. The less time you've known one another, the more intently you focus on the problems you're discussing. Over many years of marriage, the researchers concluded, "couples become less motivated in resolving disputes, their relationship theories become ossified, and they are more likely to assume that they know what their partners are thinking." So they pay less attention, don't work as hard cognitively, and they miss detecting the cues to their partners' mental states.

Psychiatrist Arnold M. Ludwig writes that his wife claims to know him better than he knows himself, which peeves him since he should be able to know himself best. After all, only *he* knows his innermost thoughts. The fact is that our mates judge us by our actions and thus find us more predictable than we expect. No matter how purposeful we think we're being, our lifemates see the patterns of how we act and begin to see those actions as dispositional traits, as who we are. Ludwig's wife has the advantage of being an observer so that she, like all alert spouses, can act like an experimenter. So it may be accurate that she knows him better. Still, expecting your mate to always read your mind or to do so at any one particular time would leave you frustrated as often as not. Nor is it normally helpful to point out that you know your lover better than he does himself—even if you're sure you do. Most people like to believe they can still surprise us. And, in truth, we can all still be surprised by what our mate does or thinks, so it's best to remain open to such possibility.

One of the oldest aphorisms is that a good relationship takes hard work. But I don't think work is the correct word. Relationships require patience and tolerance, which become habits, and they take paying attention, which is effortful. Another *New Yorker* cartoon shows a husband watching TV, and at the other end of the room his wife is talking to a friend on the sofa: "Frank and I used to work at our marriage. Now we're retired."

Retiring mentally isn't an option if you want to continue to enter flow together. Ellen J. Langer, psychologist and author of *Mindfulness,* speaks of how important it is to make the effort to *notice.* "When the target of our attention varies, it's easy and natural to concentrate and notice details and differences. When we get too used to something, it's much harder to focus on it and see it with fresh eyes. The trick is to keep looking for the new in the old."

The opposite of flow and being present in the moment are distraction and mindlessness. Leading up to my own marriage's lowest period, I once made a comprehensive list of where my time was spent. It showed me my priorities, whether they'd been conscious goals or not. Couple time was at the bottom.

There have been occasions in Barbara Greenspon's long marriage when she's had to shout, literally, for more attention to her needs. When she did that, Tom says, "We would then fight and argue about it, and I would have to think about what Barbara was asking of me. At one point I went to therapy about it." Their marriage eventually developed into a wonderfully rewarding one.

Even in passionately loving couples, it's not always easy to focus on what's going on emotionally right now. "The decision to pay attention to someone is the first act of self-limitation, the first sacrifice, the first gift we make in the name of love," writes Sam Keen. That's why it was so distressing—and so validating!—when researchers at the Indiana University School of Medicine recently reported what so many women have long suspected, that many men listen with only "half a brain." Radiologists had twenty men and twenty women, all healthy, listen to a John Grisham novel on tape, while functional magnetic resonance imaging (fMRI) measured high-speed changes in neural blood flow. In the majority of men, only the left side lit up, the half of the brain thought to be most responsible for verbal and logical activity. No credible scientist is claiming to know the full implications of this, though it is easy to speculate that perhaps women listen with more of their minds. To be fair, then, if a male says, "I *was* listening, dear, but I didn't get that bit," he may be telling the truth. Help him—and yourself—by clarifying what you meant.

Even if you miss an emotional cue in the moment, there's always hindsight. Look back—together—to figure out what happened between you so as not to make the same mistakes repeatedly. Alert couples don't have to make their parents' mistakes either. As Bob explains, "What made my own parents crazy were the same things over and over. My mother knew which button to push that would piss off my father, and my father knew which button to press to piss off my mother. And they kept using them. Jeanette and I have been very reflective about how the folks around us behaved, and we try hard not to do those things."

## THANKS FOR BEING YOU

Ten things I like about Martha. One: Her feet aren't webbed.... Okay, then start over. Martha, my dear, you are: 1. kind; 2. generous; 3. loving; 4. intelligent; 5. honest; 6. sensitive; 7. compassionate; 8. (I got stuck there at eight for a few seconds) beautiful; 9. enthusiastic; 10. hard-working. There. I had finished my assignment. I'd have the whole week to goof off.

—John Dufresne, *Love Warps the Mind a Little*

What have you noticed that's worth appreciating in your partner? A New York agent in a relationship for two years wryly shared with me her boyfriend's most "romantic" comment to her: "You never get on my nerves." She tried to take the quirky comment in the spirit in which it was offered.

Stephen spoke in a similar spirit the other day, when he described what he thinks my younger son would like in a mate: "What Kevin wants is some of the sparkle *you* have. It's a bristle-sparkle where each porcupine quill lights up at the end and you admire the beauty as you are being punctured." Rather than feeling offended at the ambivalent compliment, I enjoyed it—here was someone who is able to appreciate the opposing nuances of my personality.

Some people need—and are grateful for—appreciative comments from their spouses more than others. Ida, for instance, says that when she and Sam returned home after she gave a brief presentation at a meeting, he told her, "Do you know how beautifully you spoke? I'm proud to be your husband." "That carries you for six months," Ida says.

In some satisfied couples, you don't have to do anything out of the ordinary to get praised. Kaitlin says of her husband Mark: "He's somebody who says, when I make him a sandwich, 'Thank you so much!' I do his laundry, and he says, 'Aren't you the greatest?!' He thanks me for everything. I've always been that way with him also. I'm one of those wives who was always so grateful for what he did out in the world so I could be there for our kids. I'd say, 'Thank you—it must be so hard facing rush hour every day.'"

Margie praises her husband Frank a lot. "I'll compliment Frank about the way he looks and the way he does things that make me feel good." Frank admits he loves hearing such accolades, although he doesn't think about handing them out himself as regularly as he feels Margie would like. "It takes an active effort for me to praise. It's not that it bothers me to do it, but it wasn't done to me in a real sense as a kid, so I had to learn it."

It took time for me to catch on that Stephen enjoys being praised for any effort he makes to please me, even tidying up his own work-related paper piles. I used to think that if I gave in and made a fuss every time he did what he was supposed to do, that he'd become even more insatiable and I'd somehow spend all my energy thanking him. But we all expect to be treated with extra care around those areas in which we're most needy. Whereas I don't care if I'm thanked when I cook a tasty dinner, what I *do* relish is when my partner stops what he's doing and critiques what I've written. Then I try to remember to be appropriately effusive with my gratitude. When someone who needs praise gets it for pleasing a partner, rather than being taken for granted, he's much more likely to feel secure, loved, and willing to be generous himself more often.

Appreciation sometimes plays out in unexpected ways, reminiscent of a chess game played by mail. One afternoon, as I was reading a book by a noted sex therapist, I began to have passing doubts about the excellence of my own relationship, until I got to the part where the author admitted he sometimes isn't nice to his own wife when they're hiking and she lags behind. I thought about how at such times Stephen is *always* kind and compassionate toward me, a slacker in the recreational arts. I have dramatically slowed him down and derailed entire hikes before the halfway point with my city-bred complaints. I felt a rush of warm feeling toward Stephen. I went to where he was typing and kissed his neck and said, "I love you." He stayed focused on his screen.

About two hours later, he came into the study where I was working on my computer and asked, "What was *that* for?" I told him briefly—"You're so *nice* to me. You're nicer to me than the guy in the book I'm reading who thinks he's such a smarty-pants"—and he laughed delightedly and went off. The next morning as we left the house to get breakfast, he suddenly looked me in the eyes, kissed me, and said, "I love you."

Huh? What did I do? "Yesterday. I was busy when you came to me. But I heard you."

I think, though, that the most welcome type of appreciation—because it's unexpected—might be for some aspect of ourselves that less-loving others perceive as a flaw. As Marcel Proust wrote, "Not that the clear perception of certain weaknesses in those we love in any way diminishes our affection for them; rather that affection makes us find those weaknesses charming."

## TEN WAYS TO INCREASE MINDFULNESS

1. Schedule time for each other daily. Consider doing no work when you're home together, or at least on weekends: turn off the computer, deliberately switch mental gears and *be* together. A few focused hours a week can keep you genuinely connected. One recommended routine is to spend a couple of minutes talking just before parting each morning, becoming aware of what's going on in your partner's life that day.

2. Spend both quality *and* quantity time together. Grabbing a few minutes here and there might not keep your bond as strong as spending lengthier stretches together. Activities like tennis or bridge, taking a class together, or volunteering for the same committee can bring you closer.

3. Each of you sit down and write out, in as much detail as possible, how your partner spent the entire previous day, from waking up to bedtime. Such an exercise is akin to what artists and writers do to enhance their ability to improve memory and fine-tune detail observation. If this is difficult for you the first time you try it, you may pay more focused attention afterwards.

4. Sam Keen suggests in *To Love and Be Loved* that you pay meta-attention to what each of you usually notices and typically ignores. That is, talk about whether each of you most attends to things, people, ideas, money, family.

5. Come up with hypothetical "proof-of-life" questions for one another. Separately, compile a few items of intimate data that, if your mate was kidnapped and held for ransom, only he or she would know, thus proving his or her identity to your satisfaction. For example, what did his former girlfriend call his

bodily fluids? Where did you go on your first date? What song did her little sister sing to pester you when you visited?

6. At least once a week, thank each other for something. It might be a minor example of thoughtfulness from earlier that day (he offered to get you a snack), or it might be a kindness he performed years before, such as getting up much earlier than usual, without a hint of a grumble, to pick up your cousin from the airport. See if you can become so mindful that you find a behavior every day for which to express appreciation.

7. Next time you tell an anecdote about work or share some family gossip, purposely tell it differently. Add detail if you're usually succinct, or if you tend to meander, get immediately to the point this time. Tell your mate why this story is worth paying attention to before launching into it.

8. Play an adult version of "What's the Difference?" Choose some activity you share with your spouse, whether it's a walk around the block, a trip to the grocery store, a regular Sunday morning brunch with friends, or even...sex. This time, see how many differences you can point out. Are your friends displaying a new flag at their front door this week? Has one of the grocery clerks got purple hair today? Is your partner wearing perfume? If it's hardest to locate novelty when you play at home, each of you can *purposely* change something—a habit, a way of dressing or eating or moving—for the other to notice.

9. Add a dimension to the familiar by conferring about how your life would be different if you were from another culture, fresh off the boat, so to speak, or just arrived from another planet.

10. Be aware of and discuss the cycles of relationships in general, and notice the cycles of your own unique partnership. That way, neither of you is disconcerted by temporary shifts in closeness, nor are you likely to drift too far apart before taking corrective action.

# THE POWER OF PLAY

> Thus began their private history, the gathering of sayings and
> jokes that belonged to them, that had no currency anywhere
> else.
>
> —Jane Hamilton, *Disobedience*

Never mistake fun and play for trivial concepts. The sharing of
laughter is one of the most potent expressions—and precursors—
of intimacy there is. Play is a way of raising the stimulation level
that often results in delicious moments of flow. It is also a way of
accessing some of the creativity needed to maintain balance
within a couple. As William Betcher puts it in *Intimate Play*, "Play
can help couples to invent creative solutions. Intimate play is ide-
ally suited to the holding together of apparently mutually exclu-
sive alternatives. It embodies the flexibility and humor that
couples must cultivate in order to reconcile conflicting needs."

It's the spur-of-the-moment play that many of us would miss
most if our relationships were to end, because we could never
recapture this unique way of relating with anyone else. At the
most vulnerable heart of intimacy is where we find these playfully
outrageous exchanges. We keep this banter out of public hearing,
including all non-intimate family members. The funny animal
noises, the baby talk, the raunchy allusions, the risqué gestures,
the pretend brutishness: you can't get any more personal than
this. When outsiders witness this silly, sappy loveworld, they're

often embarrassed, if not slightly disturbed. Not until you feel utterly safe can you relax this way. And when you feel a bit unsafe, say when the two of you have been arguing, you may hold off sharing these jokey intimacies. In effect, your lover becomes, however briefly, more like a stranger than a trusted playmate.

## SCHRÖDINGER'S BUNNY: LAUGHING AT OURSELVES

Adult play isn't often studied because its nature is so private. Like Schrödinger's famous thought experiment in physics: a cat is in a special box, and it's neither dead nor alive until you open the box, so that you affect the result by opening the box. Similarly, exposing your most intimate quips to the world can be as risky as revealing your innermost fantasies. You may find a dead cat—or bunny—the next time you look.

I think that's why some of the couples I ask about their play habits tell me they had never given much thought to the subject. One or two respond, "You mean like golf?" After I'd give them an example from my own life, they would laugh and say, "Oh, sure, we do stuff like that all the time."

A shared sense of humor is regularly given credit for much of the longevity of a relationship. Laughter can be a way out of a potential cycle of negative feelings. Says Jeanette, "Our way is to say, 'Oh, don't take yourself so seriously." Another woman says her husband makes her laugh when she becomes uptight.

Sometimes an adult twist adds spice. "We feel closest when we're playing together," says Frieda. "It's nothing for us to chase each other around the house like kids. I love to pat my husband on the butt." Here she laughs from remembered pleasure tinged with embarrassment: couple play is normally as confidential as sexual intimacy—and sometimes leads to it.

"Half of our sex is play, silliness," admits Tina Tessina. "I think that's one of the things that happens to passion. You can't sustain passion over twenty years. I think it becomes humor if things go well. You don't always have the energy for that dramatic heavy breathing, but you always have the energy for a silly giggle session with someone you love."

Loving couples revel in gentle teasing that highlights differences. It's the one form of so-called disrespect—straddling the border between aggression and play—that's permitted and encouraged in secure relationships, just as long as no one's most tender spots are poked. Judging from the tales told by long-marrieds, mutuality is the key to effective and intimacy-building teasing. One husband teases his wife about her Filipino accent and her confused use of tenses. A good sport, she plays along: "There I go, I did it again."

Raleigh recalls the origin of one of his and his wife Hope's private phrases: "One time we were driving and I exhibited what one would today call road rage and Hope said, 'Don't make a specimen of yourself.' Of course she meant spectacle—but we used the phrase often for fun and to help get over disagreements."

I'll offer an example of how a joke evolves from Stephen's and my different communication styles. I had written a humorous email message to a friend, approving of something he'd done, but he wasn't sure how literally to take my comments. Stephen stepped in and sent our friend this "clarifying" message:

"Sigh. Always to be a translator for Susan. For instance, when she says, 'Honey, how would you like your scrotum bathed in lye?', it generally means, as I see it, that she's in the mood and would like me to get spiffed up."

After he showed me his message and I laughed, he said with a straight face, "I've read Deborah Tannen. I know these things."

Is teasing always harmless fun? Of course not. As Jeanette complained, "It's more like a slap when Bob starts comparing me to my mother. He'll call me 'Myrna' if I'm doing something he doesn't like. It's teasing with a point."

Howard has lately come to recognize that his teasing occasionally crosses the line into unintended cruelty. Although he insists that teasing is his way of showing affection to Jane, and he means it to be "light and fun," he admits it's probably also a stress reliever for him, especially when he purposely chooses a subject that provokes her.

"I persist in it because it's her reaction that's rewarding to me," says Howard. "She will tell me not to tease about a particular topic and I keep doing it. For instance, comments related to harming a child upset her. We'll be watching a news program about how some kid was abducted, and I'll say something like, 'Honey, what would you do if...' She gets really angry with me." Here Howard laughed a long time, seeming to get a perverse charge out of Jane's discomfort. "She has told me repeatedly that this sort of thing bugs her, yet I keep doing it. I don't have an intelligent response to that."

Howard explains that such touchy subjects are funny to him because the odds of their occurring are ridiculously low, "and I can't understand why she gets upset. At times, though, when I realize that I'm starting to make her angry and have pushed too far, I'll say something like, 'What would you do if someone came along and bashed me over the back of the head and dragged me away and kidnapped me?' And she'll respond with: 'I'd send him a thank-you letter.' And we'll both laugh and the negative emotion will be gone."

One way people add novelty to a familiar situation is to poke at it to see what will happen—and that's what Howard seems to be doing: prodding his wife's sensitivities to see how big a reaction he can cause. But while it's reinforcing to get a huge response, it's selfish to carry such teasing beyond the other person's "Stop. I mean it."

Not all of Stephen's teasing jests have been received with equanimity by me over the years. One of the worst jokes he made: I was looking in the full-length bedroom mirror during the first year we were together—I was only 36, and about twenty-five pounds lighter than I am now. "I hate being old, fat, and ugly," I said, seeking reassurance. "Two out of three ain't bad," he said. I would tell this one to various friends over the years, to show how Stephen would say anything for a joke, hoping for *their* sympathy. Oddly, I laughed when telling it, no matter how ruefully. Eventually, all semblance of pique was gone—and now when I think of it, I can see how silly and immaterial such worries were and are.

Myron, an afficionado of practical jokes, told me that when Harriet goes to the mailbox to get the mail, he locks the front door. "She has to knock to get back in," he said with impish pride. When I told him Stephen often locks me out while I'm getting the newspaper, and that I have to say "please" through the tiny window in the door to be let back in, Myron announced, "I'm going to do that from now on." (Sorry, Harriet!)

I have to admit that playing "walrus" isn't one of my favorite games. To walrus (verb transitive): commonly used as mock aggressive threat, as in "I'll have to walrus you if..." Also: walrus (noun): "The walrus doesn't like it when you..." The phrase was adopted ritually after seeing a nature program in which a greatly overweight male walrus attempted to mate with much lighter female walruses of another species, and only succeed in crushing them to death. Chez Perry, the threat is now rarely carried out, as placating efforts are now begun by the lighter one of us with great alacrity.

This brings to mind the whole notion of nicknames. One man told me, blushing at what he was revealing, "When I'm naughty, my wife calls me a monkey." Whereas in my former marriage, neither of us used pet names for the other, Stephen and I wallow in the mud of metaphoric name-calling. I was surprised to discover, though, by reading William Betcher's extensive discussion on how nicknames fit into intimate play, that we were far from the first couple to invent twinned names. Betcher writes that couples' twinned nicknames are "an umbilical cord that joins their inner worlds," and he lists the following among those he uncovered: Pussycat and Meow, Honeydew and Melonhead, Chocolate Chip and Brown Sugar, Poop and Boop, Sheepwoman and Midnight Shepherd, Plastic Chicken and Rubber Duck, and Fungus and Mildew. Ours is BunnyApe, which we use for our website and for ourselves.

Theo, the Episcopal priest, describes how he and Dennis giggle a lot, then elaborates on their unqualified comfort with one another: "I can say that Dennis is my best friend. He knows *all* of who I am, my shadow self as well as my more gifted self. And I can talk about all of that and not fear being judged. And not fear that he's going to use it against me."

Not every successful couple is as playful as the ones in the examples I've shared. For example, when I asked Laurie if she and Hamid play much together, she told me, "If I started to try being goofy with him, he'd say, 'What in the hell is the matter with you?' One time early on I did try to play a joke on him. I hid his watch, and he started looking for it, and kept looking and wouldn't go to work. He was going to be late, and I thought, Oh my, what have I done? He was furious with me. I felt bad." Here Laurie's large eyes became moist. For this couple, obviously, the serious takes precedence over the silly, and they're both happy this way. And who would argue with that?

## RELISH YOUR RITUALS

> Sometimes Bear and Katie would lie on their sides under the blanket face to face, touching each other. She would tell him he had the best, kindest, most loving face she'd ever seen. He told her he loved everything about her from earlobes to toenails...On and on it went between them, to a degree that would make you gag if you weren't one of the participants, telling each other repeatedly *I love you*, saying it as a mantra, *I love you, I love you, I love you*, until the words themselves produced a comforting soporific effect, leading Bear and Katie to sleep in a warm nest, *I love you*, covered by feathers, *I love you, I love you.*
>
> —David Martin, *Crazy Love*

When I first pondered couple rituals, I intended to divide them into "playful" and "poignant." Soon it became obvious that no such distinction exists. The frolicsome evolves into the sacred, by sheer dint of repetition. Scenarios that are originally random and insignificant, when repeated by lovers over time, develop weight and meaning. They become *necessary*.

Sometimes you know exactly where a certain ritual originated. Take what Stephen and I call the Wet Husband Alerts. When we were on a driving vacation in Ireland a few years ago, we drew each other's attention to those appealing and ubiquitous gatherings of sheep by calling out Sheep Alert. We used Minor Sheep Alert for a clump of three or fewer sheep. Back home, Stephen began calling out Wet Husband Alert after his shower, which became the signal for me to help dry him off.

One of the Greenspons' rituals is that on any birthday or holiday morning they give each other a card and gift, surprising each other with what they've kept hidden away. "Over the years, little things like that become part of the fabric of the relationship," Tom tells me. "It's a restatement of what the relationship is about. If that *didn't* happen, it would be a disaster. It's not splashy and spectacular, but it's not something you take for granted."

Another ritual is that when they cook, Barbara manages the recipe, and Tom goes shopping and is the sous-chef who chops ingredients. Barbara admits she's never thought of it as a ritual until Tom named it as such during our interview. "It's one of the times that we do something together in a particular way," says Tom. "It's stability. It's fending off the chaos to whatever extent."

The most effective couples devise ways to get their ritual needs met, whereas others may spend many years hoping that a partner will not only remember a birthday or anniversary on his own, but that he will manage to commemorate it in just the "right" way.

Christine takes no chances that her husband will forget her birthday. For thirty days beforehand, she gives him a countdown. "I don't care if you skip every other holiday of the year, just don't forget my birthday," she emphasizes.

Missed rituals can cause grief. One early Valentine's Day, for instance, I didn't buy or plan a thing, and Stephen moped for hours. At last he explained that all his girlfriends used to make a big fuss over him on Valentine's Day.

Another example: nearly every New Year's Eve, we watch television just before midnight to see the famous ball drop in Times Square. Over the years, there have been a few times we've been too tired to stay up. A couple of times we were on the road and had to settle for a quick kiss in the car. When we can, though, we watch that ball drop while we're cozily ensconced on the sofa.

This past year, the phone rang at 11:20 p.m. It was a dear friend of Stephen's who occasionally calls long-distance when he's depressed. Stephen went into the bedroom, closed the door, and spoke to his friend. I waited, watching the clock. At five minutes before midnight, I timidly opened the bedroom door, pointed at the clock, and softly interrupted the conversation: "It's five minutes to midnight." Stephen waved me away with what seemed like an acknowledging nod. Then I waited nearby as the minutes ticked away. I heard him laugh loudly several times. I decided against watching TV myself at midnight, expecting I'd feel sad doing so alone.

When he finally came out of the bedroom, at three minutes after midnight, my mood was hanging in the balance. I was disappointed but not angry. Then, seeing his smiling face, his cheerful "Happy New Year," I got upset. I said, "We missed it," and he said, "It's close enough," and then I *really* got annoyed. My negative feeling toward Stephen continued for two days until I understood that he honestly *did not know* that watching the ball drop is a serious ritual to me. He just figured that sometimes we do it, and sometimes we sleep through it, and that it's no big deal. As soon as I grasped this, my critical feelings evaporated.

Creativity is the hallmark of some couples' ritual observances. Have you considered celebrating your first kiss, your engagement, the day your home was bought, sold, or remodeled? One pair who have been married for more than two decades decided they wanted to celebrate more in their lives, so they made a list of anniversaries they weren't likely to reach, beginning with the seventy-fifth. They put the list on their refrigerator, and now whenever they feel the urge to do something special, they choose one future anniversary to commemorate. Thus, just for fun, they may go out to dinner or take a trip or buy themselves a gift to celebrate their eighty-second wedding anniversary.

Many couple rituals are brief, barely noticed as such at the time. Howard suddenly remembers that when his wife wears her hair in a ponytail, he comes up behind her and picks up the ponytail and kisses her on the back of the neck. And whenever she grocery shops, it's become a ritual for her to bring back a tidbit for Howard, perhaps a box of Devil Dogs.

Naomi told me that she and Janice share rituals about "tons of goofy stuff." "We have a two-story house, and we'll both come home and we'll be downstairs, talking about starting dinner, and either one of us will say, 'I'll go upstairs and change.' If I've said that, then she'll stop and look at me and say, 'Oh honey, don't change, I love you the way you are.' It's so silly, and we do it all the time.

"When we're in the car driving a long distance, we'll put on oldies music and sing at the top of our lungs. We also have little routines around the television. This is one of the places where we get to have points. She'll want to change the channel, and I can make a big deal over it's being my turn to choose. Either one of us can make a big deal out of letting the other one have it."

Marylis and Conrad have ritualized their Friday night date. "We go to a regular sports bar here in town and have drinks and talk about what the week was about for each of us." They also make a point of having regular times for fun: "We used to play one-on-one softball. Almost every Sunday we would go out to play, on a boat cruise or a park and hike. We're both extremely inclined to have fun. There's never anybody saying we shouldn't go out to a restaurant—it's 'Let's go.' We both want the job to go away at some point so we can enjoy ourselves."

Rituals naturally evolve with changing family configurations and the growth of children. Letitia and Lenny used to have blindfold dates much more frequently before their daughter came along. One would blindfold the other and drive somewhere. Recently, Letitia relates, she did manage to accomplish a surprise evening, though without the blindfold.

"I told Lenny to come home at seven. I had prearranged dinner reservations, and we had margaritas, and then we went down to the little place next door that he's always been wanting to go to. It's a drag club that's been there since the '50s. I kept saying, 'I'm not taking you there, I will never go there with you,' but sure enough, I took him there. We had a ball. What it boils down to is paying attention to what the other person wants."

One couple still uses a phrase they adopted years ago, "Correct as usual, King Friday," when they watched the television program *Mr. Rogers' Neighborhood* with their young children. Not only does it feel familiar and loving to share the phrase now, but it reconnects them, via their memories of their kids, to their shared family past.

Some of the most crucial couple rituals are the momentary ones that take place at transitions: the way we start the day, say good-bye, or bid one another good-night.

Theo Park says neither he nor Dennis leave the house without kissing each other. "If we're going down the stairs to go out someplace and we don't kiss on the way out, it's like something is missing. It's also a kind of... a grace note."

When Harry returns home, he yells "Hey!" to Lila, who is usually upstairs, and she calls back, "Hey!" Then they often go outside together and sit on the porch and talk about how their day has been. "His coming home is always a loving time," says Lila.

At bedtime, Sam walks around to Ida's side, covers her feet with the extra blanket, and gives her a kiss good-night. "I would be shocked if he went to bed without doing that. Before that, he tucks our little dog into her covers, and I just watch it and think, 'Oh, he's so damn nice.'"

Bedtime snuggling is high on the must-have rituals list for many couples. "When we go to bed at night," says Theo, "we spend at least fifteen minutes with Dennis lying on his side, me lying on my back, with my legs thrown over him. If I look as though I'm going to go to sleep without that, he'll nudge up to me and say, 'C'mon, you know what you're supposed to do...' Some could say that I've 'settled' for those small things from my high ideals of the romantic life, but in a lot of ways, I think those *are* the true romantic things. It's romance without the performance expectation."

Some rituals serve a useful purpose. For example, whenever Stephen walks by as I'm bending over the sink washing my face, he has a habit of gently goosing me (that's not the useful part). One time I was putting my contact lenses in and he did his usual little underhanded poke. I jumped and so did the lens perched on my right forefinger—straight into oblivion. We looked and looked but it was not to be found. Since then, Stephen quietly sings a wordless bit of what sounds like sacred cathedral music when he notices me dealing with my lenses. That reminds him *not* to reach out that tempted finger, and meanwhile reminds me of the forever lost lens but also of all the gooses of Christmases past.

One of the more unusual rituals I was told about was this one: Tina and Richard alternate saying the fourteen short lines of their self-written wedding vows to each other every time they make love, after resolving conflict, or for any reason at all. "In good health,/to the mutual benefit of all/manifesting the creative energy/for happiness in the here and now...." Tina adds, "Once a year we ritualistically renew our vows, asking 'Do you want to do another year of this? Can you handle another year of me?'" She laughs, adding, "We don't take each other for granted."

## THE FLOW OF NOVELTY

Even in Paradise it's impossible not to remember now and then that you like a slightly stiffer breeze and have never altogether cared for wisteria.

—Scott Spencer, *Endless Love*

Flow is more likely to occur in love, as in other realms, when you're not bored by sameness or strained by overwhelming challenge. To spend time in that gratifying median between stagnation and stress, couples develop their own favorite ways of novelty-seeking.

If common sense doesn't convince you, consider what experimental research has shown to be true: when you both participate in novel and arousing activities, the level of your satisfaction with your relationship rises. In the honeymoon years, *everything* is novel. But if nothing changes after that, your excitement level declines. Neuroscientists, too, have found that when all you do is the same old thing, no matter how intoxicating it used to be, the dopamine system in your brain—the part that relates to rewards—just waits there quietly. To get those dopamine neurons firing, unpredictability is required.

Essentially, two methods have been suggested to combat relationship boredom, both more complex than they appear initially. They seem to conflict—but do they? One option is to "vary the rhythm, speed it up or slow it down, do something *different*," as Stephan Rechtschaffen suggests in *Time Shifting*.

Similarly, based on several thousand questionnaires and interviews with couples both happy and no longer so, Ayala M. Pines concluded that—no surprise!—the more variety, the less burnout. Some would say a Wednesday date is not exciting, as they need more spontaneity. For each couple, it's whatever increases the level of emotional arousal just enough to keep things perking along. Pines enumerated some of the ways couples create variety: traveling, partaking in people-related activities (in some couples, one of the partners is more extroverted and is constantly meeting people and introducing them to the other), learning new skills, pursuing physical activities, giving parties, supporting political causes.

Or you could turn this advice sideways by "reflecting on what one is *already doing*!" as Stephen A. Mitchell suggests in *Can Love Last?* I like one of Mitchell's more fanciful phrasings: "The sandcastles of romance demand, by their shifting nature, continual rebuilding."

Thus you can either do something new, or do the same thing differently. Begin especially to pay attention to what you *are* doing, notice its nuances, and consider making slight purposeful changes to what has become habitual. Initiate a frank conversation: does one of you long for the excitement of hang-gliding, a foreign vacation, or a new job, while the other finds all the stimulation needed in a change of salad dressing, a fresh throw pillow, or the new season of a favorite television series? Some couples are able to reconcile even such divergent preferences by searching for areas of overlapping interest.

In my relationship with Stephen, we seem to thrive on pocket-sized upheavals: renting a video, attending a party, taking a brief trip, celebrating our own daily rituals, a birthday, fussing over a cold. Nothing earthshaking or terribly risky is needed or wanted. I'm amused when I come across scribbled lists that Stephen and I have compiled periodically of all the fun things we'd enjoy doing together, most of which we never manage to do. Yet spending that hour brainstorming and daydreaming is a stimulating activity in itself.

How long you've been together, by the way, isn't clearly related to burnout. Non-burnouts, who are the exception, must have more than longevity (or brevity of time together, for that matter), accounting for them. Psychologist Pines's research question became not why do couples last, but why do some of them stay in love? "In a 'stirring-the-oatmeal' love," she writes, "people find meaning in the little joys of day-to-day living with an intimate partner." That's flow—noticing the exceptional in details others might overlook.

Even if tedium is a risk once you achieve an ongoing sense of security, I don't think most of us would choose to return to the early days of our relationships, when we were so anxious about losing our newly found love. Pines points out, however, that even in long-term very happy pairings, there always remains the danger of loss. What is needed, of course, is balance. Pines calls this a "roots and wings" love, combining permanence and security with emotional, physical, and spiritual intensity. "Some couples seem able to live with this particular compromise quite happily," she writes, "looking at their relationship as a creative challenge. The intensity of such a relationship does not derive from the hope that it will give meaning to life, but from the realization that it actually does, and that one's mate is indeed 'the one.'" That's loving in flow.

Another way to keep your relationship fresh is to focus on your own self-actualization and growth. "I've been married ten times to the same woman," says Mimi Schwartz's husband, according to her memoir. As you reinvent yourself, so does your relationship. Burned-out couples studied by Pines found their mates intellectually boring, even if they seemed smart to others. You have to wonder if those mates are indeed terminally boring or whether one who feels burned out experiences the entire world as a huge yawn.

Among the couples with whom I spoke, as you might expect, boredom is a non-issue. Typical is Lou Owensby, who, though she may get bored with certain aspects of her life, is never bored with Norman. She says he's perpetually intellectually interesting and stimulating. Numerous couples echoed that sentiment.

It's a fact that most of us begin to lose the ability to thrill our partners with the wit and wonderfulness that used to excite them. We get habituated to one another and the qualities that were once stimulating may begin to feel overly familiar. According to social psychology's gain-loss theory, once we've become accustomed to a certain high level of liking from someone, they lose the power to "reward" us. So we're more likely to perceive a "gain" when we get liked or praised by a stranger than a loved one. When I praise my son, I may hear, "You're only my mom." While husbands rarely say outright, "You're only my wife," that's what's going on internally. A gain is more powerful a reward than a constant level of liking. But just take away some of the esteem you've been used to getting from your steady trusted mate, and see how much it wounds. Think of it this way: you can indeed hurt the one you love but you can't offer that much of a reward by merely continuing to love—and behave toward one another—in the exact same way. It's a matter of com-plexification: taking a joke or a ritual and varying it just enough to freshen it.

For some, loving in flow has more to do with utter comfort than with crackling creativity, especially if those cozy days are a welcome reprieve from an otherwise too-frantic life. Howard, familiar with being "in the zone" from when he was involved in athletics, says he was never aware of experiencing this kind of flow with another person before he met his wife. Love and lust and all that, but not flow. Now the flow episodes in his marriage occur a few times a week: "It might last all evening or all day. Not infrequently, we'll have days where for the entire day neither of our brows crease, we laugh, and we're completely in tune. In fact, sometimes I'll say to her, 'Wow, we're really in the zone today.' Time becomes a non-issue."

## ROLES AND THE POSTMODERN COUPLE

> I will say that one feature I like about men is that they can usually figure out how small appliances work.
>
> —Charles Baxter, *The Feast of Love*

One of the ways couples keep themselves from rusting of bore-dom is to subvert the traditional roles society foists on us from infancy. It's the antithesis of living and loving in flow to restrict yourself to the stereotype that insists men act one way and women are supposed to think, feel, and behave another way. Androgynous men and women have the flexibility to be either aggressive and competitive or gentle and nurturing—and anything in-between—depending on what the situation calls for.

A bit of evidence for this claim comes from research completed at Loyola College, where a group of married couples were divided into sex role categories. It was found that the androgynous couples (those who score above the group median on both masculine and feminine items on a questionnaire) were happier in their relationships than those who adhered to traditional sex roles or were mismatched (as, for example, a traditional husband with a more modern wife). A conclusion borne out by many of the couples I interviewed is that novelty and flow are more likely if each of you explore and exploit both your so-called masculine and your traditionally more feminine traits.

Role flexibility sometimes means you choose to behave in the familiar, expected way but with a non-traditional consciousness. When, in private, an ardent feminist temporarily takes on the role of a geisha, or a confirmed male wimp pretends to be a bully, they can enjoy this ironic subversion of their own backgrounds. Along these lines, researcher Judith S. Wallerstein found in her study of egalitarian marriages that husbands in such marriages would sometimes like to be teased and seduced by an old-style temptress, rather than have sex with a so-called equal. I think a number of well-adjusted couples have figured this out for themselves and try on roles they wouldn't want their neighbors or colleagues to know about.

Playing with power can be invigorating—and erotic. It's no secret that in many marriages, one partner may be a lot stronger than the other. But even when the conclusion is foregone, both partners, whatever their genders, may feel a *frisson* from the reminder. Jeanette laughs loudly when she tells me how she delights in being grabbed and tickled by her husband, and how they both enjoy it equally when she grabs and tickles him. "Every now and then he'll tackle me and we'll wrestle," she adds, "and I'll squeal, 'Don't hurt me, don't hurt me!'"

Theo and Dennis look the part of gay men, Theo tells me over the phone. "We're stylish, wear earrings, probably have a certain softness of manner, at least against a classic male stereotype."

When they tease one another, which they do a lot, says Theo, "We'll start to wrestle and I'll joke, 'Don't do that, you're going to get hurt,' which I say in a sing-songy way. Because it's obvious he's much much bigger than I am. He's six-foot-two and I'm five-foot-nine."

In my house, too, we like to play around with notions of strength. Stephen reluctantly attended a required workshop at the fitness center at his college last semester. That night, as we got into bed, he said, "They have a lot of weight machines there. I might make use of them."

"That would be really good for you," I said, "except that you might develop big muscles and then you'd be able to overpower me."

He swivelled his head around slowly. "Overpower you? *Anybody* could overpower you. A *bug* could overpower you."

Often, though, the male's upper body strength is the only part of the stereotype the couple comes close to fitting. According to Frank Pittman, "The traditional masculine stereotype, when taken literally, produced something close to an obsessive-compulsive psychopathic workaholic tyrant...The feminine stereotype, when taken literally, came close to being a passive-aggressive guilt-producing hysteric martyr and victim." Such roles may suit courtship better than life, Pittman suggests, making it hard to get along with someone who's been trained so differently. Still, keeping in mind that those "me man, you woman" scenarios, however Neanderthal, may play a cherished role in some courtships, it may be possible to resurrect such games in the intimacy of your own four walls without humiliating anyone.

Besides its boring predictability, a frustrating byproduct of remaining stuck in your culturally assigned roles is that if one of you is always helpless, the other can't ever show helplessness. How much more fair and more satisfying it can be to take turns acting childlike, needy, or vulnerable.

Jim and Zhita consider their own role-playing as a bit of a joke. "When I think of what we take on as household responsibilities, for example, or social responsibilities," explains Zhita, "we're very traditional and sort of amused about that. I think that's the key to it, that we're doing it voluntarily. For example, food preparation has evolved to where I'm the primary person, yet I also know that if I didn't enjoy doing that, Jim is perfectly capable. Conversely, I don't even consider doing fix-it kinds of things I used to do myself when I was single. 'Dear? Can you fix the light switch, hang the pictures?'"

A few months after I married my first husband, my car ran out of gas on the way home from work. My father had always taken my car to the gas station for me. It only took that one incident to recognize that my husband wasn't interested in replicating my father's caretaking, and I learned to buy gas.

In recent years, since I don't drive a lot, Stephen took over the task of keeping the tank filled. Being taken care of in this way is a treat. I've learned not to underestimate the value and power of the old ways to make you feel cared for, as long as other people's preferences aren't rigidly enforced. Stephen even fixes things around the house, sometimes—certainly, I almost never do. That role got dropped into his lap even though he'd never had it before. The behavior's very strangeness to him made it less fraught with reverberations from the past.

Another example is that George was thrilled with the role he enacted with Norma, whom he married when he was forty-two and she was thirteen years younger.

"She was vulnerable, and I felt like a daddy to her," he relates. "That was a big part of our relationship, but we also related on an adult-to-adult basis where we'd discuss the latest news. She didn't have a good relationship with her own father. I was real affectionate with her and we were both hungry for that. It was the biggest attraction. Norma kept looking to me for guidance, for support and counsel, since she'd never had that, not that I had either, but at least I'd been independent for so long that it looked like I had. We could switch roles around so that she'd take over in some situation where she had more confidence than I did, such as when we visited Europe. Yet, the sweetest purest moments came out of that Daddy/little girl role playing. It was like we were two parts of a jigsaw puzzle."

Jorge speaks to me of picking and choosing among the roles to which the culture of his ancestors would have limited him. "I'm extremely masculine, but I do a lot of stuff that perhaps my father or cousins wouldn't have done. When I feed the baby, I think I feel *more* manly. This is my offspring—I love him."

You don't have to be revolutionaries to reject the culturally scripted roles you were handed in childhood. Nor is it possible to design new roles and never think about them again. Regardless of the revised script you decide to follow, there will inevitably be blanks requiring decision-making. Does the feminist *have* to work for pay? Who, of the full-time working wife and the full-time working husband, gets a much-needed back massage first? What if, no matter how liberated and forward-thinking you are, being cherished *still* means your mate washes and puts your underwear away for you? The details are ours to define with love, a consistent assumption of good will, and a sustained and sustaining belief that there are very few rules you *must* obey once you're both inside and the front door is closed.

# *19* THE IMPERFECT ROCK TUMBLER OF TIME

The whirligig of time spins on. The world grows older. People live their lives, each life filling all the time available and yet—on the grand, cosmic scale—taking up less time than the tick of the clock.

—Kate Atkinson, *Human Croquet*

I glance at the calendar and realize our anniversary is coming up. I say to Stephen, "In only two weeks, we'll actually have been married nineteen years, and we've been together twenty."

When he responds, "We're in it for the long haul," I'm not sure this metaphor captures the romance of our lives quite sweetly enough, so I say, "You make it sound like long-distance trucking!"

"I was thinking more like sled dogs pulling a fat man."

"And we're the fat man?"

"We're both the fat man and the sled dogs."

"C'mon, we should be celebrating..."

"But I *am!*"

## MADE FOR EACH OTHER

Our story had begun, had already found its tone and style, and the more often one of us talked about our meeting one winter night in a taxi, the more it sounded like the creation myth of our love. Gradually, as the anecdote was repeated, our chance meeting came to resemble an hour of destiny.

—Jens Christian Grondahl, *Silence in October*

You have no doubt heard a divorce's inevitability explained with the words, "We were just so different." What nonsense. Members of a couple are *always* unlike, whether they turn out to be maladjusted or stunningly attuned. There are no infallible guidelines to tell us which two individuals *should* be a good match. Every example has a counter-example; for every two people who married and then split up due to their incompatibilities, you'll find two who are at least as opposite yet unable to conceive of themselves as being satisfied with anyone else.

Through enjoying blissful times and contending with woeful ones, the best couples come to feel they're a good fit, even a perfect match. What's most amazing is that they arrive at this insight by *knowing* one another—a far contrast from falling helplessly in love with a stranger.

The rock tumbler theory of marital bliss helps explain what's going on. At first, all the rough edges of your respective personalities, when struck together, create sparks and often tears. But you are no longer the same people you were once you've shared a decade or two, gaining insight into yourselves and each other; debated the same issues repeatedly; passed through disillusionment and the four-year or seven-year or nine-year itch; survived the rearing of children, stepchildren, teens; and navigated challenges both prosaic and possibly relationship-threatening. Your rough edges are smoothed by the tumbling of life and time. Now when you bump up against each other, no one is left scratched and bleeding.

All that smoothing doesn't mean you've lost your individuality. You may have heard that husbands and wives grow more alike over time. That's been shown to be a myth by a study that found partners maintain the same degree of similarity over a twenty-year span, based on tests of personality, values, and attitudes. Still, it's by sharing experience that we don't become *more* unlike. Siblings are forced to share an environment and therefore try hard to differentiate themselves from one another, whereas committed couples *choose* a common environment and experiences. Even if you don't have a lot in common earlier, after many years of living in tandem you'll share a great deal.

And yet the no-longer-sharp-edged differences between them contribute to the getting-along process for many couples. Lou Owensby says, "We've been *very* good for each other. Norman brings a certain stability and integrity. With my perfectionism, I have to know exactly how it's going to end up before I get started, and he brings a sense of 'it's not the end of the world—if we don't like it, then we'll just change it,' that kind of thing. He has really loosened me up a lot."

Laurie and Hamid are dissimilar in many obvious ways, but after twenty-five years together, their commonalities are even more telling: they're both educated, and they share a mission, as she tells it, to make the U.S. public aware of the shabby stereotype of the Arab culture and people. They both write and share community involvements. They've faced financial setbacks as a team.

Values that coincide help many couples feel connected no matter how their interests or temperaments may differ. Zhita tells me that she and Jim are "very, very different." But overriding everything is that there's never been any question between them about "the basics: how you treat people, how you feel about people, what your sense of fairness is." They also have congruent tastes about artistic matters and how they like their surroundings to look. "We enjoy being affected by each other's awarenesses or tastes, so we have always had a very eclectic setting which we particularly enjoy. Seldom do we come away from the theater and one of us loved the play and the other hated it. It continues to be amazing to me."

As different as Harriet and Myron are, she tells me that if she met a man who more resembled herself, "I'm sure I would disdain him." Harriet, a poet, admits she'd be delighted if Myron, a retired doctor, were a little more flowery, a little less logical. But she recognizes how well he stabilizes her: "He's my ballast."

When I ask Myron about this issue of fit, he says, "Sometimes I wish she were a little more realistic. I'm much more cynical about situations and she's the optimist and she gets herself built up with great expectations. But I wouldn't have it any other way. Our marriage is as good as I ever expected and as good as I've ever wanted."

When Judith S. Wallerstein interviewed fifty couples with long, happy marriages, she found that "above all, they shared the view that their partner was special in some important regard and that the marriage enhanced each of them as individuals. They felt that the fit between their own needs and their partner's responses was unique and probably irreplaceable."

The idea of irreplacability opens a fascinating line of inquiry. Philosopher Solomon wonders whether you would feel compelled to swear lifelong devotion unless the two of you already sense that you could just as well love someone else. Are we set up to love a type, a certain combination of characteristics? Perhaps we come across a likely example of this type and then decide to commit to *this* individual before some other example shows up.

Are we this exchangeable? When you look at many singles ads, you certainly don't get an impression of people who are seeking quirky individuality. Would a nice fresh Stephen clone be as good as or better than this old original? As Solomon points out, you can replace a ring, but not the one you bought for your wedding. And indeed, Stephen's ring was stolen a couple of years ago, and we haven't yet had the heart to go out and try to replace it. It wouldn't be the *same*. It wouldn't be the one we argued over when we went ring-shopping the first time, it wouldn't be the one he held up to show how nicely it paired with mine when we were in that early showing-off-your-matching-rings phase of the relationship.

And if a ring is irreplaceable because of the history it has accrued, how much less replaceable is a person? If you had a perfect adult clone, I suppose you could start breaking the person in all over again, and this time not make all the same mistakes, but would you do it? I wouldn't want to. Who we are *now* is composed of how all those mistakes were transcended. We are our history, our coupled memories.

# THE NARRATIVE OF US

> We agreed on a certain narrative of our meeting, a narrative which spun out its thread in this way: both of us trapped on the subway one night when it rumbled to a stop between 96th St. and 72nd St., both of us reading, coincidentally *The Lover* by Marguerite Duras, straphanging, talking and giggling...though there were no actual straps (it was a train that had only poles and transverses), and though I was actually reading Djuna Barnes....
>
> —Rick Moody, *Demonology*

Your personal "narrative of us" begins when you both make the internal shift from "I" to "we." It is then expanded over the years by all your shared memories, including the inaccurate ones. Connected couples repeat the details of their adventures together as a way to make a story, to create order out of the chaos of human experience, and to be able to feel secure about predicting the future. The more you revisit a past event, the firmer it sticks in your mind. Such memories become part of the chemical makeup, the actual biology of your brains.

When Stephen and I took a walk recently on a Griffith Park horse trail near our home, we had to walk single-file at one point, which put him right behind me. He made a brief comment about a video camera, and I immediately knew, and showed with a twisty grin, that he was obliquely referring to a playful prank he pulled nearly twenty years ago when he was similarly walking behind me, filming me without my knowledge. He then commented how pleasing it is that the two of us speak the "same language," often with few words exchanged.

Stories can be both used and misused, though. My ex-husband still repeats to other family members tales that star me as a prime boob, such as how I grossly overspent on a fancy car seat/high chair combination and how I accidentally sold at a garage sale a St. Christopher medal his mother had given him. Stories can connect and stories can separate, and sometimes similar stories can lead to either result. "The old stories may become as boring and stale as old jokes," Sam Keen writes. "Or revisiting a common past may become a part of the liturgy of relationship that is as pleasurable as the often-repeated dance of sexual communion."

Sharing stories provides not only pleasure, but also the stability needed for a well-coordinated life. When couples married fifty years or more were studied, it was found they had shared the same vision of how they wanted to live their lives. In other words, they were a good match all along in the ways they imagined their future.

Couples who have similar perceptions of how their lives are going are the happiest. It's not about how long you're married, but more a matter of constructing a congruent story together, from the earliest days. If either of you has forgotten essential parts of your joint past—say, what went on during your first date—it may mean the two of you have diverged and are living separate lives. Take heed: when newlyweds were analyzed over a five-year period, it was learned that husbands and wives in the marriages that failed during that span gave conflicting accounts of their lives together.

"In unhappy marriages," writes Phyllis Rose in *Parallel Lives*, "I see two versions of reality rather than two people in conflict. I see a struggle for imaginative dominance going on. Happy marriages seem to me those in which the two partners agree on the scenario they are enacting, even if...their own idea of their relationship is totally at variance with the facts." Don't fret if your stories aren't entirely identical. They never are. You might even see each other in a more flattering light than you see yourselves. The stories told by satisfied partners often put their mates in a somewhat idealized light, helping explain and excuse negative behavior. It's a terrific asset to have someone so much on your side that he or she acts like an agent and speaks ebulliently about your good points.

Everybody sees themselves as unique. Confides Lou Owensby, "We're strange in a lot of ways." When I interviewed creative writers for *Writing in Flow: Keys to Enhanced Creativity*, many of them told me they felt "different," odder than others in their thoughts and habits. Yet there's a lot of overlap among creative individu-als. Similarly with couples, "the narrative of us" requires a degree of idiosyncrasy. None of us wants to be just like everyone else. And the way we ensure we're *not* is to invent our lives out of care-fully—if not necessarily consciously—constructed stories.

If you are interested in thinking about how you and your partner have concocted your unwritten narrative, you might want to start with yourself. Write a brief autobiography, or make a couple evening of it and tell your own stories to each other. Another enlightening and enjoyable exercise is to pretend you're going to write a biography of your mate and find out all you can. How does he see his life? If it were to be made into a play or film, what genre would it be? Can you agree on appropriate names for the stories of your separate and then your married lives?

Try to come up with a metaphor for your relationship over time. Besides flow itself, see if any of the following are particu-larly evocative: merry-go-round, roller-coaster ride, tapestry, speeding train, maze, job, drama, contract, biological imperative, social construction, match made in heaven. During our early love chats, Stephen said he didn't need anyone else because our love was a cornucopia offering constant freshness and variety. Years later, I asked him what he thought about the pop creed of "surrendering to marriage." "Nah," he said, ever-teasing, "more like 'broken on the wheel of marriage.'"

Play with the idea of scrapbooking your lives together. Once I gathered all the tiny detritus of a special weekend, from tickets and receipts to a tiny pine cone, and put it in a fancy box we'd bought on that same weekend. Consider making up separate photo albums by theme or vacation, instead of waiting until you have time to put them *all* in your regular album, a task that can feel overwhelming. Themed digital online albums are another alternative.

When Stephen and I began giving ourselves what we then called Fun Days and later came to call Off Days, I decided to keep a related memento book. In it, I label each page by the date and then tape in ticket stubs and any other paper mementos with a line or two that brings back the quirkiness of that particular day. When I was a teen, I'd keep the more standard romantic effluvia of dates, such as pressed flowers. Now it's more likely to be: "We couldn't find our car and panicked, but then realized there were *two* Level Bs." I read of a couple who turned their den into a virtual shrine to themselves, beginning with a bulletin board of love souvenirs that overflowed all over the walls.

Above all, don't feel you ought to turn history-making into a major project. So many busy couples keep track of the *firsts* of their days together, or of the obvious special days like anniversaries, but then neglect to take much notice of the fun-to-reminisce-about times that pop up unexpectedly. Compiling a scrapbook with actual pages isn't even necessary: all you have to do is keep your emotional scrapbook full by frequently reminiscing together.

## THE END IS NEAR

> We only appear to be rooted in time. Everywhere, if you listen closely, the spitting fuse of the future is crackling.
>
> —Carol Shields, *Unless*

Last year my cousin Rose lost her husband of twenty-one years to prostate cancer when Morty was 52. Throughout the two years of their struggle, she anguished over losing him before they'd have their long-awaited chance to sit around in a warm climate and reminisce over their vacation albums. From one of Rose's emails: "We have gotten very bad reports on Mort in the last two weeks and have seen six doctors. We both are crying these days. I don't want to give up hope but we feel basically hopeless. I tell you that my heart is breaking. We snuggle at night and hold onto each other all the time."

After he died, Rose told me that the past two decades with Morty now seem like a dream. Some may have seen that Bob Newhart comedy a few years ago where, after several seasons playing an innkeeper, in the last show of the series, Newhart's character awoke after a night's sleep and found he'd dreamed the past few years and was now lying next to the wife he'd had in a previous series. I am sharply aware that I, too, may awake someday to an empty bed (no, it won't be filled with my ex-husband, unless life really *is* a perverse fiction), and the years I've spent with Stephen may feel like nothing more than a dream.

All of life is like that, though, isn't it? When my first son was five days old, my father pointed out, "Five days. Soon it will be five weeks, five months, then five years." And it's already been thirty-one at last count. I kept a few of my babies' diaper pins, and now I use them to pin a towel around my shoulders while I dye away my graying hair. A friend of ours, Marguerite, wrote a lovely poem that has stuck with me. In it, she's at a laundromat and wonders what a young man thinks of her lingerie on the hanging stand. And then she remembers that she's 80.

If we could only realize what we have while we still have it, if we could behave *every day of our relationship* the way a character does in Scott Spencer's novel, *Endless Love,* "I was like a tourist—a *dying* tourist—on a twilight tour of Europe. Each sunset, each spire, each cobblestoned path, each lobby, each glass of local beer is monumental, tragic, and unparalleled."

The couples I interviewed are able to appreciate—right here and now—the amazingness of what they have. Harriet, for instance, tells me that she and Myron talk a lot more about their relationship these days than they used to. "We have more time to do it, and less time, since we're growing so old."

Theo Park's partner Dennis recently lost his mother to Alzheimer's; Dennis's father has Parkinson's. One of Theo's jokes to Dennis is, "Great, which am I gonna get? How are you going to disappear on me?"

"But I have no doubt," adds Theo, more seriously, "that we'll have twenty more good years together. This is where my faith comes in. It's not faith that because we love each other we're going to live long lives, but I believe that if I die tomorrow, I've done what I need to do. And he will grieve and then he will go on and do whatever he needs to do next, and vice versa."

Bob's experience as a young doctor taught him about the vulnerability of life. "When I was a medical student, I would see patients who, though not much older than me, were very sick. You just start to realize that life is too short to make too complicated. We had to work hard at our relationship for years, and every decade we've gotten better."

And Lila, whose husband is coping with cancer, doesn't ask for too much: "Sometimes when Harry stays out late, I'll get up and come sit in here and look out my front window. I can see the main road, I can see a field and some trees out there, and you can raise the window, and at night you can see the sky and just hear the traffic in the distance, and I just think, who could ask for more than this? Since he's been sick, we try to enjoy every day, and that doesn't mean we do something big. We just enjoy it."

For some it's an ongoing struggle to push aside thoughts of what will come later. Sherry Suib Cohen has been married more than thirty years and still gets goose bumps when her husband walks in the door. "I feel so knocked out by him that I cannot wait to see him at the end of the day. I wouldn't want to live without him, literally. Certainly as I get older, I'm more terrified of the years passing. But I've always, after the first couple of years of my marriage, felt that I could not, would not survive, would not want to survive. I'm a powerful woman, you have to understand that—strong, very strong—but that's my dirty little secret.

"I can't imagine my life being joyful anymore, even though I have wonderful children and fabulous grandchildren. And I have strong relationships with friends from college, and I have editors that I love. But all of it is contingent on knowing that he's here to talk about it all with. That sounds, I'm sure, weak. It's terror every time he's a little late.

"Every single morning of my life I wake up—I don't exaggerate—every single morning I wonder, 'How much longer do we have?'" She finishes, the wretchedness in her voice easing up slightly, "Somehow it soothes me when he says, 'As much as we want.'"

Which reminds me of what a wise character in a Peter DeVries novel says: "Uppermost among human joys is the negative one of restoration: not going to the stars, but learning that one may stay where one is."

At times, I think of the now-painted-over markings on the arched kitchen wall that delineated how tall my boys were growing. It was the usual ritual of "stand up straight," mark, measure, gloat at added inches. A marriage has some of those same elements: all the markings, the milestones noted, are now painted over, no longer visible to the naked eye but still in memory. They make us what we are, each mark and the uneven spaces in-between. If we're among the fortunate, we arrive at a place where we can relish *being*. It's a good place, this long peaceful plateau.

Mostly we tell time by the recurring seasons: another school year begins, another Halloween, another soft echoing of auld lang syne in the distance. Or the daily benchmarks: the ecstatic first cup of coffee, the freshly unfolded newspaper. Lately I've felt an odd pang each time I refill Stephen's seven-day Prozac container from the big bottle. The weeks have been following each other so quickly. Monthly, I turn the page on the kitchen calendar to reveal the new picture. A moment of freshness, undergirded by a sense of the thickening pile of already-experienced scenes—and here it is fall *again*, almost time to choose the next year's calendar. And always remembering, at new calendar time, how excited I became in third grade when Mrs. Millander provided us with tiny calendars to paste onto drawings of our own. I hoarded more than one, loving those miniature packets of months, already in love with the possibilities of time, so confident that the future would always be open-ended.

Now though, other scenes more often crowd out those innocent ones. One we're all sadly familiar with is that of two people holding hands as they leap from a flaming skyscraper. It is easy to imagine them a couple. Somehow the idea of being connected to another person—physically connected—takes some of the sting out of the unacceptable.

I've already chosen the person I want to grip tightly when the endgame begins. Every morning, threaded through Stephen's groggy half-alert "Morning, Doodle," and my responding "Hi there," is the sense, lately, of our repeating this endlessly, until the end. We hurtle, all of us, in slow motion from buildings of unknown height, with the lucky ones clasping the hand of someone we love. We don't look down. Instead, we abandon ourselves to the impossible beauty of the time we have, transcending time. We ponder the fleeting images in the clouds, and we make up games to play along the way.

# EIGHT INSIGHTS ABOUT LOVING IN FLOW

To sum up the major findings of this book, here are eight insights learned from and lived by couples in the happiest long-lasting relationships:

1. **Know thyself:** self-knowledge helps you create and sustain happy relationships with others.

2. **Adapt your attitudes:** happy couples know how to love well. They have shaped the malleable parts of their personalities and are open, honest, flexible, compassionate, nonjudgmental, and generous with one another.

3. **Motivation matters:** happy couples don't fear commitment and are resilient in the face of challenges.

4. **Focus and pay attention:** happy couples learn to communicate, focus on what matters, and appreciate one another.

5. **Loosen up and let go:** happy couples assume goodwill of one another, and they accept flaws and mistakes and move on.

6. **Find balance:** happy couples are open to change, are intimate and have healthy boundaries, know how to benefit from both novelty and ritual. A loving in flow relationship is profoundly fair, often in ways that cannot be perceived from outside the couple.

7. **Realize that time waits for no one:** those in loving in flow relationships treat each other and each day together as precious and irreplaceable.

8. **Know that time is also a friend to loving in flow:** it helps couples put the trivial into big picture perspective.

# NOTES

## INTRODUCTION: THE GARDEN OF DORIAN GRAY

xiv **Mihaly Csikszentmihalyi**—*Flow: The Psychology of Optimal Experience* (NY: HarperPerennial, 1990); *Beyond Boredom and Anxiety: Experiencing Flow in Work and Play, 25th Anniversary Edition* (San Francisco: Jossey-Bass, 1975/2000).

**nearly decade-long research**—Susan K. Perry, *Writing in Flow: Keys to Enhanced Creativity* (Cincinnati, OH: Writer's Digest Books, 2001).

xv **Carl Rogers**—*Becoming Partners: Marriage and its Alternatives* (NY: Dell, 1972), p. 201.

xvi **findings of a recent study that 63 percent**—David Popenoe and Barbara Dafoe Whitehead, *The State of Our Unions: The Social Health of Marriage in America* (New Brunswick, NJ: National Marriage Project, 2002), p. 19. Survey conducted by the National Opinion Research Center of the University of Chicago.

xvii **Abraham Maslow**—*The Farther Reaches of Human Nature* (NY: Penguin, 1971).

**William James**—*The Varieties of Religious Experience* (NY: Penguin, 1982).

**I sought out, by a variety of means**—I asked a wide network of friends and colleagues for referrals to exceptionally happy couples who have been together for at least ten years. Each of these couples was asked if they knew of other potential interviewees. I then asked each willing individual, "On a scale of one to 100, how happy or satisfied are you in this relationship?" I interviewed fifty-one individuals who are members of thirty-eight couples, each of whom gave themselves a score of eighty-five or above (two-thirds in the final group indicated ninety-five or above). Quite a few of the couples are well-educated professionals; half are from various cities in California; the other half live in ten other states, three each in Florida, New York, and Minnesota, and the rest from other states in the South, Northeast, and Midwest. Respondents' ages range from thirty-two to eighty-seven. Their relationships vary in duration from ten to fifty-eight years, with twenty-five of them having lasted between ten and twenty-nine years, and the rest for thirty years or more. I conducted interviews in person or by telephone, and, in four instances, via email or letter. I sought out diversity related to crises overcome, as well as in matters of sexual orientation and ethnicity.

When I did speak separately with both members of a couple, their perceptions of the relationship were generally congruent. (Evidence suggests that it's possible to get a fairly accurate picture of a relationship from talking to one partner. See Mark Attridge, Ellen Berscheid, and Jeffry A. Simpson, "Predicting Relationship Stability From Both Partners Versus One," *Journal of Personality and Social Psychology*, 1995, Vol. 69, No 2, 254-268.) When studying changes in marital satisfaction, psychologists found that "with rare exceptions, spouses' trajectories did not differ." (Benjamin R. Karney and Thomas N. Bradbury, "Neuroticism, Marital Interaction, and the Trajectory of Marital Satisfaction," *Journal of Personality and Social Psychology*, 1997, Vol. 72, No. 5, 1087).

## CHAPTER 1: IN THE BEGINNING ARE THE WORDS

7 **Luck (even science agrees)**—David T. Lykken and Auke Tellegen, "Is Human Mating Adventitious or the Result of Lawful Choice? A Twin Study of Mate Selection," *Journal of Personality and Social Psychology*, 1993, Vol. 65, No. 1, 56-68.

## CHAPTER 2: INTIMATIONS OF REALITY

16 **Tessina, the author of**—Tina B. Tessina and Riley K. Smith, *How to Be a Couple and Still Be Free* (Franklin Lakes, NJ: New Page Books/Career Press, 2002, Third Edition), among others.

19 **Author Mimi Schwartz**—*Thoughts from a Queen-Sized Bed* (Lincoln, NE: University of Nebraska Press, 2002), p. 10.

23 **Robert C. Solomon**—*Love: Emotion, Myth, & Metaphor* (Amherst, NY: Prometheus Books, 1990), p. xxxiii.

26 **point out authors Richard Schwartz, M.D.**—Richard Schwartz, M.D., and Jacqueline Olds, M.D., *Marriage in Motion: The Natural Ebb and Flow of Lasting Relationships,* (Cambridge, MA: Perseus Publishing, 2000), p. xv.

    **Karen Kayser**—*When Love Dies: The Process of Marital Disaffection*, (NY: Guilford Press, 1993), vii, 19-23.

27 **in a memoir, *Coming About*—**Susan Tyler Hitchcock, *Coming About: A Family Passage at Sea,* (Dobbs Ferry, NY: Sheridan House, 2002).

28 **To cite a recent study**—Blaine J. Fowers, Eileen Lyons, Kelly H. Montel, and Netta Shaked, "Positive Illusions About Marriage Among Married and Single Individuals," *Journal of Family Psychology*, 2001, Vol. 15, No. 1, 95-109.

29 **Stephen A. Mitchell**—*Can Love Last? The Fate of Romance over Time* (NY: W. W. Norton, 2001), p. 108.

    **it's been found that being (reasonably) idealized**—Sandra L. Murray, John G. Holmes, and Dale W. Griffin, "The Benefits of Positive Illusions: Idealization and the Construction of Satisfaction in Close Relationships," *Journal of Personality and Social Psychology*, 1996, Vol. 70, No. 1, 79-98. Also: Sandra L. Murray and John G. Holmes, "The (Mental) Ties That Bind: Cognitive Structures That Predict Relationship Resilience," *Journal of Personality and Social Psychology*, 1999, Vol. 77, No. 6, 1228-1244.

30 **One study found that among those**—William B. Swann, Jr., Chris De La Ronde, and J. Gregory Hixon, "Authenticity and Positivity Strivings in Marriage and Courtship, *Journal of Personality and Social Psychology*, 1994, Vol. 66, No. 5, 857-869.

31 **author Sherry Suib Cohen**—Sherry Suib Cohen, *Secrets of a Very Good Marriage: Lessons from the Sea* (NY: Penguin Books, 1993).

32 **Sam Keen**—*To Love and Be Loved* (NY: Bantam, 1999), p. 184.

    **Rick Moody short story**—"The Carnival Tradition," in *Demonology* (NY: Little, Brown & Co., 2001), p. 173.

**CHAPTER 3: COPING WITH CONFLICT**

33 **Frank Pittman, an Atlanta psychiatrist**—*Grow Up!: How Taking Responsibility Can Make You a Happy Adult* (NY: Golden Books, 1998), p.1,

38 **Linda E. Olds**—*Metaphors of Interrelatedness: Toward a Systems Theory of Psychology* (NY: State University of New York Press, 1992), p. 97.

39 **Matthew McKay, Patrick Fanning, and Kim Paleg**—*Couple Skills: Making Your Relationship Work* (Oakland: New Harbinger Publications, 1994), p 199-200.

40 **Andrew Christensen suggests**—Andrew Christensen and Neil S. Jacobson, *Reconcilable Differences* (NY: Guildford, 2000), p. 180.

    **It has been found that having good self-control**—Eli J. Finkel and W. Keith Campbell, "Self-Control and Accommodation in Close Relationships: An Interdependence Analysis," *Journal of Personality and Social Psychology*, 2001, Vol. 81, No. 2, 263-277.

42 **presence of children: it's been found**—Lauren M. Papp, E. Mark Cummings, and Marcie C. Goeke-Morey, "Marital Conflicts in the Home When Children Are Present Versus Absent," *Developmental Psychology*, 2002, Vol. 38, No. 5, 774-783.

    **Studies have found that some men**—John M. Gottman, "A Theory of Marital Dissolution and Stability," *Journal of Family Psychology*, 193, Vol. 7, No. 1, 57-75.

45 **Doris Wild Helmering**—*Happily Ever After: A Therapist's Guide to Taking the Fight Out & Putting the Fun Back into Your Marriage* (NY: Warner, 1986).

**Christensen and his co-author**—*Reconcilable Differences*, p. 103.

50    **psychiatrist Peter D. Kramer**—*Should You Leave? A Psychiatrist Explores Intimacy and Autonomy—and the Nature of Advice* (NY: Scribner, 1997), p. 144.

**Patrick O'Leary novel**—*Door Number Three* (NY: Tor/Tom Doherty Associates, 1995), p. 75.

**psychologist and marital researcher John M. Gottman**—*Why Marriages Succeed or Fail* (NY: Simon & Schuster, 1994), p. 219.

## CHAPTER 4: THE NO-FAULT APPROACH

53    **Thich Nhat Hanh**—"True Presence," in Mark Robert Waldman (Ed.), *The Art of Staying Together* (NY: Jeremy P. Tarcher/Putnam, 1998), p. 189.

**Research has consistently found**—Frank D. Fincham and Thomas N. Bradbury, "Marital Satisfaction, Depression, and Attributions: A Longitudinal Analysis," *Journal of Personality and Social Psychology*, 1993, Vol. 64, No. 3, 442-452; also Thomas N. Bradbury and Frank D. Fincham, "Attributions and Behavior in Marital Interaction," *Journal of Personality and Social Psychology,* 1992, Vol. 63, No. 4, 613-628.

54    **Psychologists studying newlyweds**—Joseph Veroff, Elizabeth Douvan, and Shirley J. Hatchett, *Marital Instability: A Social and Behavioral Study of the Early Years* (Westport, Connecticut: Praeger, 1995).

55    **psychologists who adhere to constructivism**—e.g., George A. Kelly, *A Theory of Personality: The Psychology of Personal Constructs* (NY: W. W. Norton, 1955/1963).

**Kim Paleg and Matthew McKay**—*When Anger Hurts Your Relationship: 10 Simple Solutions for Couples Who Fight* (Oakland, CA: New Harbinger, 2001).

57    **in Haruki Murakami's novel**—*The Wind-Up Bird Chronicle* (NY: Vintage Books, 1997), p. 27.

**asserts Jeffrey Kottler**—*Beyond Blame* (San Francisco: Jossey-Bass, 1994).

58    **notes psychiatrist Frank Pittman**—*Grow Up!*, p. 196.

**In a *New Yorker* cartoon**—*The New Yorker*, 8/13/01, p. 46.

59    **Some studies have found**—F.D. Fincham and T.N. Bradbury, "Perceived responsibility for marital events: Egocentric or partner-centric bias?" *Journal of Marriage and the Family, 51,* 27-35.

**rather than a 'you',' suggests Andrew Christensen**—*Reconcilable Differences*, p. 177.

63    **According to Andrew Christensen**—*Reconcilable Differences,* p. 124.

## CHAPTER 5: TALKING ABOUT TALKING

68    **article about John Gottman's marriage research**—Jane E. Brody, "To Predict Divorce, Ask 125 Questions," *New York Times*, 8/11/92, B5-6.

69    **Ayala M. Pines claims that**—*Keeping the Spark Alive: Preventing Burnout in Love and Marriage* (NY: St. Martin's Press, 1988), p. 142-143.

70    **Christensen and Jacobson note, if both of you**—*Reconcilable Differences*

**psychologist Robert Kegan**—*In Over Our Heads: The Mental Demands of Modern Life* (Cambridge, MA: Harvard University Press, 1994), p. 120.

71    **Matthew McKay**—*Couple Skills*, p. 59.

73    **psychologist John Gottman**—John Gottman with Nan Silver, *Why Marriages Succeed or Fail* (NY: Fireside, 1995); *The Seven Principles for Making Marriage Work* (NY: Three Rivers Press, 2000).

76    **Psychologists suggest that**—Tamara Goldman Sher and Donald H. Baucom, "Marital Communication: Differences Among Maritally Distressed, Depressed, and Nondistressed-Nondepressed Couples," *Journal of Family Psychology*, 1993, Vol. 7, No. 1, 148-153.

## CHAPTER 6: CRACKING THE CODE

77  **Julie K. Norem**—*The Positive Power of Negative Thinking* (NY: Basic Books, 2001); see also Gabriele Oettingen and Doris Mayer, "The Motivating Function of Thinking About the Future: Expectations Versus Fantasies," *Journal of Personality and Social Psychology*, 2002, Vol. 83, No. 5, 1198-1212.

78  **Andrew Christensen observed**—*Reconcilable Differences*, p. 199.

81  **magazine article about subtle abuse**—Julius Rosen, "Subtle Abuse: How Couples Get into Trouble," *Mothering*, Fall 1992, pp. 108-111.

82  **Charles N. Seashore**—Charles N. Seashore, Edith Whitfield Seashore, and Gerald M. Weinberg, *What Did You Say? The Art of Giving and Receiving Feedback* (North Attleborough, MA: Douglas Charles Press, 1992), p. 29.

87  **Deborah Tannen**—*You Just Don't Understand: Women and Men in Conversation* (NY: Ballantine, 1990).

90  **Michael P. Nichols**—*The Lost Art of Listening: How Learning to Listen Can Improve Relationships* (NY: Guilford, 1995), p. 70.

92  **Howard J. Markman**—Howard J. Markman, Scott M. Stanley, and Susan L. Blumberg, *Fighting for Your Marriage* (San Francisco: Jossey-Bass, revised 2001).

   **the technique, per Gottman**—*The Seven Principles for Making Marriage Work* (NY: Three Rivers Press, 2000).

   **Andrew Christensen, too, focuses**—*Reconcilable Differences*

97  **reported in *Cognition in Close Relationships***—C.K. Scott, R.W. Fuhrman, and R.S. Wyer, "Information Processing in Close Relationships," In G.J.O. Fletcher & F.D. Fincham (Eds.), *Cognition in Close Relationships* (Hillsdale, NJ: Erlbaum, 1991), 37-67.

## CHAPTER 7: HOW DO YOU DRIVE ME CRAZY?
## LET ME COUNT THE WAYS

103  **character in Evelyn Waugh's**—*Brideshead Revisited* (Boston: Little, Brown, 1946), p. 164.

104  **a recent study**—Carolin J. Showers and Suzanne B. Kevlyn, "Organization of Knowledge About a Relationship Partner: Implications for Liking and Loving," *Journal of Personality and Social Psychology*, 1999, Vol. 76, No. 6, 958-971.

111  **"Things My Girlfriend and I Have Argued About."**—http://homepage. ntlworld.com/mil.millington/things.html

## CHAPTER 8: BEYOND THE CHORE WARS

114  **Australian sociologist**—Ken Dempsey, "Women's and men's consciousness of shortcomings in marital relations, and of the need for change," *Family Matters*, No. 58, Autumn 2001.

115  **Researchers looking directly**—Nancy K. Grote and Margaret S. Clark, "Perceiving Unfairness in the Family: Cause or Consequence of Marital Distress?" *Journal of Personality and Social Psychology*, 2001, Vol. 80, No. 2, 281-293.

   **According to Ayala M. Pines**—*Couple Burnout: Causes and Cures* (NY: Routledge, 1996), p. 214.

116  **In some relationships, it's been found**—Ken Dempsey, "Women's and men's consciousness of shortcomings in marital relations, and of the need for change," *Family Matters*, No. 58, Autumn 2001.

117  **Gregory J. Popcak**—*The Exceptional Seven Per Cent: The Nine Secrets of the World's Happiest Couples* (NY: Citadel Press, 2000), p. 10.

120  *Hot Buttons: How to Resolve Conflict and Cool Everyone Down*—Sherry Suib Cohen, (NY: HarperCollins, 2001).

## CHAPTER 9: THE COUPLE'S MANIFESTO OF LOVE

133 **Research has shown that such a cooperative attitude**—B.I. Murstein, M. Cerreto, and M.G. MacDonald, "A theory and investigation of the effect of exchange-orientation on marriage and friendship," *Journal of Marriage and the Family*, 1977, 39, 543-548.

135 **psychologists call reciprocation wariness**—Norman Cotterell, Robert Eisenberger, and Hilda Speicher, "Inhibiting Effects of Reciprocation Wariness on Interpersonal Relationships," *Journal of Personality and Social Psychology*, 1997, Vol. 62, No. 4, 658-668; and Jennifer Wieselquist, Caryl E. Rusbult, Craig A. Foster, and Christopher R. Agnew, "Commitment, Pro-Relationship Behavior, and Trust in Close Relationships," *Journal of Personality and Social Psychology*, 1999, Vol. 77, No. 5, 942-966.

136 **psychologist Ayala M. Pines**—*Keeping the Spark Alive*, p. 68.
**Peter D. Kramer**—*Should You Leave?*, p. 255.

137 **Pepper Schwartz**—*Peer Marriage: How Love Between Equals Really Works* (NY: Free Press, 1994), p.15 [later renamed *Love Between Equals: How Peer Marriage Really Works* (NY: Free Press, 1995)].

140 **Phyllis Rose**—*Parallel Lives: Five Victorian Marriages* (NY: Vintage Books, 1984), p. 8.

142 **Dutch social psychologist and his American colleagues**—Paul A.M. Van Lange, Stephen M. Drigotas, Caryl E. Rusbult, Ximena B. Arriaga, Betty S. Witcher, and Chante L. Cox, "Willingness to Sacrifice in Close Relationships," *Journal of Personality and Social Psychology*, 1997, Vol. 72, No. 6, 1373-1395.
**Eric J. Cohen and Gregory Sterling suggest**—Eric J. Cohen and Gregory Sterling, *"You Owe Me": The Emotional Debts That Cripple Relationships* (Far Hills, New Jersey: New Horizon Press, 1999), p. 184.

## CHAPTER 10: SEX (MORE OR LESS)

147 **Stephan Rechtschaffen**—*Time Shifting: Creating More Time to Enjoy Your Life* (NY: Doubleday, 1996), p. 112.

152 *Conjugal Bliss*—John Nichols, *Conjugal Bliss* (NY: Henry Holt and Co., 1994), p. 54.

156 **Jane Hamilton, in her novel *Disobedience***—(NY: Doubleday, 2000), p. 221.
**Diane Ackerman**—"The Cuddle Chemical" in Mark Robert Waldman (Ed.), *The Art of Staying Together* (NY: Jeremy P. Tarcher/Putnam, 1998), 30-33, 34.
**Robert J. Sternberg**—*Cupid's Arrow: The Course of Love Through Time* (Cambridge, UK: Cambridge University Press, 1998), 39-40.

157 **a poll of 1000 married adults**—*The Times* (London), 12/18/2001.

160 **Karen J. Prager**—*The Psychology of Intimacy* (NY: Guilford, 1995), p. 235.

## CHAPTER 11: SEX REDUX (KEEPING IT FRESH)

165 **Pepper Schwartz**—*Peer Marriage*, p. 107

167 **One journalist**—Alexandra Penney, "Is It Possible To Have (Good) Sex With the Same Person for 20 Years?, *Ms.*, June 1985, p. 52.

170 **David Schnarch writes**—*Passionate Marriage: Sex, Love, and Intimacy in Emotionally Committed Relationships* (NY: W.W. Norton, 1997), p.190.

171 **Jhumpa Lahiri short story**—"A Temporary Matter," in *Interpreter of Maladies: Stories* (NY: Houghton Mifflin, 1999).

173 **David Schnarch points out**—*Passionate Marriage*, p. 83.

176 **a recent *NY Times* article**—Frank Rich, "Naked Capitalists: There's No Business Like Porn Business," *The New York Times*, May 20, 2001.
**explains Stephen A. Mitchell**—*Can Love Last?*, p. 130-31.

177 **Ellyn Bader and Peter T. Pearson**—Ellyn Bader and Peter T. Pearson with Judith D. Schwartz, *Tell Me No Lies: How to Face the Truth and Build a Loving Marriage* (NY: St. Martin's Press, 2000), p. 31.

183   **David Schnarch's discussion of differentiation**—*Passionate Marriage*, p.18.

## CHAPTER 12: HITTING BOTTOM

191   **Mimi Schwartz describes**—*Thoughts from a Queen-Sized Bed*, p. 27
197   **Frank Pittman's** *Private Lies*—*Private Lies: Infidelity and the Betrayal of Intimacy* (NY: W. W. Norton, 1990).

## CHAPTER 13: THE CLICHÉ CRISIS

205   **author of** ***Dreaming Your Real Self***:—Joan Mazza, *Dreaming Your Real Self: A Personal Approach to Dream Interpretation* (NY: Perigee, 1998).
206   **Psychiatrist Peter D. Kramer**—*Should You Leave?*, p. 64.
207   **in a** ***New York Times*** **article**—Joseph Hooper, "Now Infidelity Comes Out of the Closet," *The New York Times*, 4/29/99, p. B1, B9.
208   **recent reputable surveys**—such as *Sex in America* (NY: Warner, 1994); M. W. Wiederman, "Extramarital sex: Prevalence and correlates in a national survey," *Journal of Sex Research*, 34, 1997, 167-174.
      **One source suggests that**—S.P. Glass, and T.L. Wright, "Clinical implications of research on extramarital involvement, in R. Brown and J. Field (Eds.), *Treatment of sexual problems in individual and couples therapy* (NY: PMA Publishing, 1988), pp. 301-346.
      **a survey of couples therapists**—M.A. Whisman, A.E. Dixon, and B. Johnson, "Therapists' perspectives of couple problems and treatment issues in couple therapy," *Journal of Family Psychology*, 11, 1997, 361-366.
      **Pittman divides them into**—*Private Lies*.
210   **conditions, say social psychologists**—Craig A. Foster, Betty S. Witcher, W. Keith Campbell, and Jeffrey D. Green, "Arousal and Attraction: Evidence for Automatic and Controlled Processes," *Journal of Personality and Social Psychology*, 1998, Vol. 74, No. 1, 86-101; also D.G. Dutton and A.P. Aron, "Some evidence for heightened sexual attraction under conditions of high anxiety," *Journal of Personality and Social Psychology*, 23, 1974, 510-517.
213   **Psychology backs him up**—Robert J. Sternberg, *Cupid's Arrow*, 140.
217   **Some say only a tenth or so**—M.P. Farrell and D. Rosenberg, *Men at Midlife* (Boston: Auburn House, 1981); W. Gallagher, "Midlife Myths," *The Atlantic Monthly*, May 1993, 51-68 (Gallagher quotes Ronald Kessler, a sociologist and program director in the survey research section of the University of Michigan's Institute for Social Research).
      **Levinson, on the other hand, found**—Daniel J. Levinson, *The Seasons of a Man's Life*, (NY: Ballantine, 1978), p. 199.
224   **Cohen and Sterling write**—*"You Owe Me"*, p. 164.
      **forgiveness researchers found**—Michael E. McCullough, Everett L. Worthington, Jr., and Kenneth C. Rachal, "Interpersonal Forgiving in Close Relationships," *Journal of Personality and Social Psychology*, 1997, Vol 73, No. 2, 321-336.
225   **A fascinating study found**—Daniel M. Wegner, Julie D. Lane, and Sara Dimitri, "The Allure of Secret Relationships," *Journal of Personality and Social Psychology*, 1994, Vol. 66, No. 2, 287-300.
229   **Some studies have found that** *opportunity*—David C. Atkins, Donald H. Baucom, and Neil S. Jacobson cite several of these studies in "Understanding Infidelity: Correlates in a National Random Sample," *Journal of Family Psychology*, 2001, Vol. 15, No. 4, 735-749.

## CHAPTER 14: CHILDREN: FLOW INTERRUPTED?

231 **It has been found that relationships**—Sternberg, Robert J., *Cupid's Arrow: The Course of Love Through Time*, 146-, a study of eighty adults in stable couples found that relationships typically go through at least one hard period, during which some aspects of their lives decrease—tolerance, fidelity, acceptance of each other, for example—but they may go back up later. Judith S. Wallerstein and Sandra Blakeslee, *The Good Marriage: How and Why Love Lasts* (NY: Warner, 1996) found coping with crises to be one of the main tasks with which couples have to contend, with every couple studied facing "at least one major tragedy." Robert Levenson, a U.C. Berkeley psychologist and researcher (cited by Marge Fahey, "Communication, Friendship Help Marriages," *The Washington Times*, May 1, 2001) studied 156 long-term first marriages. Half the couples were married at least fifteen years, the rest at least thirty-five years, and all felt they'd survived being tested by challenges and crises as a couple.

**Children are especially likely**—Lawrence A. Kurdek, "The Nature and Predictors of the Trajectory of Change in Marital Quality for Husbands and Wives Over the First Ten Years of Marriage," *Developmental Psychology*, 1999, Vol. 35, No. 5, 1283-1296.

**a ten-year study**—C.P. Cowan, P.A. Cowan, L. Coie, and J. Coie, "Becoming a family: The impact of a first child's birth on the couple's relationship," in W. Miller and L. Newman (Eds.), *The First Child and Family Formation* (Chapel Hill: Carolina Population Center, 1978).

232 **Rhonda Kruse Nordin**—*After the Baby: Making Sense of Marriage After Childbirth* (Dallas: Taylor Publishing Co., 2000), p.135.

233 **researchers at the University of Washington**—Alyson Fearnley Shapiro, John Gottman, and Sybil Carrere, "The baby and the marriage: Identifying factors that buffer against decline in marital satisfaction after the first baby arrives," *Journal of Family Psychology*, March 2000, Vol. 14, No. 1, 59-70.

234 **Christina Baker Kline**—Christina Baker Kline, Editor, *Child of Mine: Writers Talk about the First Year of Motherhood* (NY: Bantam, 1998).

237 **psychologists delving into parenting**—Marion O'Brien and Vicki Peyton, "Parenting Attitudes and Marital Intimacy: A Longitudinal Analysis," *Journal of Family Psychology*, 2002, Vol. 16, No. 2, 118-127.

242 **Tom, a psychologist and author**—*Freeing Our Families from Perfectionism* (Minneapolis, MINN: Free Spirit Publishing, 2002).

247 **Pam Rillstone and Sally A. Hutchinson**—cited by Jane Brody in "Losing a Child, Before a Child is Born," *The New York Times*, August 14, 2001.

## CHAPTER 15: MONEY, ILLNESS, AND OTHER POTENTIAL CRISES

251 **a vast study of more than 600**—Shlomo A. Sharlin, Florence W. Kaslow, and Helga Hammerschmidt, *Together Through Thick and Thin: A Multinational Picture of Long-Term Marriages* (NY: Haworth Clinical Practice Press, 2000). Marriages lasting from twenty to forty-six years were studied, and findings held true across all included cultures: United States, Sweden, Germany, Israel, South Africa, Netherlands, Canada, and Chile.

**other research indicates**—Catherine L. Cohan and Thomas N. Bradbury, "Negative Life Events, Marital Interaction, and the Longitudinal Course of Newlywed Marriage," *Journal of Personality and Social Psychology*, 1997, Vol. 73, 114-128, p. 124.

**is a known stress-reducer**—M.B. Hennessy, S.P. Mendoza, W.A. Mason, and G.P. Moberg, "Endocrine sensitivity to novelty in squirrel monkeys and titi monkeys: Species differences in characteristic modes of responding to the environment," *Physiology & Behavior*, 1995, 57, 331-338.

253 **unemployed, it's been found**—Amiram D. Vinocur, Richard H. Price, and Robert D. Caplan, "Hard Times and Hurtful Partners: How Financial Strain Affects Depression and Relationship Satisfaction of Unemployed Persons and Their Spouses," *Journal of Personality and Social Psychology*, 1996, Vol. 71, No. 1, 166-179.

254 **Researchers who studied breast cancer**—Niall Bolger, Mark Foster, Amiram D. Vinokur, and Rosanna Ng, "Close Relationships and Adjustment to a Life Crisis: The Case of Breast Cancer," *Journal of Personality and Social Psychology*, 1996, Vol. 70, No. 2, 283-294.

259 **suggest the authors of** *Empty Nesting*—David H. Arp, Claudia S. Arp, Scott M. Stanley, Howard J. Markman, and Susan L. Blumberg, *Empty Nesting: Reinventing Your Marriage When the Kids Leave Home* (San Francisco: Jossey-Bass, 2001), p. 47.

260 **could be related to the quality**—Jungmeen E. Kim and Phyllis Moen, "Is Retirement Good or Bad for Subjective Well-Being?" *Current Directions in Psychological Science*, Vol. 10, No. 3, June 2001, 83-86.

264 **researchers have divided**—Jeffrey M. Adams and Warren H. Jones, "The Conceptualization of Marital Commitment: An Integrative Analysis," *Journal of Personality and Social Psychology*, 1997, Vol. 72, No. 5, 1177-1196.

**insists Frank Pittman**—*Grow Up!*, p. 158.

265 **They don't use denial**—Genevieve Bouchard, Stephane Sabourin, Yvan Lussier, John Wright, & Chantal Richer, "Predictive Validity of Coping Strategies on Marital Satisfaction: Cross-Sectional and Longitudinal Evidence," *Journal of Family Psychology*, 1998, Vol. 12, No. 1, 112-131.

**satisfaction levels go up**—Terri L. Orbuch, James S. House, Richard P. Mero, Pamela S. Webster, "Marital Quality Over the Life Course," *Social Psychology Quarterly*, 1996, Vol. 59, No. 2, 162-171.

**recent research has confirmed**—Linda J. Waite and Maggie Gallagher, *The Case for Marriage* (NY: Doubleday, 2000), p. 148. Also, of the two per cent of couples who had initially rated their marriages "miserable," about 77 percent rated them as "very happy" five years later.

## CHAPTER 16: HOLDING ON, LETTING GO

267 **Richard Schwartz, M.D., and Jacqueline Olds, M.D.**—*Marriage in Motion*, p.167.

268 **Sam Keen** - *To Love and Be Loved*, p. 171.

**Robert J. Sternberg**—*Cupid's Arrow: The Course of Love Through Time*, p. 48. (The average relationship length among those studied was 6.3 years.)

**Joel B. Bennett**—Joel B. Bennett, *Time and Intimacy: A New Science of Personal Relationships* (Mahwah, NJ: Lawrence Erlbaum Associates, 2000), p. 36.

**psychologists have dubbed "openers"**—Lynn Carol Miller, John H. Berg, Richard L. Archer, "Openers: Individuals Who Elicit Intimate Self-Disclosure," *Journal of Personality and Social Psychology*, 1983, Vol. 44, No. 6, 1234-1244.

**strength of their intimacy needs**—Karen J. Prager, *The Psychology of Intimacy*, p. 228.

271 **According to Robert J. Sternberg**—*Cupid's Arrow: The Course of Love Through Time*, p. 36.

273 **divorced couples in one study**—Catherine Kohler Riessman, *Divorce Talk: Women and Men Make Sense of Personal Relationships* (New Brunswick, NJ: Rutgers University Press, 1990), 25, 37-38.

275 **One startling piece of research**—Bella M. DePaulo and Deborah A. Kashy, "Everyday Lies in Close and Casual Relationships," *Journal of Personality and Social Psychology*, 1998, Vol. 74, No. 1, 63-79.

276 **intimacy derives more from honesty**—Jean-Philippe Laurenceau, Lisa Feldman Barrett, and Paula R. Pietromonaco, "Intimacy as an Interpersonal Process: The Importance of Self-Disclosure, Partner Disclosure, and Perceived Partner

Responsiveness in Interpersonal Exchanges," *Journal of Personality and Social Psychology*, 1998, Vol. 74, No. 5, 1238-1251.

278 **One set of researchers went so far**—Jamie L. Goldenberg, Tom Pyszczynski, Shannon K. McCoy, Jeff Greenberg, and Sheldon Solomon, "Death, Sex, Love, and Neuroticism: Why is Sex Such a Problem?" *Journal of Personality and Social Psychology*, 1999, Vol. 77, No. 6, 1173-1187; quote is from p. 1182.

**mystery," she writes in her memoir**—Sherry Suib Cohen, *Secrets of a Very Good Marriage*, p. 64.

279 **Robert C. Solomon**—*Love: Emotion, Myth, & Metaphor*, p.146.

280 *New Yorker* **cartoon**—*The New Yorker*, June 18 & 25, 2001, p. 89.

282 **Marion F. Solomon**—Marion F. Solomon, *Narcissism and Intimacy: Love and Marriage in an Age of Confusion* (NY: W. W. Norton, 1992), p. 26.

283 **Peter D. Kramer**—*Should You Leave?*, p. 87

284 **lists compiled by lasting couples**—Shlomo A. Sharlin, et al, *Together Through Thick and Thin: A Multinational Picture of Long-Term Marriages*, p. 23; Judith S. Wallerstein and Sandra Blakeslee, *The Good Marriage: How & Why Love Lasts* (NY: Warner, 1996), p. 329; and a survey commissioned by the popular magazine *Redbook* (published May 2001) found more than nine out of ten men and women—all in their thirties and married ten to twelve years—rated "respect for each other" in the top six keys to a happy marriage (p. 140).

**Robert C. Solomon agrees**—*Love: Emotion, Myth, & Metaphor*, pp. 189, 194, 196.

## CHAPTER 17: YOU LOVE WHAT YOU PAY ATTENTION TO

287 **The happiest couples, in fact**—Shlomo Sharlin, et al, *Together Through Thick and Thin*, p. 23.

288 **Cartoon in The New Yorker**—*The New Yorker*, Feb. 14, 2000, p. 32.

**One psychologist wrote**—Erich Fromm, *The Art of Loving* (NY: Harper & Row, 1956/1989), p. 104.

**Gottman's research**—*Why Marriages Succeed or Fail; The Seven Principles for Making Marriage Work*.

289 **an unexpected correlation**—Geoff Thomas, Garth J.O. Fletcher, and Craig Lange, "On-line empathic accuracy in marital interaction, *Journal of Personality and Social Psychology*, 1997, Vol. 72, No. 4, 839-850; the quote is from p. 847. Seventy-four couples were studied.

**Arnold M. Ludwig**—*How Do We Know Who We Are? A Biography of the Self* (NY: Oxford University Press, 1997), p. 85.

290 **Another New Yorker cartoon**—*The New Yorker*, October 15, 2001, p. 208.

**Ellen J. Langer**—*Mindfulness* (Reading: MA: Addison-Wesley, 1989).

**writes Sam Keen**—*To Love and Be Loved*, p. 40.

291 **researchers at the Indiana University**—Reported at the Radiological Society of North America's 86th Scientific Assembly and Annual Meeting in Chicago, November 2000.

294 **Proust wrote**—Marcel Proust, *Within a Budding Grove* (NY: Modern Library, 1998 edition), p. 262.

## CHAPTER 18: THE POWER OF PLAY

297 **William Betcher**—*Intimate Play: Creating Romance in Everyday Life* (NY: Viking, 1987), p. 24- 25.

299 **Judging from the tales**—Dacher Keltner, Randall C. Young, Erin A. Heerey, Carmen Oemig, and Natalie D. Monarch, "Teasing in Hierarchical and Intimate Relations," *Journal of Personality and Social Psychology*, 1998, Vol. 75, No. 5, 1231-1247.

301 **Betcher writes**—*Intimate Play*, p. 246-247.

308 **consider what experimental research**—Arthur Aron, Elaine N. Aron, Christina C. Norman, Colin McKenna, and Richard E. Heyman, "Couples' Shared Participation in Novel and Arousing Activities and Experienced Relationship Quality," *Journal of Personality and Social Psychology*, 2000, Vol. 78, No. 2, 273-284.

**Neuroscientists, too**—reported by Sandra Blakeslee, "Hijacking the Brain Circuits with a Nickel Slot Machine," *The New York Times*, February 19, 2002.

**Stephan Rechtschaffen**—*Time Shifting*, p. 121.

**Ayala M. Pines**—*Couple Burnout: Causes and Cures*, xi.

**Stephen A. Mitchell**—*Can Love Last?*, p. 188-189.

**Mitchell's more fanciful phrasings**—*Can Love Last?*, p. 190.

309 **isn't clearly related to burnout**—Ayala M. Pines, *Couple Burnout: Causes and Cures*, p. 174.

**"In a 'stirring-the-oatmeal' love," she writes**—*Couple Burnout*, p. 176.

310 **focus on your own self-actualization**—*Couple Burnout*, p. 212.

**according to her memoir**—*Thoughts from a Queen-Sized Bed*, p. 13.

**social psychology's gain-loss theory**—Elliot Aronson, *The Social Animal* (NY: W. H. Freeman, Sixth Edition, 1992), p. 379.

312 **research completed at Loyola College**—Maria E. Zammichieli, Faith D. Gilroy, and Martin F. Sherman, "Relation Between Sex-Role Orientation and Marital Satisfaction," *Personality and Social Psychology Bulletin*, Vol. 14, No. 4, December 1988, 747-754.

**Judith S. Wallerstein found**—*The Good Marriage: How & Why Love Lasts*, p. 260

313 **According to Frank Pittman**—*Turning Points: Treating Families in Transition and Crisis* (NY: W. W. Norton, 1987), p. 51.

## CHAPTER 19: THE IMPERFECT ROCK TUMBLER OF TIME

318 **shown to be a myth by a study**—Avshalom Caspi, Ellen S. Herbener, and Daniel J. Ozer, "Shared Experiences and the Similarity of Personalities: A Longitudinal Study of Married Couples," *Journal of Personality and Social Psychology*, 1992, Vol. 62, No. 2, 281-291.

320 **Judith S. Wallerstein interviewed**—*The Good Marriage*, p. 330.

**Solomon wonders**—Robert C. Solomon, *Love: Emotion, Myth, and Metaphor*, p. 203.

322 **old jokes," Sam Keen writes**—*To Love and Be Loved*, p. 135.

**it was found they had shared**—F.C. Dickson, "The best is yet to be: Research on longlasting relationships," in J.T. Wood and S. Duck (Eds.), *Understudied Relationships: Off the beaten track* (Beverly Hills, CA: Sage, 1995), pp. 22-50.

**It's not about how long you're married**—James E. Deal, C.F. Wampler, and C.F. Halverson, "The importance of similarity in the marital relationship,"*Family Process*, 1992, Vol. 31, No. 4, 369-382.

**newlyweds were analyzed**—Lawrence A. Kurdek, "Predicting Marital Dissolution: A 5-Year Prospective Longitudinal Study of Newlywed Couples," *Journal of Personality and Social Psychology*, 1993, Vol. 64, No. 2, 221-242.

**writes Phyllis Rose**—*Parallel Lives*, p. 7.

**stories told by satisfied partners**—Ian McGregor and John G. Holmes, "How Storytelling Shapes Memory and Impressions of Relationship Events Over Time," *Journal of Personality and Social Psychology*, 1999, Vol. 76, No. 3, 403-419.

**I interviewed creative writers**—Susan K. Perry, *Writing in Flow: Keys to Enhanced Creativity* (Cinncinati, OH: Writer's Digest Books, 2001).

325 **Scott Spencer's novel**—*Endless Love* (Hopewell, NJ: Ecco Press, 1979/1999), p. 332.

327 **Peter DeVries novel**—*The Blood of the Lamb* (NY: Penguin Books, 1982), p. 164.

# INDEX

# ABOUT THE AUTHOR

**Susan K. Perry, Ph.D.,** is a social psychologist with a special interest in positive psychology. She is the bestselling author of six books and the award-winning writer of more than 800 articles, essays, and advice columns. Her most recent books include *Writing in Flow: Keys to Enhanced Creativity*; *Playing Smart: The Family Guide to Enriching, Offbeat Learning Activities*; and *Catch the Spirit: Teen Volunteers Tell How They Made a Difference.*

As an expert on relationships and family topics, Dr. Perry has written for and been quoted in such publications as *Psychology Today, Cosmopolitan, Family Circle, Women's Health and Fitness, YM, USA Today, Writer's Digest, The Los Angeles Times, Los Angeles Magazine, Parenting, Child,* and many others. She is a contributing writer for *United Parenting Publications* and *Valley Magazine.*

An adjunct instructor of psychology at Woodbury University (Burbank, California), she has also taught at UCLA Extension and other university extension divisions. She is a writing consultant, as well as an instructor for Writer's Digest Online Workshops. Her Internet home is www.BunnyApe.com. She lives in Los Angeles with her husband, Stephen, a *New Yorker*-published poet.